THE WHITE NEGRESS

The White Negress

Literature, Minstrelsy, and the Black-Jewish Imaginary

LORI HARRISON-KAHAN

Rutgers University Press

NEW BRUNSWICK, NEW JERSEY, AND LONDON

Visit our Web site: http://rutgerspress.rutgers.edu

Manufactured in the United States of America

LIBRARY OF CONGRESS CATALOGING-IN-PUBLICATION DATA

Harrison-Kahan, Lori.

   The white negress : literature, minstrelsy, and the black-Jewish imaginary / Lori Harrison-Kahan.
       p.   cm. — (American Literatures Initiative)
   Includes bibliographical references and index.
   ISBN 978-0-8135-4782-4 (alk. paper)
   ISBN 978-0-8135-4783-1 (pbk. : alk. paper)
   1. American literature—20th century—History and criticism.   2. Passing (Identity) in literature.   3. Women and literature—United States—History—20th century.   4. Ethnicity in literature.   5. African American women authors. 6. Jewish women authors—United States.   7. Americanization.   8. Immigrants in literature.   I. Title.
PS228.P35H37   2010
810.9'3529—dc22

                                                                                        2010008515

   A British Cataloging-in-Publication record for this book is available from the British Library.

THE
AMERICAN
LITERATURES
INITIATIVE
A book in the American Literatures Initiative (ALI), a collaborative publishing project of NYU Press, Fordham University Press, Rutgers University Press, Temple University Press, and the University of Virginia Press. The Initiative is supported by The Andrew W. Mellon Foundation. For more information, please visit www.americanliteratures.org.

Contents

Acknowledgments   vii

Introduction   1

1   From White Negress to Yiddishe Mama: Sophie Tucker
    and the Female Blackface Tradition   16

2   The Same Show Boat? Edna Ferber's Interracial Ideal   58

3   Limitations of White: Fannie Hurst and the Consumption
    of Blackness   96

4   Moses and Minstrelsy: Zora Neale Hurston and the
    Black-Jewish Imaginary   143

    Conclusion   177

    Notes   185

    Index   221

Acknowledgments

Over the course of writing this book, I have made my academic home at various institutions. I would like to thank colleagues and students in the History and Literature Program at Harvard University, the Department of American Studies at Brandeis University, the English Department at Connecticut College, the English Department at Boston College, and at the University of Pennsylvania for the intellectual exchange that helped to shape the content contained herein. In the early stages of my academic career, my professors at Princeton and Columbia—in particular, Michael Wood, Ann Douglas, David Eng, and Ann Pellegrini—provided inspiration and models of scholarship that have continued to fuel my writing and thinking.

Other individuals deserve special mention for the impact they have had on my research along the way: Darren Gobert, Lydia Fisher, Cara Delay, Jessica Lang, Laura Saltz, Jennifer Sartori, Katie Kendall, Rachel Prentice, Chloe Silverman, and, for her longtime friendship and nonacademic perspective, Emily Burg. At Connecticut College, Lauren Moran and Monica Raymunt assisted with research. David Greven gave me a push when I most needed it. Ann Pellegrini and Laura Levitt helped me move further toward publication. In the final stages of this project, I was fortunate to benefit from the insights of Josh Lambert, who has been a wonderful collaborator. I would especially like to thank the members of my writing group, Kimberly Chabot Davis and Shilpa Davé, who read every word of the book (some several times over) and whose feedback and collegiality have been invaluable to my scholarship.

I owe thanks to Leslie Mitchner, Katie Keeran, and Marilyn Campbell at Rutgers University Press; to Rachel Friedman, who acquired the manuscript; and to Tim Roberts at the American Literatures Initiative. Once anonymous readers, Joyce Antler and Martha Cutter provided sage and challenging comments that led to drastic improvements; I am glad to have the opportunity to thank them by name.

I want to express my appreciation of the American Literatures Initiative and the Andrew W. Mellon Foundation for their commitment to bringing the work of young scholars into print. A Dorot Foundation Postdoctoral Research Fellowship in Jewish Studies from the Harry Ransom Center, University of Texas at Austin, and a NEMLA Summer Fellowship helped me to conduct archival research.

Finally, I am grateful for the love of my family, who readily admit that they have no idea what I do for work, but who support me unconditionally just the same. Barbara and Robert Harrison nurtured my thirst for knowledge from an early age. Jodi and Neil Harrison have always been there to share in the successes. Eileen Kahan provided babysitting, and nourishment, that allowed me to bring this book to completion. My husband, David, and sons, Cuyler and Amory, are daily reminders of the need to balance work and play. This book is for them.

THE WHITE NEGRESS

Introduction

In 1922, Jewish American writer Fannie Hurst published "The Smudge," a short story about an aging blackface actress in the process of confronting her unrealized ambitions. Having once dreamed of playing Shakespeare's Juliet, Hurst's protagonist, Hattie Bertch, finds herself irretrievably typecast as a "buxom negro" maid. Despite her discomfort with such comedic supporting roles, Hattie perseveres as a blackface performer for the sake of her illegitimate teenage daughter, Marcia, who is described, in contrast to her mother's on-stage persona, as "the color and odor of an ivory fan that has lain in frangipani." Unable to subsist on her meager stage income alone, Hattie supplements her earnings with a more lucrative pursuit: she cooks up black makeup in her kitchen and sells it to other actors. The profits from Hattie's "Guaranteed Color-fast" black cold cream enable Marcia's upward mobility, allowing her to enter an upper-class milieu of finishing schools and dinner dances that is unmistakably coded as white. As Hattie puts it, "It's my blackface that has kept her like a lily!" Yet by the story's end, Hattie relinquishes the independence afforded by her blackface enterprises when she reluctantly agrees to marry—and presumably turn her business over to—Marcia's wayward father, who had abandoned mother and unborn child years earlier. This denouement comes about because Hattie realizes that the traffic in blackness can have the opposite effect as well: it has the potential to darken Marcia's reputation and thwart her ascent into white high society. In the moment that gives the story its title, Hurst describes what happens when Hattie rushes home from the theater to plant a kiss upon her sleeping daughter: "Darkly. A smudge the size of a quarter and the color of Hattie's guaranteed-not-to-fade cheek, lay incredibly on Marcia's whiteness. Hattie had smudged Marcia! *Hattie Had Smudged Marcia!* There it lay on her beautiful, helpless whiteness. Hattie's smudge."[1]

This book takes as its premise the contradiction that lies at the heart of "The Smudge." It argues that appropriations of blackness in early-twentieth-century American culture produce and shore up white identity, while simultaneously troubling that self-same whiteness. A rare and little-known fictional representation of female blackface performance, "The Smudge" announces my principal concerns by introducing the figure of the "white negress." Throughout this book, the "white negress" takes a variety of forms. At times she is racially indeterminate or ethnically unidentified (as Hattie Bertch is); other times she is identified specifically as Jewish or mixed race. But the "white negress" is consistently an ambivalent figure, an independent working woman whose crossing of racial lines becomes intertwined with her defiance of gender and domestic norms. Posing a challenge to ideals of white femininity, the figure of the "white negress" fills a lacuna in the existing scholarship on blackface minstrelsy, which either elides gender or privileges men and masculinity. By moving women from the periphery to the center of the scholarly discourse on formations of race and whiteness, *The White Negress* demonstrates how considerations of gender and femininity complicate the paradigms that currently dominate our understandings of cross-racial performances and interminority encounters.

Like many of the key texts in the field of whiteness studies with which this book is in conversation, *The White Negress* locates its inquiries within "the black-Jewish imaginary," a realm of literary and cultural production in which Jews and African Americans imagined themselves and each other in relation to the white mainstream. The black-Jewish imaginary is an especially fruitful site for examining formations of race because it at once provides an alternative to the black-white schema that dominates American culture *and* an occasion for exploring how that racial binary comes into being. Fannie Hurst's career is a case in point. Because her engagement with black culture was seen as superseding her own ethnic background ("The Smudge," for example, is emptied of Jewish characters and themes), Hurst has stood accused of strategically using African Americans in order to make herself, in the words of one critic, "white and assimilable."[2] While the creation of this racial binary is one part of the story I tell in this book, *The White Negress* also calls for a more dynamic rendering of this narrative and cautions against constructing black-Jewish relations as a one-way street.

Centering on the lives and work of Jewish women such as Hurst, Sophie Tucker, and Edna Ferber, this book contends that their sustained engagement with questions of race and African American identity should be read in dialectical relation to their Jewish backgrounds. Because of their own membership in a minority group, these women were drawn into dialogue with African American artists, many of whom, in turn, took up questions of Jewish identity. The potential for a dialogic "call and response" between Jewish and African American women is best exemplified by the friendship between Hurst and black writer Zora Neale Hurston. In the second half of this book, I examine the complexities of this interracial relationship and place Hurst's and Hurston's fiction side by side in order to paint a well-rounded picture of interminority relations, shaped by mutual forces of influence, rather than simply unidirectional exploitation. *The White Negress* does not claim to be a comprehensive survey of black-Jewish relations among women. Instead, by taking an in-depth look at key players and representative texts, this book opens new avenues of inquiry that will yield more complex stories about Jews, African Americans, and the making of whiteness.

* * *

Hurst's "The Smudge" was not the only short story about a blackface performer to be published by a Jewish American writer in 1922. That year also saw the publication of Samson Raphaelson's "The Day of Atonement," which was inspired by the life of one of the early-twentieth-century's preeminent Jewish entertainers, Al Jolson. Jolson, the son of a rabbi, immigrated to the United States with his family in 1894, part of the significant wave of Jewish immigration from eastern Europe that began at the end of the nineteenth century. Changing his name from Asa Yoelson to Al Jolson, the rabbi's son achieved his fame as a singer of jazzy, Tin Pan Alley tunes, often performed in blackface.[3] Dramatizing the tension between religious tradition and secular assimilation, Raphaelson's "The Day of Atonement" tells the story of a cantor's son, Jakie Rabinowitz, who develops his musical talent in another direction. Instead of following in his father's path and dedicating himself to the synagogue, he leaves his Orthodox family behind to pursue a career in show business, assuming the stage name of Jack Robin and sealing his identity as a white American through a union with a non-Jewish woman.

If "The Day of Atonement" is better known today than "The Smudge," this is largely because the story became the basis of *The Jazz Singer*, the film that made motion picture history when it premiered in 1927 as the first "talkie," with Jolson himself starring in the role of his alter ego, Jakie Rabinowitz. Since then, *The Jazz Singer* has figured as an ur-text of the American entertainment industry, generating multiple remakes and even several animated versions.[4] The cultural obsession with *The Jazz Singer* is due to more than its technical innovation through the introduction of sound into cinema. A backstage tale about an immigrant boy who makes good by shucking off the burden of his past, it is a distinctly American narrative and one that often substitutes as the story of Hollywood writ large.[5] While the film's status as the first talking picture secured its place in the annals of film history, *The Jazz Singer* has remained a source of scholarly fascination for quite a different reason. With its scenes of Jolson corking up in order to perform "Mother of Mine" and "My Mammy," the 1927 film has become the most famous and best-studied example of twentieth-century blackface performance to date.

An immigrant-cum-blackface narrative, *The Jazz Singer* has generated the oppositional paradigms that currently frame most scholarship on the black-Jewish cultural imaginary. The bone of contention is this: are Jews empathetically identifying with the sufferings of African Americans by wearing the blackface mask, or is blackface an expression of racism, a form of exploitation of black culture that allowed Jews to situate themselves as members of the white majority? Irving Howe, one of the first critics to consider the prevalence of minstrelsy among Jewish performers in the early twentieth century, argued the former. In his sweeping 1976 cultural history of American Jewry, *World of Our Fathers*, Howe understood immigrant appropriations of African American culture as an assertion of Jewishness, not whiteness. He interpreted the blackface of Jolson and other performers as "a mask for Jewish expressiveness, with one woe speaking through the voice of another." For Howe, impersonating African Americans allowed these entertainers "to reach a spontaneity and assertiveness in the declaration of their Jewish selves" in a culture that often denied them free expression of their own ethnic identities.[6]

Twenty years later, in what is now the most influential study of *The Jazz Singer*, Michael Rogin's *Blackface, White Noise: Jewish Immigrants in the Hollywood Melting Pot* emphasized the process of *disidentification* above identification, arguing, contra Howe, that blackface enabled marginalized Jewish immigrants to align themselves with the dominant culture. By putting on burnt cork and then wiping it off, Jewish performers created a contrast between their theatrical identities and their off-stage or off-screen selves and, through this process of racial impersonation, became part of white America. Describing blackface as "the instrument that transfers identities from immigrant Jew to American," Rogin explains Jakie Rabinowitz's meteoric rise from cantor's son to Broadway star thus: "Assimilation is achieved via the mask of the most segregated; the blackface that offers Jews mobility keeps the blacks fixed in place. By wiping out all difference except black and white, blackface turns Rabinowitz into Robin, but the fundamental binary opposition nevertheless remains. That segregation, imposed on blacks, silences their voices and sings in their name."[7] In Rogin's reading of *The Jazz Singer*, immigrants could translate the stigma of blackface into upwardly mobile whiteness. Indeed, blackface turns out not to be much of a stigma at all. Instead, it is an exuberant display, a triumphant commandeering of African American culture that allowed its wearer to declare his position of white superiority. Heralding the emergence of the new academic field of critical white studies, *Blackface, White Noise* joined other seminal scholarship on race by critics such as Eric Lott, Toni Morrison, and David Roediger, who argued that white identity comes into being in opposition to blackness—and at its expense. Rogin's interpretation of *The Jazz Singer* substantiates Morrison's provocative claim that the rise of immigrants in American society occurs "on the backs of blacks."[8]

Although Rogin's thesis has been contested from within the field of Jewish cultural studies, it continues to provide a powerful paradigm for explaining how Jews became white folks.[9] In his recent book, *Klezmer America: Jewishness, Ethnicity, Modernity*, Jonathan Freedman questions the way this paradigm has come to dominate American and ethnic studies. Critiquing some of the prevailing scholarship, he argues that the "Jew-as-white-person model" is not "invalid," but "inadequate," obscuring as it does many other narratives, including those of Jews of color, and failing to account for the possibility of multiple and contradictory identifications.[10] Furthermore, in positioning whiteness as a fixed endpoint in a linear process of cultural assimilation, many scholars end up reifying white identity as permanent and stable, seeming to forget that the very narrative of Jews *becoming* white complicated the stability of identity and revealed its performativity in the first place. Despite the vital work critical white studies sets out to do in naming whiteness and making it visible, theories of social constructed identity that have, for example, undermined deeply engrained African American stereotypes become surprisingly static when extended to whiteness. In the introduction to

Klezmer America, Freedman returns to the prototypical example of *The Jazz Singer*, noting that readings by Rogin and others downplay the sexual ambiguity that marks Jolson's performance and thus considerably complicates his ascent into whiteness.[11]

Turning to women's racial appropriations in literature and minstrelsy allows me to tell a more complex story about encounters between African Americans and Jews in modern America that similarly takes into account the imbrication of race and ethnicity with gender and sexuality. In the extensive discussion about the role that black culture has played in ushering Jews into whiteness, relatively little attention has been paid to important differences between men's and women's experiences and to the corresponding differences in their literary and cultural representations. Both Howe and Rogin mention Jewish vaudevillian Sophie Tucker, perhaps the most famous woman to perform in the Jolson tradition, but in their respective accounts they assume that blackface operates in exactly the same way for her as it does for her male counterparts. In bringing gender and sexuality to the forefront, Jewish women's appropriations of blackness issue challenges to the "Jew-as-white-person model" by complicating white identity. Their cultural productions stage multivalent and thus highly ambivalent encounters among Jewishness, blackness, and whiteness. These complex and ever-shifting encounters of and between race and ethnicity are inextricably tied to similarly variegated performances of femininity that defy gender and sexual norms. In part, these complications are due to the fact that such cultural appropriations take place in a commercial realm that circumscribes women's full participation as producers. Unlike men, for whom the regulatory norms of masculinity *require* remunerative work outside of the home, women who participated in labor and production in the early twentieth century bore vexed relationships to standards of femininity; modernity had not broken free from the vestigial Victorian ideal that defined womanhood—and this should be qualified as white womanhood—in terms of domesticity, heterosexual passivity, and an overriding devotion to maternity.

As a story about a single working mother who is both actress and entrepreneur, Hurst's "The Smudge" provides an important alternative source for rethinking the masculinist paradigms that have dominated scholarship on blackface minstrelsy. In fictional representations and historical accounts, women performers appear to experience a deeper resistance to assuming blackface. This resistance stems in part from a social protest against the inherent racism of minstrel practices, but much more so from the ways that darkening their appearance would place them at odds with white feminine ideals. In contrast, for example, to Jakie Rabinowitz, whose stardom rests on his performances in burnt cork, Hurst's protagonist views blackface as a "smudge" that marks the demise of her stage aspirations. Hattie's commercial enterprises as family breadwinner place her firmly outside feminine norms, rendering her gender and sexuality indeterminate. As on-stage mammy, she is desexualized; her purpose is to accentuate the white beauty of the play's leading lady, who "liked to feel the flame of her own fairness as she stood there waiting for the audience to guffaw its fill of Hattie's drolleries." As blackface entrepreneur, Hattie is masculinized, which the text implies in describing how the laborious task of stirring the pots of thick face cream causes "a little arch of sweat" to come out on her upper lip "in a mustache."[12]

Although Hattie's dual commodification of blackness prevents her from achieving ideals of white femininity, the story does acknowledge how the traffic in African American culture can beget financial rewards and an accompanying rise in social status. Hattie herself may not become white, but her racial appropriations do enable the whiteness of others—namely, the leading ladies with whom she performs and her daughter, Marcia. "The Smudge" persistently employs chiaroscuro imagery to contrast dark Hattie with fair Marcia, indicating that the latter's ascent into white high society is dependent on the mother's "well-paid effort in the burnt cork."[13] Yet the story also emphasizes the fragility of Marcia's whiteness. Her upward mobility comes at the price of disguising her mother's disreputable career, her family's ambiguous background, and her own illegitimacy. Hattie's blackface may bring her daughter closer to a white feminine ideal—keeping her, as Hattie says, "like a lily"—but the twist in the plot occurs because Hattie fears that her career will not continue to whiten Marcia, but rather will blacken her.[14] Hattie's decision to forgo blackface is occasioned by the return of the improbably named Morton Sebree, Marcia's prodigal father. A mysterious and racially ambiguous figure, with skin a "rather tropical combination of dark-ivory," Morton, who hails from uncertain New Orleans stock and has most recently been living in Brazil, subtly introduces the specter of miscegenation into the story, even if the burden of blackness clearly lies with Hattie.[15] Though Morton is supposedly interested in reuniting with his daughter, Hattie suspects his ulterior motives because he finally agrees to marry her. Having squandered his family's fortune, Morton is after the money Hattie has made from her blackface cream, chastising her for handling the business in "a woman's way" and instructing her to "[i]ncorporate. Manufacture it. Get a man on the job."[16] At first, Hattie resists giving in to Morton and insists on maintaining her independence, but the dramatic climax in which she "smudges" Marcia convinces her otherwise. As a result of this incident, Hattie decides to marry Morton. It seems only sexual and domestic propriety can keep Hattie from compromising her daughter's aspirations for whiteness.

In that "smudge the size of a quarter," we see how Hattie's relationship to breadwinning through her commodification of blackness places her outside the norms of femininity, interfering in her and her daughter's opportunities to enter the ranks of white society. In "The Smudge," blackface represents the *limitations* on her sexual and financial independence, beginning with the out-of-wedlock pregnancy and single motherhood that initially propelled her to fend for herself and forced her to accept demeaning roles. The blackface number that concludes the 1927 film version of *The Jazz Singer* functions as a Hollywood happy ending in which Jakie, as Jack Robin, can have it all; in addition to the Broadway career, he has won the gentile woman and the Jewish mother, who both adoringly watch his triumphant performance. Hattie decides to leave her blackface behind, but perhaps at even greater costs. "The Smudge" ends with Hattie dreading her wedding day and the loveless marriage that awaits her; in the final lines, it remains unclear whether or not Morton has once again left her in the lurch. Sharply delineating women's limited options, a lose-lose situation produced by the dichotomy between work and matrimony, the story's resolution is achingly open-ended at best, tragically dismal at worst.

As my analysis of "The Smudge" illustrates, the critical trend to read appropriations of blackness as *solely* formative of whiteness may well have to do with the fact that the existing scholarship has focused on men. While considerations of women and gender may complicate Rogin's thesis, what then of Howe's opposing argument? Is Hurst's engagement with race and African American culture motivated by an empathetic identification with the plight of African Americans? In part, yes. Hurst's philanthropy and activism on behalf of black, Jewish, and feminist causes provide evidence of a lifelong commitment to social justice, and this political consciousness is often present in her fiction as well. But Jewish women's identification with the experiences of racism and African American suffering based on their own history of anti-Semitism is only one element in a larger story. The literary and cultural texts under discussion here may expose racial inequalities, but above all they favor themes of interracialism and pluralism, often insisting on the fluidity and illegibility of racial and ethnic identity. This resistance to ontological definition contributes further to the project of critiquing and destabilizing whiteness.

As a narrative of race mixing, "The Smudge" is indicative of the primary racial tropes that thread their way through this book. Hattie's blackface ventures may facilitate her daughter's upward movement into whiteness, but it remains unclear what the women are attempting to move *from*. Although the story maintains ambiguity about the background of its characters, Hurst's description of Hattie, with her red hair and freckles, indicates that ethnicity is not entirely irrelevant to her story. The text remains conflicted over whether Hattie's distinctive coloring qualifies her as white or detracts from her whiteness. While there had once been "a prettiness" to her freckles "because they whitened the skin they sprinkled," as she loses the beauty of youth the freckles come to function as a facial and racial stain, much the way blackface itself operates for Hattie.[17] By recoding ethnic or racial difference as class difference, however, Hurst enacts a refusal to reveal "true" identity that is similar to the Bertch women's attempt to conceal their background in order to ensure the daughter's climb up the social ladder. Describing her fight to enroll Marcia in "Miss Harperly's Select Day School for Girls," Hattie remains vague about the reasons why her daughter was nearly denied admission: "It wasn't easy. I've never told you the—strings I had to pull. Conservative people, you see."[18] Withholding specificity—she breaks off abruptly with what she "never told" Marcia—Hattie insinuates that social class was the primary obstacle in getting her daughter into this elite institution. At the same time, the specters of miscegenation and racial passing haunt this text, which hints at the possibility that its characters may be of mixed race.

Jewishness haunts this text, too, as it does much of Hurst's work that is not ostensibly on Jewish themes. A telling biographical detail, gleaned from Hurst's 1958 memoir, *Anatomy of Me: A Wonderer in Search of Herself*, sheds light on the role that the author's Jewish background played in her writing of "The Smudge." In her autobiography, Hurst, who was raised in a well-off and assimilated German-Jewish family, relates a formative incident of anti-Semitism that occurred when her mother, aspiring to higher social status, determined to enroll her daughter in a select private high school, Harperly Hall. As it turns out, the private institution that grudgingly accepted Hurst, despite what her mother called the school's *richus*, or "race prejudice," gave its name to the fictionalized "Miss Harperly's Select Day School for Girls," which Hattie's daughter attends in "The Smudge." As a pupil at Harperly Hall, Hurst was made to feel her difference from the other students, and she transferred to a public high school after a few months.[19] With "The Smudge," Hurst transposed her personal experience of near-exclusion and social ostracism due to her Jewish background on to a story about a girl who may or may not be white and whose mother's commodification of blackness at once enables and encumbers an ascent into white upper-class society. Although Hurst's Jewish heritage is often considered incidental to her writing, her fictionalization of the Harperly Hall incident is suggestive of the ways that Jewishness provides a backstory and subtext for her treatment of racial themes. Rather than simply illuminating the transformation of Jews into white folks, the absence and presence of ethnic specificity in Hurst's fiction indicate how Jewishness troubles whiteness. While the elision of ethnic particularity from the work of Jewish cultural producers is commonly read as a universalizing impulse and thus a means of whitening, this book argues that Jewish women used interracial narratives to fashion new models of pluralistic identity that called into question the black-white binary and unseated whiteness as a universal ideal.

The White Negress spans the period from the second decade of the twentieth century up until the Second World War. It thus contributes to reevaluations of modern American culture by scholars such as Ann Douglas, George Hutchinson, and Michael North, who have singled out the interwar period for the ways in which blacks and whites began to defy actively their separateness, leading to the breakdown of racial dichotomies.[20] At the same time, the turn-of-the-century influx of European immigrants led to debates about the integration of foreigners into the fabric of the nation, contributing to an amplification of nativism, on the one hand, while ushering in a new acceptance and even celebration of racial and ethnic differences, on the other. Countering ideologies of nativism and the melting pot, for example, intellectuals began to imagine a pluralistic society that would benefit from variation and diversity. In the words of Jewish philosopher Horace Kallen, cultural pluralism would bring about "a multiplicity in a unity, an orchestration of mankind."[21] In interracial encounters between African American and Jewish women, we see how these shifting ideologies of race and ethnicity coalesced with radical changes in gender roles that also occurred in these decades.

As women increasingly entered the workplace and developed professional identities, they fashioned models of New Womanhood opposed to the Victorian cult of domesticity. While the popular image of the New Woman depicted her as a white, middle-class construct, feminist critics have emphasized that many different models of female independence were in play in the early twentieth century, with recent scholarship illuminating the ethnic and racial dimensions of New Womanhood.[22] As professionally accomplished public women who led unorthodox lives outside the constraints of conventional marriage and domesticity, Tucker, Ferber, and Hurst were early-twentieth-century icons of the modern woman. I show that their Jewish backgrounds and engagement with Africans Americans and black culture were instrumental in formulating their identities as New Women. To varying degrees, Tucker, Ferber, and Hurst relied upon the labor of black women, who worked for them in service capacities. In the relationships they formed with African American women, they found both a source of identification and a means of differentiation. I explore the complexities of several of these relationships, which, though they could be classified as friendships, were unequal; the ability of the Jewish women to achieve bourgeois New Womanhood remained dependent on racial hierarchies, hierarchies that were replicated in their portrayals of cross-racial relations on stage and in fiction.

As the New Woman's demands for sexual, marital, and financial independence became intertwined with discourses of race and ethnicity, modern women also found models of feminist empowerment in black women's culture. Although this attraction to blackness rested to some degree on notions of African American women as sexually free, it would be a mistake to view Jewish women's racial appropriations as simply akin to that of "the white negro"—a figure epitomized in the work of another Jewish American writer, Norman Mailer. In his controversial 1957 essay "The White Negro," Mailer offered a portrait of the post–World War II hipster whose nonconformity is conveyed by enacting the myths of black masculinity; in James Baldwin's words, Mailer reduces the black man to a "walking phallic symbol."[23] Though no less rebellious a figure, the "white negress" performs a cross-racial identity that resists phallocentricism. While her racial crossings do at times problematically rely on stereotypical views of black femininity, these appropriations are multiply inflected in ways that both participate in and challenge blackface traditions, especially since minstrelsy was as grounded in sexism as it was racism. The figure of the "white negress" articulates a variant of New Womanhood that is distinctly racialized; she reveals how the unconventionality of the modern woman was viewed as an affront to ideals of white femininity and thus initiated a critique of whiteness as well as gender norms.

While *The White Negress* overturns previous scholarship by demonstrating that cross-ethnic identifications and tensions among women can have different valences than those among men, it is also my hope that the book's periodization will further broaden approaches to black-Jewish relations. The early twentieth century marks the first sustained contact between Jews and African Americans, as Jewish immigration and black migration brought both groups to the urban centers of the North. As a result of this contact, exchanges between blacks and Jews took place in the realm of popular culture, and African American and Jewish activists and intellectuals began to come together around the issue of civil rights. Yet it is typically the mid-twentieth-century civil rights era that gets remembered, celebrated, and scrutinized as the heyday of the black-Jewish coalition. As the civil rights era became the primary locus for most historical studies of black-Jewish relations, literary studies followed suit. The four major comparative studies of Jewish and African American literature—Emily Miller Budick's *Blacks and Jews in Literary Conversation*, Ethan Goffman's *Imagining Each Other: Blacks and Jews in Contemporary American Literature*, Adam Zachary Newton's *Facing Black and Jew: Literature as Public Space in Twentieth-Century America*, and Eric Sundquist's *Strangers in the Land: Blacks, Jews, Post-Holocaust America*—all center on post–World War II literature directly influenced by the interracial and separatist politics of the civil rights movement.[24] Illuminating a historical era that has received less attention in studies of black-Jewish relations, *The White Negress* supplies a foundation for understanding the ties that bound Jews and African Americans in the civil rights era and the tensions that drove them apart.

Although this book focuses on the black-Jewish cultural imaginary, the real affinities, conflicts, and interactions between African Americans and Jews provide important background and framework for my interpretations. I am indebted to the work of those historians who have examined the roots of the post–World War II civil rights movement in an attempt to understand the complex reasons that brought African Americans and Jews together in the fight against racial injustice. Historians such as Hasia R. Diner, David Levering Lewis, and Cheryl Greenberg have emphasized the shared sense of marginality that united members of the two groups. However, these scholars also remain attentive to the differences between the African American and Jewish experiences, demonstrating that these differences led to paternalism on the part of Jews and the reproduction of hierarchies within the very civil rights organizations that brought the two minorities together as allies.[25] This ambivalent relationship is evident in historical encounters between Jewish and black women and in the fictional interracial encounters they imagined as well. While the texts I discuss speak to the promise of collaboration and partnership between minority women, they also reveal the limitations of cross-racial identification and solidarity. These limitations often stem from the ability of Jews to claim white privilege, and in this respect this book draws on the work of scholars such as Matthew Frye Jacobson, Karen Brodkin, and Eric Goldstein, who have examined the relationship between Jewishness and whiteness. In particular, Goldstein's *The Price of Whiteness: Jews, Race, and American Identity* offers an indispensable account of the ways that American Jews constructed their identities in racial terms. Goldstein's argument that Jews are continually in the process of *negotiating* their whiteness (rather than definitively becoming white) and his contention that whiteness has its limitations as well as its privileges resonate with my findings here.[26]

The texts that I discuss in this book operate at the nexus of literature, performance, and mass culture. I begin by unearthing an early-twentieth-century tradition of female blackface performance on the stage, examining representations of minstrelsy in the memoirs and performances of Jewish vaudevillian Sophie Tucker. As I show in chapter 1, Tucker's career, even when she performed out of blackface, was strongly influenced by African American music and musicians, but it was also shaped by her Jewish background and her feminist sensibility. My analysis of her autobiography, song lyrics, performance persona, and exchanges with black women indicates that she was using both blackness and Jewishness to fashion a pluralistic, rather than purely white, American identity, while simultaneously asserting her sexual independence in defiance of traditional gender roles. By examining various permutations of the Sophie Tucker story, I hope to offset the dreary outcome of "The Smudge" with a more optimistic alternative, a narrative in which a female performer capitalized on the playfulness of the stage in the service of redefining widely accepted ideas about ethno-racial and gender relations.

Situating Tucker within scholarly debates about Jewish minstrelsy allows me to set the stage in chapter 1 for an analysis of Jewish women's literary engagements with African American culture. Chapters 2 and 3, respectively, turn to writers Edna Ferber and Fannie Hurst, who have stood charges of perpetuating egregious minstrel stereotypes on the basis of their best-known novels, Ferber's *Show Boat* (1926) and Hurst's *Imitation of Life* (1933). Because these works have been obscured by their famous musical and film adaptations and because the writers have been relegated to the category of the middlebrow, few attempts have been made to delve deeply into the novels themselves. I reconsider the charges against Ferber and Hurst by reading *Show Boat* and *Imitation of Life* closely and in the context of the writers' lives and careers. Chapter 2, for example, traces a trajectory from Ferber's treatments of Jewish identity and pluralism in her early fiction to her later depictions of African Americans and mixed-race identity. I demonstrate that *Show Boat* conforms to some established paradigms of black-Jewish cultural relations but also deviates from them due to the prominent roles of women, the uncertainty about its characters' racial backgrounds, and its metatheatrical context, which underscores the performativity of identity. In contrast to its musical adaptation, which undercuts its own progressivism by romanticizing black suffering for the purposes of white entertainment, Ferber's *Show Boat* employs multiple narratives of racial mixing in order to advance interracialism, rather than whiteness, as an ideal.

Like *Show Boat*, Hurst's *Imitation of Life* exposes the limitations of whiteness through intersecting interracial narratives: in this case, a central plot about an unequal business partnership between a white woman and her black maid and a subplot involving the maid's light-skinned daughter, who passes for white. *Imitation of Life* is often read as a facile treatment of racial issues, dismissed as another white writer's dissemination of the sentimental tropes of the mammy and the tragic mulatto. By reading this novel in the context of Hurst's career as a social activist and white participant in the Harlem Renaissance, I argue that *Imitation of Life* does not simply exploit images of black women. Instead, as a story about a white woman whose success is built on mass-producing her black domestic's waffle recipes and "Aunt Jemima"–like persona, *Imitation of Life* wavers between being a problematic reiteration of the mammy myth and an incisive exposé of the black image as a product of white fantasy. Contributing to the theme of inauthenticity announced by its title, *Imitation of Life* layers narratives of racial, gender, and ethnic passing on to one another so that it becomes impossible to decipher what is imitation from what is real—a task made even more difficult by the fact that the novel is unreliably narrated from the third-person limited point of view of its white heroine. The novel's multiple passing narratives create a system of identification in which the New Woman protagonist is aligned with racial and ethnic others who pass for white, thus further destabilizing white female subjectivity.

While Tucker, Ferber, and Hurst cannot be absolved of all accusations of minstrelsy, their work calls for a more dynamic rendering of the critical rubrics used to explain the black-Jewish cultural imaginary. Through their engagements with black culture, these women produced not an empty and static category of whiteness, but surprisingly nuanced representations of white femininity. Their lives and work attest to the fact that cross-ethnic relations can be shaped simultaneously by the process of empathetic identification and the tensions of differentiation. In my final chapter, I explore how these findings are reiterated in Zora Neale Hurston's *Moses, Man of the Mountain* (1939), a multifaceted portrayal of black-Jewish political and cultural alliances. The debate about Jewish exploitations of blackness allows me to contextualize accusations of minstrelsy leveled against Hurston, whose career was marked by her association with influential Jews, including Hurst, social activist and writer Annie Nathan Meyer, and anthropologist Franz Boas. In this chapter, I interpret *Moses, Man of the Mountain*, an expropriation of the biblical tale of Exodus that casts blacks in the role of the ancient Hebrews, as an allegory for the interethnic coalition of the early civil rights movement and a comic send-up of the Jewish blackface tradition. By concluding with an examination of a black woman writer who expropriates Jewish themes, this book underscores the interplay that takes place between these ethnic traditions and thus reframes black-Jewish relations in terms of cross-cultural exchange rather than unidirectional appropriation. In the study of comparative race and ethnicity, black-Jewish relations have largely become an occasion for exploring the production of white privilege. Filling the gender gap in the existing scholarship, *The White Negress* demonstrates that the inclusion of women's voices can also transform the black-Jewish imaginary into a site for a feminist critique of whiteness.

1 / From White Negress to Yiddishe Mama: Sophie Tucker and the Female Blackface Tradition

"The Smudge," Fannie Hurst's little-known tale about an actress's dead ambitions, was inspired by the author's attendance at a play in which a white woman performed in blackface.[1] Although Hurst did not specify the ethnicity of her blackface protagonist, in the early decades of the twentieth century some of the best-known female performers to draw on black culture for their material came from Jewish backgrounds. The list includes singers and comediennes Sophie Tucker, Stella Mayhew, Nora Bayes, and Fanny Brice, who all blacked up—or, slightly more subtly, "tanned up"—at some point in their careers and whose style of music was often referred to as "coon shouting" because it was modeled on black song (or at least white perceptions of black song).[2] Building upon my analysis of "The Smudge" in the book's introduction, this chapter highlights the case of Sophie Tucker in order to consider how the tradition of female blackface performance on the stage intervenes in current debates about Jewish minstrelsy.

I follow Tucker from her first breakthrough on the vaudeville circuit as a blackface "coon-shouter" to her long career out of blackface as a cabaret and nightclub performer. Unabashedly sexual, Tucker became known for her bawdy lyrics and suggestive performance style, a self-described "red hot mama" whose music and life choices posed significant challenges to outdated and moldering conceptions of gender and sexuality. Avowedly Jewish, yet frequently mistaken for black based on her voice alone, she was closely associated with her signature songs, "My Yiddishe Mama" and "Some of These Days," which themselves represent these different, but not unrelated, aspects of her identity. The nostalgic "Yiddishe Mama," a rare concession to sentimentality in Tucker's decidedly unsentimental oeuvre, was a paean to the singer's Jewish heritage. "Some of These Days," as she seldom let audiences forget, was written for her by the African American composer Shelton Brooks and is one of many examples of her connections to black culture and artists.

Although Tucker sang of the stereotypical Jewish mother who sacrificed her own pleasures for the sake of her children, she was far from a "Yiddishe Mama" herself. To the contrary, her songs repeatedly convey the then-revolutionary message that women, whatever their age or size, have sexual desires and the right to satisfy them, too. When it came time to pen her autobiography, it was thus Brooks's song that she adopted as her title. A narrative of the immigrant experience and a chronicle of female celebrity, Some of These Days, Tucker's 1945 memoir, offers one of the few textual representations of female blackface performance. The memoir presents a prime opportunity to explore how considerations of gender can complicate existing interpretations of blackface, revealing a more ambivalent encounter between blackness and white ethnicity. Yet Some of These Days, as its title acknowledges, is only a partial telling. This chapter thus incorporates other renditions of Tucker's story, competing and complementary accounts constructed as she continuously reinvented her public persona.[3] These personae remain tied to her engagement with African American culture and artists, as I show by analyzing the confluence and active exchange between Tucker and African American blues women such as Bessie Smith, Ethel Waters, and Alberta Hunter, who developed their own distinct and vibrant tradition of black female performance in the 1920s. Unlike Hurst's protagonist in "The Smudge," Tucker avoided being typecast as a minor blackface comic, and her career can only be described as an unqualified success. That success may be founded on and sustained by her appropriations of black culture, but it does not translate into her full assimilation into whiteness. Instead, blackface served as a somewhat painful initiation rite to the popular stage and its penchant for identity transformation, providing Tucker with a platform from which to begin a career-long complication of whiteness and of femininity. In order to understand Tucker's place within an American tradition of blackface performance, I begin by surveying this cultural institution as it evolved from the popular entertainments of the nineteenth-century minstrel show to the early-twentieth-century vaudeville stage, where it became closely associated with Jewish immigrants.

From the Minstrel Show to the Vaudeville Circuit

Since the 1990s, an exhaustive body of scholarship on blackface minstrelsy has emerged, spearheaded by scholars working within the fields of race and whiteness studies. The minstrel show, which enjoyed tremendous popularity in nineteenth-century America and is considered foundational to modern mass entertainment, featured white men who blacked up with greasepaint or burnt cork in order to impersonate African Americans, performing a variety of songs, dances, and comic sketches. The minstrel show has provided an outlet for scholars to consider how African Americans were constructed in the white imagination and, in turn, how whites imagined themselves in relation to blackness. Not surprisingly, early scholarship emphasized the undeniable bigotry of blackface minstrelsy and the ways in which it developed and transmitted a host of negative stereotypes of African Americans. "Blackface minstrelsy epitomized and concentrated the thrust of white racism," wrote Alexander Saxton in *The Rise and Fall of the White Republic: Class Politics and Mass Culture in Nineteenth-Century America* (1990), one of the first historical treatments of white American identity. This view was confirmed by the work of labor historian David Roediger, who views blackface as a principal example of the methods used by working-class men, many of them Irish immigrants, to shore up and align themselves with whiteness.[4]

Eric Lott's field-defining contribution *Love and Theft: Blackface Minstrelsy and the American Working Class* complicated the preceding studies by highlighting the ambivalence of minstrelsy. Lott maintains that blackface minstrelsy was motivated not only by an impulse to degrade African Americans but also by an erotic attraction to and fascination with blackness. Despite such contradictory impulses, for Lott, blackface minstrelsy remains an act of commodification and containment that allowed male performers and their audiences to define themselves as white in relation to a racial other. Taking an opposite tack, W. T. Lhamon argues that minstrelsy does not construct whiteness after all, highlighting instead the liberating and resistant aspects of blackface performance that made it antiracist in many of its manifestations.[5]

Despite their differing positions on minstrelsy, Saxton, Roediger, Lott, and Lhamon share a focus on men almost exclusively. Such a bias makes sense, given that early blackface acts featured male performers and drew predominantly male audiences as the nineteenth-century working-class theater was segregated along gender and racial lines. While women rarely participated in minstrelsy as performers throughout most of the nineteenth century, discussions of gender have not been absent from the scholarship. Taking note of the homosocial environment of the nineteenth-century theater, many critics have considered questions of masculinity and male sexuality. Due to its all-male context, spontaneity and ad-libbing, and the fact that white men were performing under the cover of blackness, minstrelsy made permissible topics such as homosexuality and masturbation that were taboo on the Victorian stage and in print. In the "social unconscious of blackface," performers and audience members found "a homoerotic charge," and, as Lott has famously argued, the minstrel show functioned as a carnivalesque space that allowed for the expression of cross-racial same-sex desire.[6]

Nor did the absence of female performers translate into the absence of female representation. Adding further complexity to its racial crossings, the minstrel stage was a showcase for female impersonation, an issue taken up by scholars who have emphasized the resulting misogyny and containment of women. As Marjorie Garber writes, "a black-impersonating female impersonator summed up and disempowered (or emasculated) two threatening forces at once."[7] The popular "Lucy Long," a song cited by almost every scholar of minstrelsy, was representative of the requisite "wench" number that depicted women as either objects of coquettish flirtation or shrewish wives. Such songs provided opportunities for men to boast of their sexual exploits, openly voicing male desire for pleasure, while keeping women firmly confined to boundaries. Lucy Long, the recipient of the singer's affection, is a disempowered possession; she is warned that if she "makes a scolding wife" (that is, attempts to assert any power through speech), she will be "tote[d] ... down to Georgia" and "trade[d] ... off for corn."[8] Similarly, another commonly cited feature of the minstrel show is the women's rights stump speech, which used malapropisms facilitated by black dialect to ridicule female suffrage. Nineteenth-century minstrelsy portrayed women and African Americans as objects of derision in order to express and contain anxieties about race and gender and thus asserted the dominance of white men.[9]

By the end of the nineteenth century, as the minstrel show evolved into the more heterogeneous amusements of the vaudeville stage, African Americans and women began to carve out spaces for themselves in American theater. Yet the end of the minstrel show as the dominant form of mass entertainment and the newfound acceptance of talented African American performers did not signal the end of blackface. Many black entertainers, such as West Indian comedian Bert Williams, were compelled to perform from behind the burnt cork mask. Although black minstrels often claimed to be more authentic than white ones (Williams and his partner, George Walker, called themselves "The Two Real Coons," for instance), black-on-black minstrelsy also created opportunities for resistance, since the minstrel mask could be employed to expose the fallacy and inauthenticity of white racist depictions of African Americans.[10] At the same time, acts in which whites performed in blackface, romanticizing the old plantation South to the tune of "Mammy" and "Swanee," continued to generate laughs, pathos, and applause. As it was carried over to the vaudeville stage, minstrelsy became a specialty of Jewish immigrants, including women.

Spanning roughly from the 1880s through the 1920s, when it was displaced by the new technology of cinema, vaudeville enjoyed a heyday that coincided with the influx of immigration from eastern Europe and with corresponding debates about the place of racial and ethnic minorities in American society. Several studies have made note of this confluence, touching on the role that Jews, in particular, played as performers, theater owners, and audience members.[11] A systemized big business that reached to the major urban centers of the nation, vaudeville developed in response to the diversification of American audiences, which now included not only new immigrants but also women and children. Vaudeville houses marketed themselves as sanitized, family-friendly alternatives to the minstrel show's immediate predecessors, the burlesque halls and concert saloons that offered a standard fare of lewd humor and sexual titillation, centered on the display of scantily clad and disrobing women. As Andrew Erdman has shown, such claims to decency and refinement were often overstated, and vaudeville can better be understood as "navigating the boundary between naughty and respectable," creating a form of entertainment that would appeal to and be suitable for various members of its diverse audience.[12] Catering to a clientele that transcended gender, class, ethnic, and, at times, racial lines (while most theaters remained segregated, some admitted African Americans to sit in separate gallery sections), vaudeville developed its reputation as a purveyor of heterogeneity. Shows were comprised of music, dance, acrobatics, magic, gender and ethnic impersonations, novelty acts, melodrama, and comedy, with a female solo performance usually serving as the highlight. While blackface minstrelsy had once been the order of the day, vaudevillians served up a wide range of racial and ethnic impersonations, with dialect comics doing turns as Hebrews, Italians, Dutch,

Irish, Chinese, and Native Americans. These impersonations traded on caricature and crude ethnic humor, but they also gave shows a polyphonic quality, and, for many performers, opened up spaces to craft their own representations.[13]

While critics such as Michael Rogin, Harley Erdman, and Jeffrey Melnick have focused on Jews in the entertainment industry who used performance as a means to make their own difference invisible, facilitating their assimilation into the white mainstream by the 1920s, there is ample evidence to suggest otherwise.[14] Provocatively titled *Jewface*, a recent compilation of tunes from the vaudeville era indicates that the so-called Hebrew comedians were extending and adapting minstrel conventions to performances of Jewish identity, largely based on antiSemitic stereotypes. Jewface's descent from blackface is evident in quips like "All Cohens look alike to me," a pun on "All Coons Look Alike to Me," a popular minstrel song made more notorious by the fact that its composer, Ernest Hogan, was African American.[15] In what may be the most comprehensive study of Jews in vaudeville thus far, Ted Merwin demonstrates that Jews remained highly visible as Jews during the Jazz Age. Variety stage headliners included Al Jolson, Eddie Cantor, George Jessel, Sophie Tucker, Belle Baker, and Fanny Brice, the last of whom went on to become a main attraction of the Ziegfeld Follies. Merwin goes "beyond blackface" to illuminate the explicitly Jewish content of their acts, from Baker's "Eli, Eli," Cantor's "My Yiddisha Mammy," and Tucker's "My Yiddishe Mama" to Brice's repertoire of Jewish girls in "Sadie Salome, Go Home," "Second-Hand Rose," and "Oy, How I Hate That Fellow Nathan." For Merwin, many of these performances display ethnic pride, loudly declaring the performers' Jewish identities.[16] Far from rendering Jewishness invisible and enacting assimilation, these performers were working out images of Jewish ethnicity on the stage. Like African American minstrels, they simultaneously laid a tentative claim to authenticity and challenged stereotypes through exaggerated performance.

Drawing similar conclusions to Merwin's, Pamela Brown Lavitt questions previous interpretations of Jewish minstrelsy by directing attention to women performers specifically. In her article "First of the Red Hot Mamas: 'Coon Shouting' and the Jewish Ziegfeld Girl," Lavitt examines two Jewish Ziegfeld Follies stars, Nora Bayes and Anna Held, who vocally performed "encrypted" blackness since it was not portrayed visually as in blackface, but through the singing of "coon songs," the genre that also secured Tucker's fame. Reading their gendered performances as asserting "white Jewish ethnicity," rather than constituting a category of empty whiteness, Lavitt argues that these women represent a transitional period in which Jews were "crossing from 'black' to 'white' from race to ethnicity." Directly countering Rogin, she concludes that "coon shouting did not so much separate Jews from blacks" as "joined them at the hip in performance history."[17]

It is not incidental that Lavitt arrives at these conclusions by turning to representations of the female body. The vaudeville stage has also been a crucial locus for scholars Susan Glenn and M. Alison Kibler, whose studies of female performers explore how the presence of women in American theater undermined the nation's gender and cultural hierarchies. Working in a venue that encouraged and rewarded identity transgression, women used the stage to challenge traditional gender roles and conventional ideals of feminine beauty. Amid the social upheavals of the fin de siècle, "female performers became agents and metaphors of changing gender relations," writes Glenn, who finds in female spectacle the emergence of New Womanhood and the foundations of modern feminism.[18]

Both Glenn and Kibler are further attentive to the ways in which the racial masquerades that take place in vaudeville contribute to women performers' abilities to live up to and defy established gender ideals. Opening her book with a discussion of the "Sarah Bernhardt Effect," referring to the French actress who made a number of sensational appearances in the United States between 1880 and 1918, including several vaudeville runs, Glenn illustrates how the reworking of conventional femininity is bound up with discourses of ethnicity and race, and specifically with the interplay between Jewishness and blackness. Though her background was shrouded in some mystery, Bernhardt's alleged Jewishness was integral to her star persona, allowing her to play upon notions of the Jewish woman as the sexually exotic *belle juive*, or beautiful Jewess. In her 1907 memoir, *My Double Life*, Bernhardt also drew an important link between her unconventional femininity and blackness. Discussing a hairdresser's attempt to tame her disobedient curly locks, the actress describes her hair as that of a "white negress." The term is worthy of some consideration. After all, why not simply liken her hair to that of a "negress"? How is the adjective "white" functioning in this appellation? In the context of this story about her hair, an aspect of her appearance that is somewhat mutable (though, in the episode, it is also intimated that the only option may be to shave it all off), "white" serves as a reminder of her *potential* distance from "negress." Though she is classified in racialized terms, the qualifier hints at an ability to shape her identity in a way that would de-racialize her, retaining her white-ness and eliminating the negroid. Her unruly curls, a physical feature often associated with Jewishness as well as blackness, can be made to conform to standards of feminine obedience. But it is equally significant that Bernhardt strongly resists such a taming, reveling instead in disor-der and insisting that rebelliousness is the source of her appeal.[19] As the autobiographical anecdote suggests, Bernhardt's feminine mystique de-rived from being simultaneously identified with blackness, Jewishness, and whiteness.

The same might be said of another "white negress," Sophie Tucker, whose identity—and, more important, the multiple narratives she con-structed about it—continually defied easy categorization. In addition to negotiating between her Jewish immigrant and American identities, and between black and white through her "coon shouting," Tucker also bridged male and female domains. Her unconventional life choices—beginning with her decision to pursue show business over domestic-ity—are reflected in her lyrics and her suggestive performance style, both of which display her sexual agency as well as her refusal to abide by standards of female behavior, ranging from sex and marriage to dress and dieting. Although early in her career Tucker compared herself un-favorably to her French predecessor and counterpart, stating, "I can't be a Sarah Bernhardt and be fat," Tucker's weight would become to her public persona what Bernhardt's hair was to hers: an outward emblem of her resistance to conformity. As she later put it, "Without a little fat here and there, mostly in the right places, I just wasn't Sophie Tucker!"[20] Like Bernhardt, Tucker played up and reveled in her status as an unruly woman, while simultaneously moving among the categories of Jewish-ness, blackness, and whiteness in ways that highlighted and heightened the unruliness of gender and race.

Blackface, White Negress

In tune with Glenn's argument that female performers broke the mold of Victorian womanhood to forge images of modern femininity, scholars of Jewish women's cultural history have claimed Tucker as a feminist foremother. For these scholars, Tucker is the first in a line of iconic female entertainers, extending from her non-Jewish contemporary and some-times rival Mae West to singers and comediennes known for their Jewish pedigrees and styles, such as Totie Fields, Belle Barth, Barbra Streisand, Bette Midler, and Joan Rivers (a line that could be further extended to

include, most recently, Sandra Bernhard and Sarah Silverman).[21] June
Sochen and Joyce Antler, for example, view Tucker as a reformer—"an
early prophet of women's liberation," in Sochen's phrase—who used entertainment to challenge sexual double standards, bringing discussions
of female sexuality into the public sphere.[22] In her study of Jewish comediennes, Sarah Blacher Cohen identifies Tucker as the "pioneer" taboo
flaunter; the first Jewish woman to treat sex with savvy, good-natured
humor, she became a "comic assaulter of Gentiles' puritanical society."[23]
In his autobiography, Eddie Cantor fondly remembered Tucker singing
"the words we used to write on the sidewalks," and Tucker herself, in
her usual forthright manner, declared "sex" to be "funny, not necessarily
intense and tragic the way the playwrights such as Ibsen made it out to
be."[24] With her irreverence for sexual mores, Tucker exemplifies broader
claims that Jews contributed an openness about sexuality to American
culture. While scholars such as David Biale have explored the impact of
Jewish-authored eroticism on late-twentieth-century American culture,
from the fiction of Philip Roth and Erica Jong to the comedy of Lenny
Bruce and Woody Allen, this phenomenon can be traced back to the
notable Jewish presence in vaudeville with its affronts to Victorian standards of morality, especially as they applied to women.[25]

Just as this book asks how considerations of gender complicate
our understanding of minstrelsy in the black-Jewish imaginary, it is
equally important to consider how race and ethnicity impacted Tucker's shattering of sexual conventions. Like the self-conscious edginess
of Bernhard and Silverman today, Tucker's taboo breaking cannot be
separated from the carnivalizing of racial tropes that takes place in the
interstices between Jewishness and blackness. As someone who got her
start in blackface and went on to emulate African American performers and modes of performance, Tucker's sexual frankness often appears
to be channeled through her appropriations of black sexuality. Thus,
the tendency might be to argue that blackness gave Tucker a mask for
free expression, as it did for nineteenth-century white minstrels and
Mailer's "white negro." Yet while Tucker should not be fully pardoned
of minstrelsy's offenses, her engagement with black culture cannot be
reduced so easily to caricature. She frequently displayed an uneasiness
about inheriting minstrelsy's legacy, and many of the narratives that
she constructed can be read as rejoinders to the forces of containment,
inherent in the blackface tradition, that placed limits on women's expression of agency and sexual desire. By infusing her act with Jewishness as well as blackness, Tucker succeeded in subverting the sharp

dichotomy between black and white as well as prevailing attitudes about gender and sexuality.

Tucker's rise to stardom speaks to the anxieties about and fascination with racial difference in the early decades of the twentieth century, a period paradoxically marked by deep racism, nativism, and anti-Semitism and by a celebration of the faddish exoticism of racial and ethnic differences. Born Sonya Kalish in 1884, Tucker immigrated to the United States as an infant and grew up in an Orthodox Jewish community in Hartford, Connecticut, where her family's kosher restaurant became the site of her earliest performances. Soon after her high school graduation, in what would become the first in a series of defiant acts, Tucker eloped with the twenty-year-old Louis Tuck; their son, Albert, was born two years later. Motherhood and an unhappy marriage did not sit well with Tucker, who found herself back in her parents' restaurant, working in the kitchen and entertaining the customers with her singing. Among the patrons were Jacob Adler and Boris Tomashevsky, leading figures of the Yiddish theater, who encouraged Tucker to join their troupes. Bolstered by their encouragement, Tucker decided instead to pursue the spotlight in American theater. Leaving her small son behind with her family, she set off on her own for New York in 1906. Despite rough beginnings, in just a few years Tucker managed to establish herself as a vaudeville sensation, an imposing presence with her hefty size, stylish gowns, and belting voice. Her decades-long career spanned multiple musical trends—including, in her own catalog, "coon shouting, ragtime, jazz, swing, the hep-cat, jitterbug, and zoot-suit"—all of them indebted to the influence of black cultural forms.[26] These shifting trends were also reflected in the changes in her billing. Initially labeled the "World-Renowned Coon Shouter," Tucker went on to become known as the "Mary Garden of Ragtime" (a reference to the popular opera diva of the time), the "Queen of Jazz," and "The Last of the Red Hot Mamas." Tucker's metamorphoses did not only occur across the duration of her career but also within individual performances; her solo act required her to move among personae and styles, combining "coon songs" with Jewish music, friendly banter with blue jokes and hot numbers peppered with subtle and not-so-subtle double entendres.

Although Tucker's brief foray into film was an admitted failure, her aptitude for self-invention enabled her to continue as a nightclub and cabaret performer after vaudeville's demise, with bookings up until her death in 1966.[27] Published in 1945, her autobiography, *Some of These Days*, recounts the vicissitudes of her career in the first half of the twentieth century. Written in an upbeat voice that exudes the same sassy, confident tone as her singing, *Some of These Days* combines show business memoir with immigrant narrative to draw parallels between the identity shifting of her theatrical career and the process of reinvention undergone by the new American, developing an analogy that underscores the performativity of ethnic identity. Reviewing the book, BBC critic Wilson Midgely cautioned, "if it's literature you're looking for, don't look this way," but he went on to call *Some of These Days* a "brilliant record" of immigration in which Tucker's success on the stage is shaped by "the ancestral pattern of which she was made."[28]

Opening the autobiography with the story of her birth, which occurred en route from Russia to Poland as her mother was in the process of immigrating to the United States, Tucker establishes herself as a figure of in-betweenness, a mediator between cultures, born between the Old World and the New. In explaining that she "was born on the road," Tucker clarifies that the road to which she refers is not "the Orpheum, the Pantages, Keith, or any of the other circuits I've traveled since," alluding to the correspondence between her passage to America and "the road" of the traveling vaudevillian, where she achieved her fame and ostensibly solidified her transformation from immigrant into American.[29] Continuing this parallel between life's beginnings and the self-makings that occur through popular entertainment, Tucker describes multiple rebirths in the course of her narrative. Her continuous reinvention suggests that her identity is never quite stable and exposes the complexities in the processes of identity formation, transformation, and cross-identification.

In *Some of These Days*, Tucker's shifts in racial, ethnic, and gender identity can be traced through changes in her name, further underscoring the performative tenet that language, including acts of naming, constitutes identity. While most immigrants' names were Americanized upon arrival in the United States or after immigrants found the nominal sign of their ethnicity to be detrimental to attaining social and economic opportunities, Tucker's initial name change occurred even before she and her family set foot on American soil. Fleeing his inscription into the Russian military, Tucker's father, Charles Kalish, immigrated to the United States ahead of his wife and unborn daughter, becoming friends with an Italian AWOL named Charlie Abuza along the way. When Abuza suddenly died, Tucker's father "prudently helped himself to the Italian's papers and moniker" in order to elude the Russian authorities. "Don't ask me what the United States Immigration officers made of an

Italian who couldn't speak anything but Russian and Yiddish," Tucker sardonically reflects. "But it was as 'Charles Abuza' that Papa got into this country, and found a job in Boston."[30] Here, Tucker alludes to the dichotomy established between Americans and foreigners, whereby European immigrants, whatever their country of origin, became undifferentiated masses. In the United States, Tucker's family made no attempt to reclaim their former name or Anglicize their adopted Italian moniker; when her father opened a kosher eating establishment in Hartford, he called it Abuza's Home Restaurant. By detailing this episode, Tucker establishes not a narrative of assimilation through name changing, but rather the replacement of one ethnic identity with another—if in name only, since the Abuzas settle in a Jewish community and continue to observe Orthodox religious practices. The adoption of the name "Abuza" may serve as a disguise for her family and a partial shedding of their Jewish heritage upon their immigration, but it also operates more as a complication of their identity rather than a clear-cut sign of impending Americanization.

Significantly, however, Tucker's name changing does not end there. She goes on to discuss several other name changes, which are related more to gender than ethnic identification. Early in her narrative, she becomes "Sophie Tuck" when she runs off to marry Louis Tuck. Quickly growing dissatisfied with her marriage, she runs off again—this time alone to New York in order to make her way in show business, creating a scandal in her community when she leaves her child behind. Upon getting her first job singing in a café, Tucker again changes her name. Since "Mrs. Tuck didn't sound right for a singer," she tells the manager her name is "Sophie Tucker," and "[r]ight like that a career was born." The first of several theatrical rebirths for Tucker, this moment differs from her previous renamings, which were dictated by patriarchal convention (that is, her name was changed to coincide first with that of her father and then with that of her husband). In contrast, this *self*-naming brings Sophie Tucker, the fiercely independent, no-holds-barred performer, into being. As notable as the elongation of her name from Tuck to Tucker is the elimination of "Mrs.," a sign of her sexual independence and fledgling feminism. Although Tucker married two more times, she continued to keep the stage name she conferred upon herself; in fact, in a further reversal of gender norms, one of her husbands, disappearing into the shadow of her fame, became known as "Mr. Sophie Tucker."[31]

While Tucker was to develop a reputation as a sexual free spirit, manifest in lyrics that express her resistance to marriage and traditional gender roles, early in her career she was better known for her crossing of racial lines. Her first major breakthrough was facilitated by her adoption of blackface. In contrast to many of the costuming and publicity decisions to which she credits herself, Tucker's induction into minstrelsy cannot be easily categorized as an incident of self-making, since it was dictated by a man, and, significantly, was a role she tried hard to resist. As Tucker tells it, when she auditioned for an amateur night at a Harlem theater, the manager declared, "This one's so big and ugly the crowd out front will razz her. Better get some cork and black her up. She'll kill 'em."[32] According to Kibler's study of women on the vaudeville stage, female performers not only defied traditional gender roles through their pursuit of the spotlight but also defied standards of feminine beauty due to their less-than-svelte figures, darker skin tone, or more mannish appearances. Often, this failure to conform to ideals of femininity derived from their ethnic difference, since most of the performers were from immigrant backgrounds. In this case, "so big and ugly" was likely the manager's coded reference to physical characteristics associated with Tucker's Jewishness. In line with Rogin, Kibler argues that blackface became a way for women such as Tucker to emphasize their white beauty beneath the makeup. However, it is clear from Tucker's first performance in burnt cork that blackface does not operate in this way. Appearing on stage with her face smeared with cork, black gloves, a red bandanna covering her blond hair, and lipstick "painted" in a "grotesque grinning mouth," Tucker may win over her audience, but after the show she struggled to remove the cork, "to get the nasty mess out of my ears and eyes" and "the roots of my hair"—a struggle that reduced her to tears.[33] As in Hurst's "The Smudge," blackface functions for Tucker as a shameful stain that could not be easily wiped away after a performance; it compromised her already precarious respectability as a woman, and she became, to her Jewish community back in Hartford, "a whore, in the unvarnished language of the Scriptures."[34] Examining this episode, Antler argues that the painfulness of blackface lay in its denial of Tucker's femininity, not her ethnicity, but the two aspects of her identity are perhaps more intimately intertwined than it first appears.[35] Tucker was made to black up because her looks did not conform to ideals of white womanhood, and the strategies of resistance that she developed in response challenged definitions of both whiteness and femininity. It was by openly expressing her ethnicity that she began to issue that challenge.

Despite the pain it caused her, Tucker's successful blackface debut accelerated her ascent from amateur shows to the vaudeville circuit. Billed as a "Refined Coon-Shouter" and a "Manipulator of Coon Melodies," she seemed doomed, however, to the fate of typecasting that befell Hurst's fictional Hattie Bertch and other real-life performers like Jewish actress and singer Stella Mayhew, whose girth similarly led her to spend twelve years performing in blackface, typically in mammy roles. Pleading with managers to "leave off the black," complaining that the recalcitrant cork was staining her white clothes, Tucker repeatedly tried to resist this forced appropriation of blackness. At one point, she attempted to lighten herself by changing to "high-yellow," or mulatto, makeup, but was warned by a more seasoned blackface comedian that "[u]p North they don't know anything about the high yellow. Here you're either black or white."[36] Because Tucker's resistance was not voiced as a direct protest against the racist underpinnings of minstrelsy, her refusal to embrace blackface can itself be read as an expression of her desire for whiteness. Tucker seems to have fallen victim to the adage "damned if you do and damned if you don't," charged with racism for perpetuating offensive stereotypes and for trying to break free of the blackface yoke. If Tucker endeavored to prove herself white through blackface (or through its shedding), this determination became coupled with—and was, perhaps, even dependent upon—a desire to undercut the rigid binary between black and white.

As her act evolved, Tucker finally did hit upon a formula that allowed her to simultaneously proclaim her whiteness and to challenge this racial dichotomy when she began making a habit out of removing her glove to expose her white skin at the conclusion of her performances. Upon first glance, this gesture appears to reinforce the causal relationship between blackface and the immigrant achievement of whiteness posited by Rogin, lending support to the notion that, for women as well as men, blackface helped to construct white identity. Yet a careful analysis of Tucker's narration of this innovation indicates that the whiteness she exposed to her audience was ethnically marked. In fact, the removal of the glove evolved because she found her "greatest difficulty was convincing the audience I was a white girl": "My Southern accent had got to be as thick and smooth as molasses. When I would pull off one of my gloves and show that I was white there'd be a sort of surprised gasp, then a howl of laughter. That season I started interpolating Jewish words in some of my songs, just to give the audience a kick."[37] Tucker's account is full of surprising contradictions. Although Antler claims that Tucker resented blackface because it disguised her femininity, not her ethnicity, keeping her "from appearing as herself, like the prettier girls," in examining this episode, she also suggests that Tucker incorporated Yiddish "to declare . . . who she really was."[38] In transposing the desire for femininity on to a declaration of her Jewish roots, Tucker reveals how these aspects of her identity work together to complicate whiteness and its relationship to blackface. Since spectators supposedly knew that the performances they were attending were not authentic, Tucker's difficulty in persuading the audience of her whiteness may indicate a failure to distinguish between the illusion on the stage and the performer's identity behind the mask, but it may also allude to the fact that, as a Jewish immigrant, her white identity was not a given. Tucker did not simply dispute the many misreadings she encountered throughout her career, but instead took pleasure in confounding audience expectations, as suggested by her decision to insert Yiddish words into her act. It is further unclear how to read the Jewish inflection of her performance. On the one hand, it is possible to understand the expression of her Jewish identity as added confirmation of her whiteness. On the other hand, her statement that the Yiddish words were intended to "give the audience a kick" suggests that her Jewishness functions as yet another troubling of her ethnic identity. The shifts in her performance—from black to white to Jewish—unsettle notions of whiteness and racial difference, as well as their relationship to one another.

Even when Tucker finally succeeds at getting out from under the blackface mask, her white identity remains unstable, becoming more, rather than less, complex. According to her account of events, the blackface phase of her career came to an end due to a fortunate accident in which her wardrobe trunk was lost, forcing her to go on stage without makeup or costume. This modification in her act is again facilitated by a male manager who reassures the initially distraught Tucker that "[a] good-looking, hefty squaw like you don't need black-make-up."[39] Although Tucker appears unperturbed by this comment, insisting that "a good-looking hefty squaw" is "quite another bill of goods" than "so big and ugly," it is significant that the description carries with it a racial resignification of its own. The unusual word choice did not go unremarked by Tucker; in the draft of her autobiography, she inserted the parenthetical comment, subsequently removed, "funny he called me a squaw."[40] At times used as a general disparaging term for a woman, comparable to "broad," the word "squaw" originated as an ethnic slur for Native American women. Images of Jewish and Native American women would comically clash in Fanny Brice's performance of "I'm an Indian," in which she sang the part of the "yiddishe squaw" Rosie Rosenstein. Alan Trachtenberg argues that Brice's song and other Jewish vaudeville routines with western motifs, like Edward Meeker's memorable "I'm a Yiddishe Cowboy," depict Jews as outsiders who were simultaneously adapting their identities to become part of a national narrative—in Brice's case, by aligning herself with "native" Americans, rather than "alien" immigrants.[41] Tucker's reassignment—from the woman whose appearance was "so big and ugly" that she needed to be concealed behind blackface to the "good-looking hefty squaw" who could appear without it—may bring her closer to Americanness, but through an identity that remains distinctly racialized and decidedly "other."[42]

Tucker's description of her first appearance out of blackface continues to complicate matters, displaying her whiteness while muddying its representation. Walking out on stage without her usual disguise—an experience she compares to the near-nakedness of appearing in "tights and a G-string"—she explains to the audience (who supposedly is anticipating a blackface act), "You-all can see I'm a white girl. Well, I'll tell you something more: I'm not Southern. I grew up right here in Boston, at 22 Salem Street. I'm a Jewish girl, and I just learned this Southern accent doing a blackface act for two years."[43] Although Tucker states that the audience can "see" she is white, the monologue that follows implies that they might need more than ocular verification; furthermore, it is unclear from this monologue what it is exactly that makes her white. She intimates that her geographical roots uphold her claims to identity, since she relies upon her Northern upbringing to prove that she is "a white girl." This dichotomy between the North as white and the South as black simultaneously echoes and problematizes the notion that in the North "you're either black or white." As with the removal of her glove, Tucker immediately follows the revelation of her whiteness with a declaration of her Jewish identity, supporting Merwin's claim that Jewish vaudevillians maintained their visibility as Jews, rather than effacing their ethnicity. Like the earlier incorporation of Yiddish words into her blackface act, it is unclear exactly how this announcement of her Jewish background functions: does it counter her claim to be a "white girl" or legitimate her whiteness, at the very least making her not-black?

This uncertainty about how to read Tucker's declarations of Jewishness is, I argue, precisely the point. Tucker may have been, in Antler's words, declaring "who she really was," but the ambiguity as to what exactly *Jewishness* is undermines existing interpretations of blackface minstrelsy. Contrary to Rogin's argument that blackface "wipe[d] out all difference except black and white," Tucker's continual reminders of her immigrant background, staged in conjunction with her blackface and "coon shouting," muddled, rather than retained, "the fundamental binary opposition." In contrast, too, to Rogin's claims that minstrelsy bestowed unfettered mobility upon Jewish performers, Tucker's experiences reveal that burnt cork—the "nasty mess" that could not be easily removed after her act—also operated as a restrictive force, especially for women.

By 1909, after three years of making her name in blackface and being hailed as an innovator of "coon shouting," Tucker began voicing strong opposition to the theatrical legacy that had been passed down to her. In that year, the *Cleveland Dealer* ran an interview with the "dialect singer" in which she confessed that though she once "had a pretty fine opinion of [herself] as a Negro impersonator," she now realized that the type she was impersonating was itself a fabrication of the stage and had little basis in reality. Tucker was disillusioned of her self-conception when she took her first trip to the South and noted that audiences there did not respond to her act with the same enthusiasm as Northern ones. She took it upon herself to conduct an investigation of her own. "I began to walk about the streets and study the Negro character of the South intimately," stated Tucker. "I realized how far away I and other performers were from the real thing. The conventional stage representation is a descendent from minstrel shows, and that which I considered a real impression of a living race was nearly all a stage creation. During my trip South, I found many interesting and admirable points about the Negro of the South that would make good material for the stage."[44] Though blackface, in one form or another, would remain in vogue for at least two more decades, Tucker's realization was, in many ways, a timely one. Her objections to blackface minstrelsy echoed the slowly shifting tides of the nation's racial ideologies. The year 1909, for example, marked the founding of the National Association for the Advancement of Colored People (NAACP), one of whose stated objectives was to combat negative media representations of African Americans. Yet it is also significant that Tucker's rejection of minstrelsy did not extend to other uses of blackness as fodder for spectacle. She implies in the interview that, while she would forsake theatrical traditions whose intent was to burlesque, she would instead take her cues from more direct observation of African Americans. As I discuss in the following sections, she does go on to seek ways to incorporate "interesting and admirable" attributes of black culture into her stage artistry, producing what might be described as Afro-Semitic performances that continued to trouble rather than stabilize her relationship to whiteness.

Mammy Act or Sister Act?

Even as Tucker began distancing herself from the wearing of burnt cork, vowing to be "through with blackface forever," she did not wholly separate herself from appropriations of blackness, given her style of music and performance.[45] Out of blackface, Tucker not only continued to shout "coon songs," but she also expanded her repertoire to become one of the first non–African American women to sing the blues and dance the shimmy. The inclination may be to align Tucker with other Jews in the music industry who took their inspiration from black music. According to Melnick, male composers such as George Gershwin and Irving Berlin solidified their own identities as white Americans by acting as intermediaries between African American culture and the white public. Like these men, Tucker unquestionably benefited from a racial system in which whites avidly consumed African American culture as long as it came in white packaging. The story of W. C. Handy's legendary "St. Louis Blues" exemplifies the racial dynamics of commercial entertainment. Though "St. Louis Blues" was a signature song for black chanteuse Alberta Hunter, who popularized it on stage, Tucker became the first woman to record the song in 1917. It turned out to be a hit, further boosting Tucker's career, but not necessarily opening doors for black women like Hunter who originated and developed the blues genre.[46]

Though inevitably shaped by racial hierarchies, Tucker's relationship with African American performers and musicians does appear to be more interactive than it was for many Jewish men in the industry. In contrast to the fabled "little colored boy" whom Irving Berlin was rumored to keep in his closet to aid him in writing his music,[47] Tucker's access to black culture can be attributed to documented exchanges that were, at times, reciprocal rather than solely exploitative. In her study of early-twentieth-century African American women performers, Jayna Brown writes that "Tucker's case furnishes one of the strongest arguments for the historical precedent of cross-racial/interclass alliance," while also noting that this instance of "relatively mutual respectful recognition" was "perhaps the exception and not the rule."[48]

An admirer and champion of black talent, Tucker took advantage of her increasing fame to promote actively African American musicians and to oppose outmoded theatrical conventions held over from minstrelsy. In addition to featuring songs by Jewish Tin Pan Alley composers such as Berlin, she debuted the work of African Americans such as Shelton Brooks and the songwriting duo of Noble Sissle and Eubie Blake.

FIGURE 1. Sophie Tucker appears on a 1915 sheet music cover. Popularized by Tucker, "It's All Your Fault" was written by a songwriting team that included the famous black duo of Noble Sissle and Eubie Blake (Music Division, Library of the Performing Arts, New York Public Library, Astor, Lenox and Tilden Foundations).

She was also one of few performers to appear on stage in integrated acts at a time when the theater was just beginning to push the boundaries of segregation. The stage functioned as an important testing ground for the extension of such boundaries, especially through black-Jewish couplings, many of them still circumscribed by minstrelsy. In the Ziegfeld Follies, numbers featuring Bert Williams alongside Fanny Brice and Eddie Cantor satirized commonly received ideas about race, exposing its fluidity rather than affirming its fixity. In the 1916 Follies, for example, Brice, a first-generation American and descendant of European immigrants, sang the comic novelty song "Nijinsky" while a blackfaced Williams parodied the leaps of the Polish-Russian ballet dancer in the role of *Scheherazade*'s Golden Slave. For the dramatic finale of the 1919 Follies, Williams and Cantor both donned blackface, sharing the stage as Tambo and Bones in a rendition of Irving Berlin's "I Want to See a Minstrel Show" accompanied by the "Follies Pickaninnies."[49]

While Tucker incorporated black women into her performance routines, usually as backup dancers or comic foils, her defiance of racial boundaries was not limited to what took place on stage. Nor, as it turned out, did she protest the indignities of blackface only for herself. Emboldened by her new power as a headliner, Tucker began to dictate her own terms. When the performer Ida Forsyne, known for her Russian dances and Topsy routine, appeared in Tucker's act, Tucker defied the management and insisted that the black woman go on without burnt cork. Aware of Forsyne's difficulty finding work as a chorus girl in an industry that offered few opportunities for African Americans to begin with and even fewer for dark-skinned dancers, Tucker stepped in and employed her coperformer as a maid for two years.[50]

Forsyne was one of several black women employed by Tucker who allowed her to gain proximity to black culture and acted as go-betweens with other African Americans in the entertainment world. Tucker frequented black clubs, such as the integrated Dreamland Café in Chicago, looking for material. There, she was particularly impressed by the work of Alberta Hunter, a soloist with the fabled King Oliver's Creole Jazz Band. Recalling that Tucker "sent her maid, Belle, for me to come to her dressing room and teach her songs," Hunter refused Tucker's presumptuous request that she make herself available, but she did not necessarily shut down the possibility of exchange, allowing Tucker's piano player to "come over and listen and get everything down."[51] Tucker had more success with Ethel Waters, who agreed to Tucker's offer to pay her "a little money" in exchange for private singing lessons.[52] Rather than simply unidirectional theft, there is evidence of give-and-take between Tucker and blues women such as Hunter and Waters, who were also known to attend Tucker's performances. Hunter may have refused to be at Tucker's beck and call, but she admitted that Tucker influenced her as well and that she was "crazy about her as a singer."[53] Blues historian Daphne Harrison concludes that, in this era of "constant borrowing, stealing, or co-optation of style, content, and material," the two women drew from each other: "Tucker sought the rhythms, emotional expressiveness, and black dialect inflections and Hunter learned stage presence and the use of sexy innuendoes from Tucker."[54] One has only to listen to Hunter's hilarious ribaldry in songs such as "Two-Fisted Double-Jointed Rough and Ready Man" and "My Handy Man" from her comeback in the late 1970s and early 1980s to hear echoes of Tucker's lusty and playful repartee; but one hears, too, Hunter's incomparable ability, well into her eighties, to take thinly disguised innuendo to the next level through her characteristic yelps and winking asides.

The relationships Tucker formed with women of color, even when they were employed as her backstage maids, added texture to her appropriations of black culture. Unevenly balanced though they were, many of these were genuine friendships, buttressed by the shared difficulties of surviving in a male-dominated business. Tucker remained sympathetically aware that the obstacles and double standards were much more stringent for black women—indeed, almost impossible to overcome, which is why so many of these women found themselves waiting on white actresses. A significant portion of *Some of These Days* is devoted to one of these women in particular, Mollie Elkins, who, until Elkins's death from cancer in 1930, was Tucker's closest friend and confidante. (Not incidentally, the woman who became one of Tucker's closest friends after Elkins's death was the Chinese American physician Mom Chung, famed for taking in World War II soldiers and entertaining them in her celebrity saloon.[55]) Tucker's narration of her friendship with Elkins reveals the Janus-faced quality of her interchanges with African Americans, illuminating how these cross-racial associations had the effect of both reifying and unsettling racial categories. Tucker's success was undoubtedly enabled by Elkins's support, making Tucker the beneficiary of a discriminatory racial system that severely curtailed opportunities for black women; yet their companionship, in many ways, defied the strictures of the color line.

Tucker and Elkins met in 1909 when Tucker landed her first—and what would become her only—spot in the famed Ziegfeld Follies.

Dressed in a leopard-print suit, she starred as the Jungle Queen in the second-act number "Moving Day in Jungle Town," leading a coterie of jungle girls, white hunters, and men dressed as animals. The upbeat number with its rhythmic dancing and cameo by a Teddy Roosevelt impersonator was a crowd-pleaser, but Tucker became a victim of her own success. According to her account, Follies stars Nora Bayes and then her replacement, Eva Tanguay, were fearful of being upstaged by Tucker, and Tanguay eventually conspired to have her fired from the show. Disappointed by her conflicts with the show's female luminaries, Tucker, wandering backstage, came upon Elkins, a veteran of black vaudeville who was supporting herself as a ladies' maid. Desperate for someone to talk to, Tucker thrust aside their racial differences, musing, "Black or white, what does it matter?" In further defiance of the color line, the two women became fast friends, bonding over the shared disappointments of their theatrical careers. The initial encounter is marked by another renaming when Elkins, in an effort to console Tucker, begins calling her "Patsy," explaining that the "patsy" is the one "nobody paid no mind to" but who would become "the hit of the show."[56] The nickname, which stuck throughout their twenty-year friendship, turns out to be prophetic while also pointing to the disparity of their careers. Tucker eventually overcame this low point to make it big in vaudeville, due, in no small part, to Elkins's forgoing of her own ambitions in order to devote herself to her friend's advancement.

Although the two women met at a time when Tucker was still occasionally working in blackface, the sequence of events as Tucker portrays them in her memoir suggests that Elkins's entrance into the narrative occurs almost concurrently with Tucker's shucking off of burnt cork. This slightly doctored chronology leaves the impression that Elkins became a replacement for blackface, providing Tucker with an embodied form of blackness against which she could assert her whiteness. However, this reading is complicated by the fact that Tucker often emphasizes the likenesses between the two women. Their similarities are enhanced by a fact that Tucker often notes: fair-skinned Elkins is light enough to "pass anywhere as white." Describing their friendship, Tucker writes, "We might have been any two girls off for a day at the beach, instead of two adventurers with wildly beating hearts and hopes too big and glittering to put into words."[57] Though Tucker highlights their interchangeability, a conjoining rather than contrasting of selves, it is, after all, Tucker who ultimately lives out their shared ambitions, effectively taking on the black woman's role and identity when a prejudicial system interferes in Elkins's own stage aspirations.

In a reversal of the patronage system, Elkins initially becomes Tucker's "benefactress."[58] The more experienced and financially secure ladies' maid aids Tucker in restarting her career after she loses her coveted spot in the Follies. Lending the unemployed actress money, as well as clothes, jewelry, a suitcase, and makeup, Elkins in effect transfers part of herself to Tucker through this exchange of material belongings. In a draft version of Tucker's memoir, the gown Elkins lends her for her comeback becomes "'our' dress."[59] Elkins even goes so far as to lend herself; wisely ensuring her indispensability, she proposes that she begin accompanying Tucker on the road as her dresser, insisting, "It'll make you look important. Your personal maid."[60] While Elkins initially poses as a maid, over time it becomes increasingly difficult to see her as anything other than Tucker's personal maid, especially when the performer begins earning enough money so that she can afford to pay her friend. The language Tucker uses in her memoir, referring to Elkins with the possessive, "my Mollie," to indicate her affection and her ownership, further establishes their hierarchical relationship as mistress and servant.

The hierarchy also appears to be reinforced when Tucker begins incorporating Elkins into her act, an event she again claims to be fortuitous rather than planned. Realizing in the midst of a performance of the Dixie melody "My Southern Rose" that she had forgotten to request a chair for the number, Tucker called to Elkins from the stage to supply one for her. "Out came Mollie, toddling as only colored people with their inborn sense of rhythm can," Tucker renarrates the scene. "Toddling to her own humming, and grinning broadly. . . . The audience began to laugh. 'Here's yo' chair, honey chile,' and off she toddled, to a roar of delighted laughter."[61] Ensuring that Elkins receives credit for this scene-stealing cameo, Tucker requested that she come out and take a bow at the end of the act. Although Tucker writes that Elkins's performance is due to an "*inborn* sense of rhythm," there is a striking contrast between Elkins's stage persona and the refined and well-spoken woman Tucker depicts as her companion throughout her memoir. In this scene, Elkins, hamming it up in the role of the mammy, functions as a comic prop for the white actress. Though her appearance on stage presumably serves to highlight Tucker's whiteness, we should recall that the fair-skinned Elkins—minus the toddling, grinning, and dialect—would easily be mistaken for another white woman. The cultural construct of the mammy typically operates by means of vivid contrast with white womanhood—the juxtaposition created, for example, when amply pro-portioned Mammy (Hattie McDaniel) tightens the corset of the slender Scarlett O'Hara (Vivien Leigh) in the film classic *Gone With the Wind*. The big-boned Tucker side by side with the more conventionally beauti-ful, white-appearing Elkins presents more of a visual conundrum.

Just as Tucker insisted on crediting Elkins for her on-stage role, few renditions of Tucker's life story neglect the influence of her close friend, whose memory continued to be invoked even years after the black wom-an's death. A 1961 *Daily News* article on Tucker's serial marriages, for example, makes reference to Elkins, describing her as the star's "maid, companion, friend, and booster."[62] "I wish I had a penny for every time I have mentioned the name Mollie from the day she left me," Tucker wrote in her notes for her memoir. "I have never stopped wishing she were with me."[63] In 1953, at Tucker's star-studded Golden Jubilee, celebri-ties gathered to pay tribute to their colleague by re-creating the story of her fifty years in show business. Standing out amid entertainers such as George Jessel, Eddie Cantor, Milton Berle, Tallulah Bankhead, and Ger-trude Berg was Ralph Bunche, intellectual, diplomat, and activist, who had recently become the first African American recipient of the Nobel Peace Prize for negotiating an Israeli-Arab armistice. Adding his voice to the mix by narrating the tale of a friendship formed in defiance of racial barriers, Bunche describes Elkins as an "angel from heaven," a "friend during rough times," and recalls how she "nursed" the "sick and penni-less" Tucker "like a sister."[64]

One of the most poignant moments in *Some of These Days* takes place not at Tucker's sickbed but at Elkins's deathbed, where Tucker keeps vigil in the midst of a grueling performance schedule. With faint echoes of the white woman's teary farewell to her black servant in *Imi-tation of Life*, Tucker relates the memory of holding Elkins's "thin and wasted" hand as the dying woman declares her love for her "Patsy," closes her eyes, and, with a final sigh, takes her leave. Fittingly, given Elkins's transference of her own identity to Tucker, the memoirist eu-logizes her longtime companion with these words: "She took a piece out of my life when she went."[65] Like many of the episodes between Elkins and Tucker, this valediction conveys the ambivalence underly-ing their cross-racial relationship, wavering between a sentimentalized sob story in which Elkins takes a final bow for the lifetime act of self-sacrificing mammy, and a touching tribute to a friendship whose bonds were sealed by a legitimate sense of sisterhood. As I discuss in the fol-lowing section, Tucker's public engagement with black blues culture was fraught with ambivalences similar to the ones that categorized this personal relationship.

When a Red Hot Mama Sings the Blues

Elkins's role in Tucker's life story becomes even more pronounced when we consider that Tucker owes the very title of her autobiography and perhaps the most significant breakthrough of her career to the other woman's influence. Encouraging Tucker to work directly with African American musicians—indeed, shaming her by asking, "since when are you so important you can't hear a song by a colored writer?"—Elkins introduced her employer to Shelton Brooks, then an unknown composer.[66] In 1911, Tucker debuted what would become her trademark song, Brooks's "Some of These Days," to overwhelming applause, winning her, in the words of one newspaper account, "overnight fame and a nation of admirers" as well as an engagement at the Palace Theatre, New York's top vaudeville house.[67] The benefits of this collaboration were mutual, as the debut turned out to be an important break for Brooks, who was to become known for standards like "Darktown Strutters' Ball." Yet Tucker acknowledged that the songwriter's race prevented him from achieving recognition anywhere near her own. In a poetic tribute to the song that "helped" her "more than friend or kin," Tucker recalls her first encounter with "Some of These Days" when "a chap whose skin was dark" approached her with the now famous melody. Rhymes Tucker, "I assure you, his name isn't in headlines or in books / But it's engraved on my heart, Shelton Brooks."[68] Periodically in public appearances, Tucker would trot out her original copy of Brooks's sheet music, carefully preserved, in order to express her gratitude to the musician whose composition came to define her celebrity image.

Somewhat deceptive in its simplicity, Brooks's song does not at first appear to be as blatant in its expression of female agency as some of Tucker's later music, but a closer examination reveals "Some of These Days" to be highly representative of her unsentimental approach to love and her predilection for overturning conventional relations between men and women. The song's message is directed at a man who has thrown a woman over. Rather than passively accepting this fate or bemoaning her lost love, the woman retaliates with a warning:

Some of these days
You'll miss me, honey.

Some of these days
You're gonna be so lonely.
You'll miss my hugging.
You're gonna miss my kissing.
You're gonna miss me, honey
When I'm far away.

As the last line quoted above implies, the singer has no intention of wait-ing around in the hope that her man will return; in fact, she will be the one to move on. Tucker's original 1911 recording unequivocally makes this point when the woman, deciding "two can play at this game," hops a train and leaves town, while the man, realizing his error, returns to an empty house.[69] As sung by Tucker, "Some of These Days" displayed the big voice of a fully confident woman who knows her own worth and recognizes that her lover will regret the mistake of leaving her behind.

The motif of the woman who resists passive victimhood to best the man at his own game crops up repeatedly in Tucker's oeuvre. "I Know That My Baby Is Cheating On Me," one among many of Tucker's pointed critiques of monogamy, builds to the revelation, "But maybe, my baby, don't know that I'm cheating too." Here, as elsewhere, Tucker sings not only of her inability to be fooled by her lover's indiscretions but also of the man's foolish ignorance that women can assert their own sexual agency—as she puts it, "this prim-rose path is no one-way street."[70] Tuck-er's career-making venture with Brooks was thus historic for more than its cross-racial collaboration: "Some of These Days" became Tucker's sig-nature number because it helped launch her reputation as a performer who flouted gender conventions, especially by singing freely of women's sexual desires. Tucker was already moving in this direction by the time of her collaboration with Brooks, gaining notoriety for songs like the whorehouse number "There's Company in the Parlor, Girls, Come on Down" and the "Angle Worm Wiggle," whose accompanying lascivious gyrations led to back-to-back arrests on charges of obscenity in 1910.[71]

When Tucker compared her first experience of walking on stage with-out blackface to wearing nothing but "tights and a G-string," the analogy was, in many ways, an apt one. The postblackface phase of her career was defined by her adoption of a risqué persona that contrasted sharply with her minstrel character, which was based on the "absence of overt (het-ero-)sexual appeal."[72] While Tucker's declarations of her Jewish identity worked to disrupt the implied racial binary of the blackface tradition, the continued complication of identity that occurred after her blackface phase translated into performances of unabashed sexuality, further establishing her distance from ideals of white womanhood. As Linda Mizejewski points out in her study of female performers in the Ziegfeld Follies, it was the conventionally beautiful, svelte, and glamorous chorus girls who became icons of national womanhood; Jewish women, like Brice and Tucker, provided the inverse relation that produced the whiteness of these "Glorified American Girls," as they were billed. In comically rendering Jewishness and ethnicity on the Follies stage, Brice was the "embodiment of everything the Ziegfeld Girl was forbidden to be," writes Mizejewski.[73] Tucker may have made only one ill-fated appearance in the Follies, but Mizejewski's conclusions are applicable to her public persona as well. Tucker's continued association with blackness and her persistence in reminding audiences of her Jewish background made her a point of contrast, enabling the coding of idealized female sexuality as white and nonethnic. Predating and running parallel to various other constructs of New Womanhood, such as the flapper and the vamp, Tucker articulated an emancipative model of female sexuality that feminist critics have read as transgressively empowering. Borrowing from jazz argot to reinvent herself as a "red hot mama," Tucker adapted themes from working-class black women's blues to project a racialized sexuality; the persona she created thus facilitated her subversion of gender norms by positioning her in contradistinction to white feminine ideals. A consideration of Tucker's engagement with blues culture thus further complicates the oppositional paradigms that interpret Jewish appropriations of blackness as either motivated by shared identification with suffering or an exploitative desire that enables the achievement of whiteness.

The central motif of "Some of These Days"—what Peter Antelyes calls the "two timer, two-timed"—contains seeds of the genre that would develop between 1910 and 1930 into black women's blues.[74] While blues women persistently sang of being "done wrong" by men, Hazel Carby has compellingly argued that they were able to transform such mistreatment into statements of female agency and empowerment, often by using strong vocal intonation to parody feminine weakness that might be expressed in lyrics. Blues women simultaneously signified on the heartaches of heterosexual romance to address issues of race and class, expressing the plight of being poor and black in a white-dominated world. Even when composed by men, the blues became associated with a vibrant tradition of black women's orality, inseparable from their interpretations by a generation of singers that included Alberta Hunter,

Ethel Waters, Ma Rainey, Victoria Spivey, Ida Cox, Bessie Smith, Clara Smith, and Mamie Smith. Observing the autonomy and frank eroticism expressed by both the style and subject matter of blues singers, Angela Davis locates in their music the origins of contemporary black feminism. For blues scholars such as Davis, Carby, and Daphne Harrison, blues women constituted themselves as sexual subjects through song, rejecting men and marriage, celebrating women's mobility and decrying domestic entrapment, and enacting violence as rebellion against and lesbianism as an alternative to compulsory heterosexuality.[75]

More than any other non–African American woman of her time, Tucker is closely associated with this tradition of female blues singers, many of whom she knew personally and whose performances she sought out, admired, and imitated. Her story is inseparable from the history of the blues and from the racial disparities of commercial entertainment that shaped this history. While she became, as previously discussed, the first woman to record the blues in 1917 with Handy's "St. Louis Blues," her lack of availability several years later led to the first blues recording by a black woman. In 1920, composer Perry Bradford approached General Phonography Company with his idea for race records that would be marketed to African Americans. Although Bradford intended for a black singer to record his compositions, the head of the record company had other ideas, hoping to sign Tucker. According to different reports, Tucker turned out to be either ill or under contract with another label. Thus, in a landmark event for music history, African American stage-show performer Mamie Smith, whose style resembled Tucker's due to her experience in black vaudeville, was asked to record Bradford's "Crazy Blues" in Tucker's place. The song became an instant hit, leading to a million-dollar industry of race records and ushering in the blues craze, dominated by black female singers, that corresponded with the Jazz Age and the Harlem Renaissance.[76]

Even as the blues became the rightful domain of black women, however, Tucker's name continued to be associated with black music and its artists. While some fans may have casually referred to Tucker as the "Jewish Bessie Smith," in an ironic reversal, African American vocalists Ada Ward and Sarah Martin both advertised themselves as "The Colored Sophie Tucker."[77] Meanwhile, Tucker, once "The Mary Garden of Ragtime," had refashioned herself by 1916 as "The Queen of Jazz" with her all-male band, the Five Kings of Syncopation. "Contrary to recent published statement," one review informed its readers, the Five Kings "are not Creoles, but regular Jewish boys, and good-looking."[78] Recalling her time with the Five Kings in her memoir, Tucker writes, "I worked the boys to a frazzle. I was a regular Simon Legree."[79] Although Tucker appears to lay claim to whiteness by identifying herself with the infamously heartless slave owner from Harriet Beecher Stowe's *Uncle Tom's Cabin*, her white identity remains fraught by the ambivalence of her gender identification. Tucker may crown herself "queen," but in becoming a Legree, she identifies with masculinity (an association reiterated by friends and co-workers who frequently called her "Boss," in part to denote her reputation as diva). By 1924, Tucker was underscoring her female sex appeal by adapting black slang to pronounce herself a "red hot mama." As the Jazz Age came to a close in 1929, she signaled the end of the era by reinventing herself as "the Last of the Red Hot Mamas"— a sobriquet that would remain firmly affixed for the rest of her career. Though the foreign press tended to refer to her as an "original" American "'blues' singer," this was not a mantle Tucker claimed for herself.[80] Interestingly, none of her billings explicitly mentioned the blues, in part because the term conjured melancholy associations that did not mesh well with Tucker's upbeat, fun-loving persona. Instead, she was more apt to be perceived as the "blonde banisher of the blues."[81]

Given her appropriations of black music in its many forms, it is not surprising that Tucker is viewed as an interloper by African American intellectuals and chroniclers of music history. It is likely that Zora Neale Hurston had Tucker in mind when she lamented "what the world has suffered from the white damsels who try to sing Blues."[82] As scholars often note, the blues are a distinctly African American form. They are the outcome of the "peculiar social, cultural, economic, and emotional experience of" African Americans in the United States, according to Amiri Baraka in his seminal work of music criticism, *Blues People*. For Baraka, "the idea of a white blues singer seems an even more violent contradiction of terms than the idea of a middle-class blues singer." Angela Davis likewise argues that the forthright sexuality of the blues derives from "an ideological framework that was specifically African-American," connected to the postemancipation experiences of former slaves who had been prohibited from the sovereignty of sexual partnerships.[83]

Even as they defend the sanctity of blues and jazz as uniquely African American art, inseparable from a diasporic history of oppression and protest, many critics acknowledge that white emulation of black music has been a source of pride, providing evidence of black cultural achievement and supremacy. In his 1977 dissent from the black arts movement, J. Saunders Redding captures this ambivalent response when he looks back at the Jazz Age to lambaste white appropriations of black music and simultaneously to suggest that such cultural usurpation may have its upside in approximating an integrationist ideal. Redding begins by taking to task white jazz musicians such as Paul Whiteman and torch singers such as Tucker who played and sang black songs "without even a nod in the direction of the Negroes who composed them." (Redding's complaint is not entirely valid; as I have discussed, in appearances and recordings, Tucker frequently paid tribute to black composers, especially Brooks.) Describing African Americans' reactions to this phenomenon as "an unequally proportioned mixture of pride, amusement, and contempt," Redding explains that the response was "amused and contemptuous" because Tucker and other white singers "could not match the individual talents and sensibilities—to say nothing of the special American Negro consciousness—of Rainey, Smith, and other Negro artists and entertainers." He goes on to argue, however, that pride largely canceled out scornful amusement because the creations of African Americans were "being accepted as genuine and authentic expressions of American national culture."[84] The pride many African Americans felt in the white appropriation of their music may be due in part to an important distinction noted by Baraka when he compares white attraction to black music during the Jazz Age to the previous blackface and minstrel traditions. While minstrelsy "sought to burlesque certain facets of Negro life (and, superficially, the music associated with it)," white blues and jazz musicians of the 1920s were drawn to black music because they found it "emotionally and intellectually fulfilling."[85] Black critics may disparage the kind of cultural theft of which Tucker stands accused, but beneath the disparagement lies an awareness that such cross-cultural contact testifies to the ways that African Americans have indispensably contributed to and shaped American culture.

Although it is important to consider her music as derived from black sources, it would be a mistake, as I have suggested, to label Tucker a blues singer. Tucker covered and even originated blues songs, but it was rare for her to sing the classic twelve-bar blues associated with African American musicians. Nor, as Redding observes, do Tucker's renditions articulate a black consciousness, or double consciousness, which was conveyed through effects of call and response and signifying enabled by the formal properties of the blues. For Tucker, the blues were one part of her variety act, and it might be more accurate to describe her performances as bluesy or blues-inspired, or, better yet, as the fusion of black women's blues with a tradition of Jewish women's comedy and vaudeville

showmanship. What interests me here is how this synthesis enabled a rebellion against regulatory norms that gains much of its force from—and
would not be possible without—its interethnic framework.

Even Tucker's songs that do not technically qualify as blues were infused by a feminist sensibility that derives from her engagement with
black women's oral culture. Noting that blues women rarely sang about
being wives or mothers, Davis describes the female protagonists of the
blues as "independent women free of the domestic orthodoxy of the prevailing representations of womanhood through which female subjects
of the era were constructed."[86] Similarly, Tucker's persona is never tied
down by domestic responsibilities or by marital, or monogamous, commitments. "No One Man Is Ever Going to Worry Me" proclaims the title
of one her songs, while another announces, "I Ain't Taking Orders from
No One." For the rambling women of the blues, the ability to hop freight
trains and travel was often an imaginary protest against gender and
economic constraints that prevented most black women in this period
of migration from moving about as freely as men did. Tucker likewise
assumes the character of a woman whose mobility rivals that of men, as
summed up by titles like "Mama Goes Where Papa Goes (Or Papa Don't
Go Out Tonight)" or, more boldly, "Stay at Home Papa (Your Mama's
Going Out Tonight)."

Characterized by a sassy realism about heterosexual relationships that
eschews the romantic or the sentimental, Tucker's songs, like those of
her black contemporaries, function as anthems of female independence.
Ethel Waters's pronouncement in "No Man's Mamma Now" that "I can
come when I please / I can go when I please" is echoed, for example, in
Tucker's "I'm Living Alone":

> I'm a one-ticket gal, free as the breeze
> I go where I like, I do as I please
> When I lock up my apartment, I've got all the keys
> I'm living alone and I like it.
> If I wanna play gin, I stay up and I play gin
> I come home when I want to and when I walk in
> There's nobody growling at me, "Where the hell have you been?"
> I'm living alone and I like it.

In an era where more and more women were entering the workplace,
"I'm Living Alone" also advocates women's financial autonomy, noting, "No man buys my dresses or pays for my minks / If I get a new
hat trimmed with posies and pinks / There's no darling husband yelling

take it off it stinks."[87] Such lyrics do more than enact fantasies of female emancipation; beneath this is also a trenchant feminist critique of the puritanical codes of morality dictating sexual and familial conventions. For example, in encouraging women to view their husbands' adultery as an opportunity to do the same, to see it as "the chance / That you've been waiting for years," Tucker's many songs about infidelity move beyond blaming men to a universal questioning of the unrealistic expectations of long-term monogamy and, with that, the institution of marriage.[88] This critique of matrimony as a cultural norm is made clear in another hymn to independence, "Me and Myself." Contrasting her situation with "married folks who don't get along," she expresses her contentment at being unattached for she is always able to "get along with me and myself."[89]

While Tucker and black blues women renounced marriage and, in fact, any dependent heterosexual relationship in their music, this renunciation did not extend to sex. Tucker's representations of female eroticism and sexual agency have much in common with the frank treatments of sexuality in the music of blues women.[90] In the lyrics of songs by Bessie Smith, Clara Smith, and others, sexual desires were thinly coded through imagery (Clara Smith's "Whip It to a Jelly") and passionately expressed with just the faintest hint of teasing ambiguity (Bessie Smith's "I'm Wild About That Thing"). Food, as the first example suggests, was a ubiquitous metaphor. "I need a little sugar in my bowl," croons Bessie Smith, only to get more explicit with "I need a little hot dog between my rolls."[91] In the blues, a good man may be hard to find, but a hard man is usually good to find. Contrary to most popular music of the time, the blues allowed women to voice the craving for and fulfillment of physical pleasure, while transforming men into sexual objects. One of the best examples of this is "My Handy Man," a song recorded in the 1920s by Ethel Waters and Victoria Spivey, which uses double entendres to signify on the old joke that men are only useful for their handiness around the home. Through references to masculine chores, like cutting the lawn ("Never has a single thing to say / While he's working hard / I wish that you could see the way / He handles my front yard"), as well as traditionally female ones ("he threads my needle, creams my wheat"), the blues singer creates a litany of sexual acts aimed at woman's erotic satisfaction.[92]

Like black female blues singers, Tucker's expressions of female sexuality had to walk a fine line between upholding stereotypes of exotic promiscuity and claiming empowered agency. For women performers of the era, the double entendre provided a way to assert control over and through language, to be naughty without appearing smutty.[93] Given vaudeville's prohibition against "vulgarity" (a line Tucker frequently crossed, asked to remove songs like the seemingly innocuous "Who Paid the Rent for Mrs. Rip Van Winkle When Rip Van Winkle Went Away?" from her act), more practical concerns also motivated her preference for insinuation over explicitness.[94] She typically works through implication, encouraging her listeners to fill in what's left unsaid, as in the aptly titled "Oh! You Have No Idea." Just as blues women strategically employed satire and irony as a guise for social protest, Tucker's use of wit and humor, which Sarah Blacher Cohen views as part of a larger tradition of subversive Jewish comediennes, prevents her affronts to sexual ethics from moving into the territory of the salacious.[95] In snappy one-liners, she counsels other women: "When your red-hot papa's steam-pipe gets cold, tears won't heat it up," or "Love is like home-cooking, good and wholesome, but all men like a little piece of mutton on the outside now and then."[96] A more graphic example of wordplay can be found in her riff on the axiom "And I believe in giving tit for tat / That's the way I live / And I'm entitled to a hell of a lot of tat / For what I've got to give"—lines later lifted by Kander and Ebb's vaudeville-homage musical *Chicago*, transported to the same-sex setting of the woman's prison cell, and subsequently immortalized on film by Queen Latifah as Matron Mama Morton.[97]

Not only are men sexually objectified in Tucker's music, but they typically lack the stamina to compete with her own insatiable appetites. She sings of men whom she leaves "bruised" and "crippled," or about the Hollywood star she made love to "a year ago in January" and who is still "unconscious yet."[98] As in the "tit for tat" line, Tucker comically draws attention to her own body in order to boast of her sexual capaciousness; she admits, for example, that it "takes more than good looks to satisfy a girl my size" or proposes that her extra "meat" means "there's more schmaltz to sizzle when" she "turn[s on] the heat."[99] In constantly poking fun at her weight, while contending that her extra pounds enhance her desirability, Tucker challenges conventional notions of female attractiveness. In "I Don't Want to Get Thin," she explains,

> Why should I when I'm all right as I am?
> Those slender-waisted mamas make me laugh
> My goodness, men like to see a little fore and aft.
> I don't want to reduce
> Furthermore, what's the use?
> When the men follow me around like Mary's lambs.

The girls who talk of dieting
Jeez, they get on my nerves.
If you want to keep your husband straight
Show him a lot of curves.[100]

In the blues, references to body type, more so than skin color or other racially defined physical features, provided commentary on white beauty standards. Singing "I'm a big fat mama, got the meat shakin' on my bones [2x] / And every time I shake, some skinny gal loses her home," the blues woman espouses pride in the physicality of her body.[101] Tucker works in a similar vein of protest humor that transforms into an asset what the dominant culture constructs as weakness.

With the above reference to "schmaltz," Tucker continues the tradition she began with the insertion of Yiddish words into her blackface act. Often conveyed linguistically and interspersed as jokes between and in the midst of songs, Tucker's allusions to her Jewish background provide comedic overtones that augment the multidimensionality of her performance. In "I Don't Want to Get Thin," her accompanist corrects her claim that she'll "eat anything" by reminding her, in reference to kosher dietary laws, that she "won't eat ham." Tucker responds, "Well, we'll leave politics and religion out of it."[102] But Tucker rarely left her Jewish identity out of it. In her performances, Jewishness did not simply represent who Tucker "really was"; instead, it functioned as another complicating ingredient that bedeviled attempts to pin down her identity. Perhaps there is no better example of this than the spicy, ethnic stew of "There's Something Spanish in My Eyes," in which she slyly revises her own origins to the sound of castanets: "My mother is Jewish / My father is Irish / Which proves that I'm Spanish / And I love you." Like so many of Tucker's songs, this one, too, is a declaration of womanly passion, and the resistance to ethnic definition becomes intertwined with her sexual self-representation, building to the rousing finale: "I'm your chiquita / Your sweet senorita / Your hot kosher meat-a / I love you."[103]

Comparing Tucker with her fellow singer-comedienne and friend Fanny Brice, Sochen argues that both women succeeded by "blending the particular with the universal," which allowed them to connect with gentile as well as Jewish audiences. For Sochen, the universality of their performances depended on transposing racial and ethnic histories and traits on to representations of femininity. Herein, for Sochen, lies an important contrast between the two: while Brice took on the identity of the female victim, hapless in love, always waiting for the man who was sure to be her downfall, Tucker was the self-reliant sexual "aggressor."[104] Like Tucker, Brice got her start as a "coon-shouter," once claiming that her residency in Harlem (she lived for a time on 128th Street) gave her inside knowledge of "proper" black pronunciation.[105] In her first amateur appearance, she sang "If the Man in the Moon Were a Coon."[106] Her 1910 performance of another "coon song," "Lovie Joe," led to her long-term employment with the Ziegfeld Follies, where her comedic talents were honed in Yiddish, not black, dialect portrayals. Although Brice, who changed her name from the ethnic-sounding Fania Borach, did not grow up speaking Yiddish and had to learn it for her roles, she always insisted that her Jewish comedy derived from a strong racial identification. In response to accusations that she was "standing apart" from or mocking Jews, she insisted, "I *was* the race, and what happened to me on the stage is what could happen to them. . . . They identified with me, and then it was all right to get a laugh, because they were laughing at me as much as at themselves."[107] Yet biographer and theater historian Barbara Grossman identified in Brice the constant struggle to "be accepted, admired, and respected by [the] dominant culture."[108] For Brice, acceptance meant assimilating to dominant norms of white femininity, from her well-publicized nose job (earning the quip from the perpetually acerbic Dorothy Parker that she "cut off her nose to spite her race") to her aspirations to break free of ethnic comedy in order to pursue serious, unaccented dramatic roles.[109] In the story told by Grossman, Brice saw Jewishness as limiting, more than invigorating, her art; she may have triumphed by blending the particular with the universal, but her ultimate wish was to transcend her ethnic roots, to forsake the particular for the universal.

Tucker, in contrast, remained unfazed by occasional reviews complaining, for instance, that her "'Yiddish' asides" were "funny to a relatively small proportion of the average audience" and "not at all in keeping with" her "attempts at artistic presentation."[110] More so than combining the universal with the particular, Tucker blended elements of different minority cultures in ways that unsettled whiteness as the universal norm. Nor, contrary to Sochen's claims, can her carnivalization of racial and ethnic tropes be separated from her upending of gender and sexual conventions. In African American culture, Tucker found models of female comportment and empowerment that were outside of, indeed opposed to, genteel white America. By co-opting blackness, she constructed alternatives to the standard-bearers of white femininity, while also creating an image that countered prevailing stereotypes of Jewish womanhood themselves shaped by the desire to imitate mainstream American ideals.

Analyzing early-twentieth-century stereotypes such as the "ghetto girl," Riv-Ellen Prell showed that largely negative representations of Jewish women resulted from the anxieties of assimilation, the "fight to become American." The "ghetto girl," for example, arose from the immigrant desire to approximate bourgeois respectability through consumption; yet her attempts to copy the latest styles, for instance, led only to garish imitations. In such stereotypes of Jewish women, materialistic desires displaced sexual ones (leading, ultimately, to the stereotype of the frigid Jewish American Princess [JAP], the butt of many a sexist Jewish joke, who can only reach orgasm with her father's credit card in hand). Writing of the excessive consumerism of the stereotypical Jewish woman, Prell also explains that "her wanting was never connected to her own productivity."[111] Because the ghetto girl's working-class identity placed her uncomfortably at odds with middle-class norms of domesticity, a related stereotype emerged of the "Jewish Woman in Search of Marriage," who pinned her hopes for mainstream acceptance on finding a man to provide for her. In Prell's analysis, popular culture portrayed Jewish women as anxiously aspiring to, but always remaining at a distance from, the comforts and securities of white, middle-class America.

In some respects, Tucker's identity as "aggressor" may appear to align her with negative portrayals of Jewish women who were (and are) often depicted as loud, pushy, excessive, and gaudy. However, in firmly rejecting marriage and actively voicing sexual desire, Tucker challenged the dominant stereotypes of Jewish womanhood of her time. Rather than substantiating the popular misconception, Tucker's identity supports Susan Glenn's argument that immigrant Jewish women—especially those employed in the garment industry and active in labor movements—were instrumental in constructing notions of working-class New Womanhood.[112] While Tucker does not disassociate herself from materialistic desires, her self-sufficient approach to consumerism differs from the modus operandi of Prell's ghetto girls. In Some of These Days, Tucker confesses her obsession with fashion, emphasizing the importance of "dress[ing] smart"; however, far from a slavish imitator, she is a trendsetter whose styles were intended to push boundaries of feminine respectability rather than adhere to them.[113] Wearing a tight sheath skirt with side slit or claiming that she was the first woman to sport pants in the United States, Tucker uses dress to portray herself as scandalously ahead of her time, in revolt against prevailing conventions of sexuality and gender. Tucker celebrates consumerism not because it leads to assimilation, but because, for her, it is couched in an adamant refusal of patriarchal dependence. In "Me and Myself," she explains, "When I find that I need a lot of new clothes / I don't have to run over to any fat old tyrant in Oxford bags / And call him Darling when I'd like to kill him / Myself sez to me, Soph . . . you need a lot of new clothes / . . . And I go out and buy just what I want."[114] Tucker may need a man to satisfy her carnal needs, but the material ones she takes care of on her own; her wanting is connected to her own productivity. While the stereotype of the ghetto girl, like its later manifestation in the JAP, depicted Jewish women as failed (because over-the-top) imitators of white bourgeois culture, Tucker constructed herself in opposition to middle-class domesticity, embracing indecency rather than aspiring to gentility. Through her cross-racial mimicry, she formulated a critique of patriarchal and puritanical conventions and acted out a fantasy of sexual and economic liberation in which women were equal to men. While her success was predicated on her enduring engagement with black culture, it was not contingent on her assimilation into whiteness because she refused to accept the terms of white femininity. Instead, as I address in the final section, Tucker's identity continued to rest on a pluralistic enactment of Jewish ethnicity as well as blackness.

A Colored Voice, a Matza-Soprano

From "Some of These Days" to her adaptation of the central tropes of black women's blues, Tucker's career continued to be defined by her association with black music and African American producers. Rather than affirming her identity as white, Tucker's affiliation with African American culture often led her to be mistaken for black. Unlike her negative response to blackface, Tucker did not resist such racial misrecognition. Instead, she capitalized on and took pride in her "'colored' voice," as one review described it, and her ability to pass vocally.[115] In her memoir, she recalls a concert in Holland where her initial appearance on stage caused the audience to gasp and cry out in Dutch, "My God! she's a white woman!" Tucker is amused to learn that the audience assumed that she was a "colored star" based on her "syncopation and deep voice" and that shopkeepers advertised her records as "By the American Negro Singer— Sophie Tucker."[116] In Jean-Paul Sartre's 1938 novel, *La Nausée* (*Nausea*), Tucker's ability to transcend racial categories becomes a vehicle for a literary and philosophical meditation on the instability of identity. At the novel's conclusion, diarist-protagonist Antoine Roquentin sits in a café, indulging his existential crisis while listening to jazz. The song is unmistakably "Some of These Days," but Roquentin assumes the hoarse-voiced singer is "a Negress" and the songwriter a "Jew with black eyebrows." Realizing that "the Jew and the Negress" have justified their existence through the creation of art, Roquentin decides that he, too, can save himself by writing a book. In *Jean-Paul Sartre and the Jewish Question*, Jonathan Judaken understands the confusion over Tucker's and Brooks's identities to be purposeful on Sartre's part, intended to have the ironic effect of emphasizing the uncertainty of being at the very moment that the existential hero has hope of combating the meaninglessness of life.[117]

While scholars such as Rogin argue that Jews became white through their commodification of black culture, these misreadings of Tucker, which persist throughout her career, provide evidence to the contrary. The close ties that Tucker maintained with Jewish culture also indicate that assimilation is not as neat and straightforward as Rogin makes it out to be. If Tucker was identified by her "colored voice," she was also, in the words of comedienne and sitcom star Gertrude Berg, a "matza-soprano."[118] Tucker's Jewish identity remained an essential component of her private life and public persona. Though she was an "American Negro Singer" to the Dutch, the publicity for her European tours more often touted her as "America's foremost Jewish actress."[119] As Tucker's career progressed, she not only continued to invoke her ethnic roots in her performance but also used her fame in the service of domestic and international Jewish causes, attempting to arrange refuge for Jews from Hitler's Germany, speaking on behalf of the new state of Israel, and raising money for various philanthropic institutions. Although Tucker might be identified as a secular Jew, known for sending out a yearly batch of Christmas cards, evidence abounds of her continued observance of Jewish holidays and religious rituals, from keeping kosher in some form (albeit laxly) to saying kaddish for her parents.[120]

Tucker's experience also refutes the claim that blackness simply stood in for Jewish ethnicity, becoming "a mask for Jewish expressiveness, with one woe speaking through the voice of another," in Irving Howe's words.[121] Instead, for Tucker, inscriptions of blackness and Jewishness comfortably coexisted. "Some of These Days," Tucker's notable collaboration with a black songwriter, often became intertwined with public statements of her Jewish identity. Decades after she debuted the song on the vaudeville stage, she used it in promotional advertisements for the Zionist Organization of America.[122] On another occasion, after inserting a Talmudic tale into a speech at a dinner for the American Federation of Actors, she apologized to the rabbi present for "muscling in on his territory," suggesting that "just for that, if he wants to, he can get up and sing 'Some of These Days.'"[123] In a 1927 recording, she added an autobiographical introduction in which she discussed how Brooks's song enabled her conversion from a "young Connecticut lass" who was "as green as grass" with "lots of nerve, no class" to a star of the stage. This introduction includes several references to her immigrant identity, from "green as grass" to the "Yiddishe hunch" that kept her from being fooled by men who promised her stardom in exchange for "dates." Although fashioned as an American success story in which the immigrant overcomes the "rough" road that was especially "tough . . . for a girl alone," the recitation serves to remind audiences of her Jewish background, rather than occlude it.[124]

In one of the more perplexing instances of blackness and Jewishness existing side by side, the same Dutch audience that mistook Tucker for a black woman also demanded that she not leave the stage without singing her popular tune "My Yiddishe Mama." First performed by Tucker in 1925, "My Yiddishe Mama" became, like "Some of These Days," a staple of her act and is evidence of the fact that she maintained a pluralistic public identity as a Jew throughout her life. Though Tucker's autobiography takes its title from Brooks's song, acknowledging the influence of black culture and artists on her life and career, the memoir is dedicated to her Jewish accompanist Jack Yellen, "a grand song writer" who wrote "My Yiddishe Mama" for her after her own mother's death. "Old and gray" with a "wrinkled brow," a fixture of a "humble East Side tenement," the archetypal Jewish mother of Tucker's ballad sacrificed her needs and pleasures to find "her jewels and treasures . . . in her baby's smiles."[125] At first glance, the sentimental song might seem a radical departure for a "red hot mama" who not only openly demanded a woman's right to sexual pleasure but also had put her career before her own child. Noting that the figure of the "Yiddishe Mama" was antithetical to Tucker (and, for that matter, to Tucker's own mother, who was committed to a variety of social causes as well as to her family), Antler concludes that "the Yiddishe mama" also "contained its outlaw opposite."[126] The lyrics create a distance from the mythical mother of "days gone by"; sitting "in the comfort of a cozy chair," the singer/daughter rejects the previous generation's version of femininity and thus must beg forgiveness for actions that went against filial expectations ("for things I did that made her cry").[127] By placing this maternal vision resolutely in the past, Tucker's "My Yiddishe Mama" paved the way for models of modern femininity that would find their expression not in the mythology of Jewish motherhood but in the utopian possibility of cross-racial sisterhood.

Yet critics have noted that "My Yiddishe Mama" relegates Jewish identity to the past as well. Even as the song's popularity indicates that "statements about ethnicity were both acceptable and commercially viable" in American culture in the 1920s, Mark Slobin argues that the tune represents the "growing Americanization" of Jewish popular song in which tradition became a figment of Old World nostalgia with "the gray-haired mother" acting "as bridge from minority to mainstream."[128] Tucker's own comments on the song in her autobiography suggest, however, that the process of Americanization was more complex than forsaking ethnic specificity for whiteness. Tucker notes that when she began singing "My Yiddishe Mama," she would only do so when "the majority of the house would understand the Yiddish." On one occasion that exemplifies further Tucker's capacity for misrepresentation, she sang the song at a Jewish benefit in England where the audience was surprised by her use of Yiddish, unsure, she writes, of "whether I was a Jewess, or whether I just learned to say those words for the occasion."[129] Eventually, however, Tucker found that the song was as well received by gentiles as by Jews, despite the untranslated words: "They knew, by instinct, what I was saying, and their hearts responded just as the hearts of Jews and Gentiles of every nationality responded when John McCormack sang 'Mother Machree.' You didn't have to have an old mother in Ireland to feel 'Mother Machree,' and you didn't have to be a Jew to be moved by 'My Yiddishe Mama.' 'Mother' in any language means the same thing."[130] Although it may convey more idealism than reality, this passage alludes to the transformation of Jews (and other white ethnics) into Americans, able to cross linguistic and cultural barriers to be understood, accepted, and appreciated by ecumenical audiences. Tucker's insistence that the Yiddish words need not be translated indicates that this process of acculturation was not necessarily a unidirectional "bridge from minority to mainstream," but had the potential to be a two-way street in which the mainstream pluralistically integrated aspects of minority culture.

In many ways, Tucker's career emblematizes this pluralistic ideal. Rather than melting down differences into a category of empty whiteness, her performances of blackness and Jewishness remind us that America would not be America without the cultural contributions of its minority people. Black and white, Jewish and American, were not opposite poles for Tucker. Her Jewish-themed novelty numbers like "At the Yiddish Wedding Jubilee" were at times referred to as "Yiddish coon songs."[131]

During a jazzy rendition of "Bluebird, Where Are You?" she improvises by switching over to cantorial rhythms, imagining how "Cantor Rosenblatt would chant the song."[132] In addition to combining Yiddish and English in numerous songs, from the sentimental "My Yiddishe Mama" to the comic "Make It Legal, Mr. Siegel," Tucker was also known to record two versions of the same song, one in English, the other in Yiddish, sometimes on opposite sides of a single album. While this gimmick befits "My Yiddishe Mama" or "My Mother's Sabbath Candles," it is more surprising that she did the same with the bluesy "Mama Goes Where Papa Goes."[133]

Proving, too, that the black-Jewish imaginary needs to be understood in terms of reciprocity rather than unilateral appropriation, scholars have noted instances of African American vocalists singing songs in Yiddish and Hebrew; oft-cited is Ethel Waters, who included "Eli, Eli" in her cabaret act.[134] To such examples of cross-cultural exchange we might add Billie Holiday, who recorded Tucker's trademark, "My Yiddishe Mama," and whose own signature song, "Strange Fruit," a chilling protest against lynching, was written in 1936 by Jewish radical Abel Meeropol under the pen name Lewis Allan.[135] While Tucker's bilingual vocalizations are apt metaphors for the duality of identity, her give-and-take with African American artists and culture causes this duality to gain in complexity, translating into expressions of multiplicity.

Tucker's failure to find a niche for herself in Hollywood may further attest to the complexity of her ethnic performance. The actress often attributed this failure to her looks; with her large size, she was far from a typical leading lady. However, her weight, as we have seen, often functioned as the physical embodiment of flagrant ethnicity that prevented her from conforming to norms of white femininity. Film historian Neil Gabler has argued that the Jewish film moguls who "invented" early Hollywood erased Jewish identity from film as they strove to redefine themselves. For Gabler, *The Jazz Singer*, with its assimilationist message about the potential of popular entertainment to transform immigrant outsiders into Americans, was considered a swan song to Jewish-themed films.[136] By obscuring Jewish (and other white ethnic) difference behind the mask of every American, Hollywood cinema appears to have promoted a more simplistic black-white dichotomy. In 1930, Tucker sang of her experience making the talkie *Honky Tonk*, which was by all accounts, including her own, a bomb. In this version of events, however, Tucker, in typical racy fashion, claims to have surpassed even Hollywood's reputation for scandal, focusing on her many sexual conquests and asserting, in the song's title, that "Hollywood Will Never Be the Same." Indeed, Hollywood might have never been the same if it had made room for someone like Tucker, whose persona was defined not only in revolt against gender and sexual propriety but also by a proclivity for moving among racial and ethnic demarcations in ways that continually troubled, rather than upheld, a black-white binary.

In contrast to those who contend that immigrants became white "on the backs of blacks," the Sophie Tucker story demonstrates that there is more ambivalence present in the relationship between white ethnicity and blackness, especially when we take into account ideologies of gender and sexuality. While I do not want to suggest that Jewish women's appropriations of blackness are unproblematic, I do believe that Tucker's narrative has a de-centering, as opposed to stabilizing, effect on whiteness and white femininity. The scholarship to date has overlooked or downplayed the role of women in the history of blackface performance, focusing instead on the masculinized "white negro." In turning to the phenomenon of the "white negress" with the "matza-soprano," "America's foremost Jewish actress" with the "colored voice," this chapter illustrates how female appropriations of blackness offer a different, more complex narrative—a narrative that has the potential to push forward a feminist critique of paradigms dominating the comparative study of race and ethnicity. More so than establishing her distance from blackness and allowing her, as a Jew, to assimilate into whiteness, Tucker's cross-racial mimicry engendered multifaceted representations of racialized femininity.

2 / The Same Show Boat? Edna Ferber's Interracial Ideal

While the heterogeneity of the early-twentieth-century stage opened spaces for the construction of new models of racial and gender identity, popular literature of the time offers another venue for exploring such shifting ideologies as they relate to the black-Jewish imaginary. The work of Jewish American writer Edna Ferber bridges the realms of literature and mass entertainment, and it was in minstrelsy that Ferber found one of her earliest sources of creative inspiration. In the first volume of her autobiography, *A Peculiar Treasure* (1939), Ferber added detail to her portrait of the artist as a stage-struck youth by describing her childhood infatuation with minstrel shows. "When the curtain went up, revealing those rows of red-and-white candy-striped satin pants, those absurd wing collars, those black faces and rolling eyes, I began to laugh in anticipation. I knew the ritual by heart," wrote Ferber. "There was always the cakewalk in the second half, as American (or as American Negro) as jazz itself." Though destined for a career as a prolific and versatile writer, rather than an actress, Ferber always considered herself a "blighted Bernhardt," and her love for the theater—and for theatricality—is evident in some of her best-known novels. Eventually, Ferber parlayed her stage aspirations into several playwriting ventures, most notably her collaborations with dramatist George S. Kaufman. Their first, *Minick*, produced in 1924 and based on one of Ferber's short stories, had little to do with race, but its casting of a "Harlem actress rather than a white girl in blackface" in the role of "colored maid" broke new ground, according to Ferber. "We thought ourselves rather daring," she recalled of this casting decision. "White and colored actors did not then ordinarily mingle. The stage has grown in that direction, at least."[1] In a shift from the somewhat mournful tone with which she earlier lamented that minstrelsy "seems to have passed entirely out of the theater," Ferber had come to take pride in her own progressive contribution to eradicating the racial segregation of the American stage.[2]

Ferber's experiences working on *Minick* led to her next project, *Show Boat*, her 1926 novel about a group of thespians living and performing on a Mississippi riverboat.[3] Epic in scale, *Show Boat* uses a multigenerational family saga to chronicle the growth of the American stage, tracing the evolution of the variety show from the floating theaters of the post-Reconstruction South to the urban milieus of Chicago and New York in the mid-1920s. *Show Boat* thus conveys in fictional form the entertainment history surveyed in the previous chapter, reiterating how theatrical traditions have been shaped by—and have shaped—the nation's racial ideologies. Like most of Ferber's novels, *Show Boat* is also a female success story, featuring a protagonist, Magnolia Hawks, who defies gender and racial conventions to rise to fame as an actress. As a child, independent-minded Magnolia disregards the rules of segregation to form close relationships with the black servants on her family's plantation-like showboat, the *Cotton Blossom*. Further flouting expectations for ladylike decorum, Magnolia grows up to become an amateur performer with the floating theater troupe. When an ill-fated union with her leading man, the gambler Gaylord Ravenal, leaves Magnolia to fend for herself and her young daughter in Chicago, she goes on to achieve renown as a "coon singer," performing the black music that she earlier learned from her African American companions.

Both the minstrel show of Ferber's youth and the rapidly evolving Broadway stage of the early 1920s are present in *Show Boat*—and not just in the performances that the characters participate in throughout the novel. Ferber's primary black figures are drawn from the interlocking nineteenth-century traditions of minstrelsy and sentimental fiction. The chief servants of the showboat—Jo, the shiftless man-of-all-work, and Queenie, the full-bosomed cook—are recycled stereotypes of the Uncle Tom and the mammy. Magnolia's closest friend, the beautiful leading lady Julie Dozier, who passes for white in order to perform on a segregated stage, conforms to the trope of the tragic mulatto, but the novel's sympathetic portrayal of this character and of miscegenation also opposes racist theatrical practices, and racism in general. Magnolia may reap the benefits of her friendships with these characters to make a name for herself first in vaudeville and then on the Broadway stage, but she ultimately sacrifices her celebrity status in favor of a return to her roots and a closer connection to black folk culture. Unlike the better-known musical adaptations, which reunite the protagonist with her wayward husband, the novel kills off Gaylord and ends with Magnolia returning alone to her childhood home in order to take over as proprietor of the showboat.

Show Boat addresses a topic that has been the subject of endless scholarly fascination in recent decades: the interplay between black and white culture. Despite the fact that Show Boat is very much a product of the 1920s, an era in which the "mongrelization" of culture was recognized and celebrated, Ferber's novel has received little attention in literary and cultural criticism.[4] Overwhelmingly, discussion of Show Boat focuses on its theatrical adaptation, with scholars in the fields of American studies and musical theater exploring both its racial politics and its pivotal role in entertainment history. In their compelling interpretations of the adaptation, for example, both Linda Williams and Lauren Berlant fit Show Boat into white melodramatic and sentimental traditions that offer the pretense of progressivism through a narrative of black suffering. As they demonstrate, such white appropriations of black pain for the purposes of entertainment end up maintaining the strictures of the color line.[5] Due to the fact that two Jewish men, Jerome Kern and Oscar Hammerstein II, were responsible for transforming Ferber's novel into the classic musical, Show Boat has also become a contested text of the black-Jewish cultural imaginary. While its attempts to espouse liberal ideologies and showcase the rich history of African American oral culture have been duly noted, the musical is also viewed as part of a long-standing tradition of Jewish appropriations that, to quote Michael Rogin, "silences" black "voices and sings in their name."[6]

One can see how a similar argument might be applied to Ferber as the novel's Jewish author. When scholars have taken note of Ferber's role as originator of Show Boat, it is usually to point out that the text marks a departure from her earlier fiction, especially her autobiographical novel Fanny Herself (1917), which drew directly on the writer's ethnic heritage and featured an explicitly Jewish heroine. As a "white negress," Magnolia Hawks may vaguely evoke famous Jewish "coon-shouters" such as Sophie Tucker (or, more likely, one of her thin and more conventionally attractive contemporaries such as Nora Bayes or Anna Held), but Ferber does not make Show Boat's heroine a Jew.[7] In fact, Jews are all but absent from Show Boat, even as the novel's time frame coincides with the increased presence of Jewish immigrants in the United States and on the stage. The absence of Jewishness in *Show Boat* serves as proof for some critics that Ferber, in universalizing her fiction, shed her Jewish identity and positioned herself as part of the white mainstream. June Sochen applies to Ferber the model of "blending the particular with the universal" that she used to analyze Tucker and Brice; she argues that *Fanny Herself* was an "exorcism" of the author's Jewish identity that freed Ferber to focus on heroines who were ethnically and religiously unidentified. In a more recent study, Carol Batker, examining the appearance of racial others in Ferber's fiction, argues that racist representations of African Americans allowed the author to situate herself as "white and assimilable."[8] Batker does not mention Rogin, but his paradigm of Jews becoming white through the exploitation of African American culture is clearly operative in her conclusions.

While *Show Boat* appears to reinforce the black-white binary through its perpetuation of stereotypes drawn from blackface minstrelsy, this chapter investigates how the text's place in the black-Jewish imaginary simultaneously complicates its racial representations. In the context of the existing scholarly debate about Jewish appropriations of African American culture, *Show Boat*'s use of blackness would be read as either the result of empathy or an unfair—and even gross—misappropriation. Yet neither of these options adequately explains the uses of blackness in Ferber's novel. Quick to point out *Show Boat*'s reprehensible stereotypes, critics have neglected much of the subtlety with which Ferber treats representations of mixed-race identity and, in particular, her nuanced deployment of the trope of passing. Ferber's reliance on the passing narrative is not a simple appropriation from African American culture; instead, her use of this trope can be traced back to texts like *Fanny Herself* and her 1918 short story "The Girl Who Went Right," both of which feature Jewish women who pass for gentile. On the surface, *Show Boat* may uphold myths of the Old South, but a careful reading of the novel in the context of Ferber's earlier fiction suggests that it also does much to expose the myth of whiteness. Nor is this novel an anomaly for Ferber. *Show Boat* sets the author off on a tour of America's multiethnic landscape. As I go on to discuss via the example of her 1941 novel, *Saratoga Trunk*, her subsequent regional fiction chronicles the nation's partially hidden history of miscegenation and interracialism in order to underscore how racial mixing is fundamental to American identity.

In contrast then to the commonly held view that Ferber transformed ethnic specificity into white universalism, this chapter argues that in novels such as *Show Boat*, Ferber displaced whiteness as a universal norm, substituting in its stead an interracial ideal. As a writer with broad popular appeal, Ferber herself may have entered the mainstream, but her fiction does not necessarily promote mainstream values or conventional modes of behavior. Consistently featuring working women who cross racial lines and flout gender norms, Ferber's writing, much like Tucker's performances, tends to unsettle, rather than stabilize, the categories of whiteness and femininity. Before redirecting attention to Ferber, it is helpful to review in more detail the legacy of *Show Boat*'s musical adaptation in order to understand how its reception continues to color the critical assessment of her work today. In fact, as I go on to demonstrate, many of the complexities of the novel, especially as they relate to race and femininity, were lost in translation from page to stage and screen.

"Jes' Keeps Rollin' Along"

Ferber may have prided *Minick*'s artistic team for its progressive casting of an African American actress in the supporting role of maid, but it was composer Jerome Kern and librettist Oscar Hammerstein II's musical adaptation of *Show Boat* that was widely viewed as breaking new ground, both aesthetically and politically, in American theater. Premiering on Broadway at the newly built Ziegfeld Theatre in 1927, Kern and Hammerstein's *Show Boat* inaugurated the genre of the "integrated book musical." In the integrated musical, song and dance are incorporated into the storyline, so that music and plot meld together to develop narrative and character.[9] As a backstage musical about theater history, *Show Boat* pays tribute in song to the vaudeville and revue traditions, even as it radically departs from the lighthearted and comic mood that dominated early musical entertainment. Taking on topics such as racial injustice, miscegenation, marital abandonment, single motherhood, and working womanhood, the adaptation of Ferber's novel proved that serious subject matter could be the stuff of which musicals were made.

As one of the first major theatrical productions to cast black and white actors side by side, *Show Boat* was an integrated musical in another sense as well. Yet the 1927 Broadway production of *Show Boat* reveals a theater very much in flux. While the show provided significant opportunities for black actors like Jules Bledsoe and later Paul Robeson, who made "Ol' Man River" its most unforgettable number, the theater had not yet been released from minstrelsy's grip. The part of Queenie, the show's stereotypical mammy figure, went to Italian American actress Tess Gardella, who was so well known for her blackface roles that she was billed as "Aunt Jemima." By the time of the show's London opening, however, Hammerstein, stating his desire for the "real thing" over an actress in blackface, chose blues singer Alberta Hunter to play Queenie opposite Robeson.[10]

Through its multiple revivals, countless regional productions, and three film versions, *Show Boat* has generated its share of controversy because of its deeply embedded racial ambivalences, evident on the levels of plot, language, music, and casting. Despite its popular success with generations of theater- and filmgoers, the musical has continually come under attack due to its romanticized view of Southern blacks, whose main purpose, according to objectors, is to provide a colorful backdrop for the white heroes and heroines. African American responses to the original Broadway production varied widely. One black theater critic praised the show for the "respectful flourish" with which it recognized black beauty and talent, noting that "the majority of the beauties, the liveliest of the dancers and the most stirring of the singers are African." In contrast, a columnist for the *Amsterdam News* reported general "disapprobation of the play" by "Negroes of intelligence or self-respect," many of whom criticized *Show Boat* for perpetuating stereotypes that "exist . . . more in white men's fancy than in reality."[11] Critics today continue to debate whether *Show Boat* is an offensive and embarrassing relic of a bygone era or an aesthetically innovative and socially progressive historical achievement, worthy of its designation as classic. Should it be condemned for its racism or lauded for its attempts (however misguided at times) to expose bigotry? Such competing views of *Show Boat* are heightened, in part, by the malleability of performance. The musical's capacity for either testing or upholding racial boundaries can be charted, for example, in ongoing debates about casting (especially in relation to the mixed-race character of Julie, who has been played on film by white actresses Helen Morgan and Ava Gardner), or in the show's opening lyrics, "Niggers all work on the Mississippi," which have been revised several times over; in attempts to find an acceptable alternative, the "n-word" was variously replaced with "darkies," then "colored folk," then "we."[12]

The debate over *Show Boat*'s racial politics reached its dramatic climax over sixty years after Ferber published her novel. In 1993, Live Entertainment Inc. attempted to update the musical for a politically correct era, premiering the lavish revival in Toronto, with plans to move the production to Broadway the following year. Local black activists launched an organized protest against the musical, arguing that it perpetuated damaging racial stereotypes and misused taxpayers' money, since the revival was slated as the inaugural show for the publicly funded North York Performing Arts Centre (now the Toronto Centre for the Arts). The show did go on, but not without some rapid-fire damage control by the producers, who altered their marketing strategies and hired African American scholar Henry Louis Gates, Jr., to write an educational guide. The majority of reviews were favorable, and the subsequent New York premiere went off without a hitch. Reviewing the Toronto production, Frank Rich wrote that "the anger this 'Show Boat' directs against racism is far more caustic than the chants and signs of the polite, ill-informed local protestors who have accused the show of racism without bothering to see it." Like Rich, many critics took the opportunity to extol both the revival and the original for their artful handling of sensitive racial issues. In *Newsweek*, for example, Jack Kroll wrote that the revival allows audiences to "feel the idealistic chutzpah of Kern and Hammerstein," whose "work is full of love for a romantic ideal that's gone, for a fraternal ideal that never arrived."[13] Such reviews, however, did little to appease protestors, with the revival leading to particular animosity between Toronto's black and Jewish communities. Black leaders held Jews accountable for the prominent roles they played in the show's production, beginning with Kern and Hammerstein and extending to the revival's director, Hal Prince, and producer, Garth Drabinsky.[14]

While most of the conflict centered on the musical, a number of commentators went to the source. Reviewing the revival for the *New Yorker*, John Lahr found much to recommend in the production itself, but "little to defend in [the] gushing bestseller on which the musical is based," taking Ferber to task for her "unconscionable racial caricatures."[15] In *Showing Grit*, a passionate lament against the revival, M. Nourbese Philip, a Canadian writer of West Indian descent, similarly held Ferber's racist depictions liable for the offenses of the musical. Illustrating how the "theft" of black culture works to advance white interests, Philip accuses Ferber's novel of emphasizing "the subservient aspect of Black life" and "omitting its long history of resistance."[16] Whereas Ferber once participated in what she perceived to be a "daring" act of resistance against segregation on stage, critics today tend to view her as propagating the racist evils of minstrelsy, an assessment that rests largely on the role she played as the creator of *Show Boat*.

To be sure, the influence of the minstrel show she so loved is evident throughout Ferber's works of prose, and especially in *Show Boat*.[17] The images of blacks with "woolly" heads, "rolling protuberant eye[s]," and oversized lips unquestionably evoke the iconography of minstrelsy. In addition to the novel's visual iconography, Ferber's black characters indulge in primitive behaviors that similarly suggest they have been transported from the minstrel stage into *Show Boat*'s fictional universe. The shuffling, singing blacks whose "mellow plaintive voices" are heard from "the levees and in cabin doorways as the boat swept by" provide the local color for Ferber's Southern tour. Although Ferber identifies the music as "the folk songs of a wronged race," the novel seems to do little to right these wrongs, as the main purpose of the black presence is to serve whites. Other than the mixed-race characters, whom I will discuss in more depth, the only black characters who emerge from the scenery to play minor roles are the chief servants, Jo and Queenie. When Magnolia's father, Captain Andy Hawks, purchases the showboat, he obtains Jo and Queenie as part of the package. Emphasizing their status as property, Queenie is conflated with the kitchen that comes to define her as mammy; the kitchen stove, for example, is described as "[b]road-bosomed, ample, vast, like a huge fertile black mammal whose breast would suckle numberless eager sprawling bubbling pots and pans."[18] Relics of the mythic plantation past, Jo and Queenie are depicted as simple, childlike, and ignorant, with vices confined to shiftlessness and drink.

Even as her novel steers clear of black villainy and extends sympathy to her African American characters as a "wronged race," it is impossible, based on such caricatures, to absolve Ferber of charges of racism. But Ferber's racism is not that of a Thomas Dixon, whose novel *The Clansman* (1905), which depicted the Ku Klux Klan as heroic redeemers of the Reconstruction South, would become the basis of another mass entertainment milestone, D. W. Griffith's film *The Birth of a Nation* (1915). Instead, Ferber's stereotypical depictions are more akin to those of the sentimental tradition epitomized by Harriet Beecher Stowe's famous abolitionist novel *Uncle Tom's Cabin* (1852), whose slave characters were themselves drawn from the author's familiarity with blackface minstrelsy as it pervaded popular culture. In turn, Stowe's narrative was taken up by that performance tradition; her story and its characters became the subject of melodrama and many minstrel acts.[19] *Show Boat* may lack Stowe's explicitly activist agenda, but Ferber's novel does acknowledge the influence of its nineteenth-century predecessor: the play *Uncle Tom's Cabin* is part of the showboat's repertoire.

Thus, much like Stowe's novel and Sophie Tucker's performances, Ferber's fiction simultaneously participates in and displays resistance to a blackface tradition. In the passage with which I began from *A Peculiar*

Treasure that verifies the likelihood of the minstrel show as a source for *Show Boat*, Ferber's ambivalences are apparent in her fascinating parenthetical qualification. Singling out the cakewalk as a representative element of the minstrel show, Ferber described it "as American (or as American Negro) as jazz itself." The parenthetical insertion at once asserts and undermines a distinction between (white) American and "American Negro." Ferber's uncertainty about whether these cultural forms are "American" or "American Negro" suggests a muddying of origins and acknowledges that black cultural forms have come to define mainstream American culture. In identifying these staples of popular entertainment—blackface routines, the cakewalk, and jazz—as "American," Ferber illuminates the multiracial mien of the national culture. Ferber's own predilection for complicating racial identity is especially evident in *Show Boat*. Stressing the mixed roots of national popular entertainment, the novel similarly disrupts distinctions between "American" and "American Negro," while also offering a surprisingly nuanced portrait of white femininity. Arguing that *Show Boat* lost a good deal of its nuance when it was adapted for the stage, I show, in what follows, that analysis of this volatile text as the cultural product of a Jewish woman challenges paradigms dominating the study of relations between Jews and blacks in American culture.

I foreground my analysis of *Show Boat* by providing an overview of Ferber's career and her vexed place in American literary history. Despite recent revivals of women's writing, particularly works by ethnic writers, Ferber remains largely overlooked, buried in the poorly tended graveyard of the "middlebrow," in stark contrast to the fame she experienced during her lifetime. Although Ferber was one of the first Jewish writers to win the Pulitzer Prize (for *So Big* in 1925) and counted herself among the literary elite of the legendary Algonquin Roundtable, her popularity as best-selling author has led her to become a straw woman of the "masscult," the term coined by Dwight MacDonald in his incendiary indictment of writers who placed commercial demands above aesthetic value. Beginning in the 1970s and continuing through several recent studies, feminist scholars have been recuperating nineteenth-century sentimental women writers such as Stowe and twentieth-century "middlebrow moderns" by highlighting their political and cultural work and rejecting the aesthetic criteria established by male critics and writers. In this spirit, it is worth revisiting Ferber's fiction, which offers a heretofore unexamined source for analyzing how considerations of gender and femininity alter theorizations of white identity in critical race studies.

Ferber Herself

Daughter of a Hungarian immigrant father and a second-generation German-Jewish mother, Ferber was born in Kalamazoo, Michigan, in 1885 (not 1887 as she claimed) and spent her childhood in the midwestern United States. Although her family did not observe religious practices beyond attending services on the High Holidays, Ferber considered her Jewish background to be formative to her identity and to her career as a writer. She described her first autobiographical installment, *A Peculiar Treasure*, as "the story of an American Jewish family in the past half-century, and as such . . . really a story about America which I know and love."[20] Despite the patriotic zeal with which Ferber claimed that a Jewish family's story represents that of the nation, the America she knew and loved was not always a hospitable place for Jews. The opening of *A Peculiar Treasure*, which dwells on the childhood years Ferber spent in the mining town of Ottumwa, Iowa, paints a bleak picture of the anti-Semitism she and her family endured, as they tried to support themselves by running a general store. Due to repeated instances of persecution, the Ferbers were eventually forced to move their store to Appleton, Wisconsin, a town they found more congenial to Jews.[21]

In addition to her secular Jewish identity, Ferber's knowledge of working womanhood was another significant influence on her upbringing and her writing. Due to her father's poor eyesight, her hard-working and indomitable mother ran the family store and later became the inspiration for the character of Fanny's mother, Molly Brandeis, in *Fanny Herself*. Ferber often helped out in the store as a clerk, but she began her own career in earnest as a journalist. She was the first female reporter for the *Appleton Daily Crescent* and later wrote for the *Milwaukee Journal*. In 1910, while recovering from a minor nervous breakdown brought on by a rigorous work schedule, she turned to fiction writing while convalescing at home. Her first published short story, "The Homely Heroine," which appeared in *Everybody's Magazine*, established her interest in writing about the lives of ordinary, working women and her refusal of traditional happy endings, including love and marriage. In the foreword to *Buttered Side Down*, her 1912 collection of short stories, Ferber explicitly eschewed the "happily ever after" ending, explaining that her stories "end truthfully, thus: And so they lived."[22]

Beginning with her first novel, *Dawn O'Hara* (1911), a partially autobiographical tale of a female journalist, Ferber's fiction testifies to the changes taking place in gender roles during the early decades of the twentieth century. Ferber went on to achieve nationwide recognition with the Emma McChesney stories, the wildly popular series following the adventures of a divorced single mother who supports herself and her son by working as a skirt and petticoat saleswoman. Heralded as a "new type" and lauded as the first businesswoman of American fiction when she made her literary debut in 1911, Emma McChesney enjoyed a five-year run in the pages of *American Magazine* and *Cosmopolitan*.[23] In *Dawn O'Hara* and the Emma McChesney stories, Ferber's New Women were Irish protagonists whose ethnic identities were mostly inconsequential to their stories. In 1917, when Ferber published *Fanny Herself*, her second full-length work about a strong working woman, she not only transformed her heroine, Fanny Brandeis, into a Jew but also made the character's Jewishness a crucial component of the narrative. Often identified as a transitional work in Ferber's career, allowing its author, in Sochen's words, to "exorcise" her Jewish heritage in order to refashion herself as an American writer, *Fanny Herself* features a protagonist who occludes her ethnic identity and passes—a narrative that is more commonly associated with the African American literary tradition and one that Ferber will resurrect in a black context when she writes *Show Boat*.

Although it is a passing novel, *Fanny Herself* does not espouse passing as a means of dealing with one's ethnic or racial difference, but rather employs the trope as a critique of melting pot ideology. Because Fanny comes to regret her decision to pass, the novel, like many African American passing narratives from this period, advocates race pride; in reclaiming her ethnic heritage, Fanny subsequently moves toward a metaphorical enactment of a pluralist ideal. Growing up in the midwestern town of Winnebago, where the Brandeises are one of the few Jewish families, Fanny initially believes that her Jewish difference is a "handicap." Thus, when she leaves the small town for Chicago after the death of both her parents, she vows that in order to "make something of herself" she will discard "race, religion, training . . . if they stood in her way." But when Fanny does do away with her background, it is to compensate for being a woman in a man's world. Embarking on her career as a buyer for Haynes-Cooper mail-order company, she presents an identity devoid of ethnic particularity in order to overcome the handicap of her gender, which is more difficult to disguise. When her boss inquires whether she is a Jew, she replies simply, "No." With her acute business acumen, Fanny quickly rises in the ranks at Haynes-Cooper, but she begins to suffer a malaise at having cut off a part of herself and is increasingly drawn to her "people," albeit through interclass identifications.[24] Moved by solidarity with the Jewish factory workers in her employ, for example, she protests their low wages. At the same time, a creative force propels her toward the ghetto, where she begins sketching its residents. The novel unfolds with a romantic resolution, and Fanny eventually reclaims her ethnic identity by acknowledging her love for an openly Jewish childhood acquaintance, Clarence Heyl. Negotiating between what Werner Sollors has termed "consent" and "descent," Fanny, in choosing to identify as Jewish (rather than having this difference imposed upon her), transforms her difference into an "asset" rather than a handicap.[25]

However, the novel's resolution is more complex than a simple declaration of racial pride. Drawing on theories of cultural pluralism that had begun to circulate between 1910 and 1920, the text suggests that Fanny will create a hybrid identity, amalgamating her new and old selves. By 1915, prominent intellectuals such as Horace Kallen and Randolph Bourne were countering rising nativist sentiment brought on by the influx of immigration. Protesting, too, the erasure of ethnic differentiation advocated by proponents of the "melting pot," they imagined instead a pluralistic society that would benefit from variation and diversity. In his essay "Democracy versus the Melting-Pot," published in the Nation in 1915, Kallen envisioned that each ethnic group could contribute its distinct "timbre and tonality" to create "a multiplicity in a unity, an orchestration of mankind."[26] Kallen's essay was followed one year later by Bourne's "Trans-national America" in the Atlantic Monthly. Employing textile imagery to describe the United States as "a weaving back and forth, with ... other lands, of many threads of all sizes and colors," Bourne warned against "attempts to thwart this weaving, or to dye the fabric any one color, or disentangle the threads of the strands."[27] Resolving the tensions between assimilation and differentiation, Kallen and Bourne imagined a "wider and richer and more beautiful" entity constructed from a plurality of differences.[28] Both Kallen (who was Jewish) and Bourne (who was not) viewed Jews as emblematic of cultural pluralism and "transnationality." Bourne, for example, authored a version of his philosophy titled "The Jew and Transnational America." In "Democracy versus the Melting-Pot," Kallen prized the ability of Jewish immigrants to develop a distinct culture on American soil, describing them as both "the most eagerly American of the immigrant groups" and "the most autonomous and self-conscious in spirit and culture."[29]

The influence of such theories on Ferber is in evidence in Fanny Herself, especially as the main character participates in fairly heavy-handed didactic debates early in the novel about how to define her Jewish identity

if it cannot be understood as either a race or a religion. Rather than elid-
ing her Jewishness or making it the dominant feature of her identity,
Fanny ultimately effects a metaphorical interweaving that is highly suggestive of Bourne's notion of transnationality. In setting her story in the
apparel industry, Ferber uses fashion as a material metaphor to challenge essentialist notions of identity. The narrator, for example, reflects
on Fanny's reinvention as a sartorial transformation: "How could she
think it possible to shed her past life, like a garment? . . . She might don
a new cloak to cover the old dress beneath, but the old would always
be there, its folds peeping out here and there, its outlines plainly to be
seen."[30] Rather than describing Americanness as the "cloak" disguising
essential Jewish identity beneath (as nativists were wont to do), Ferber
portrays both the old and new selves in terms of dress.[31] And if these
selves are represented in material terms, they have the potential to be
woven together, as in Bourne's analogy.[32]

Fanny's talent for weaving together supposedly mismatched elements
is initially represented by the line of women's clothing she creates for
Haynes-Cooper. Hiring a haute couture designer to fashion inexpensive
dresses aimed at the average, middle-class woman, she campaigns for
styles that erode class barriers and combine masculine and feminine elements. By the novel's end, Fanny begins to apply the technique of combining contradictory elements to her own life. Although she worries that
she and Clarence are an incongruous pair, she allows him to persuade
her that their lack of compatibility is an advantage. In attempting to arrive at a strategic reconciliation of their differences, the couple decides to
live simultaneously in the country and the city, traveling between Heyl's
home in the mountains of Colorado and Fanny's comfort zone, the urban centers of Chicago and New York. Finally, when Fanny decides to
quit her job in order to follow her passion for art and become a newspaper cartoonist, her shift in occupation is not described in terms of one
identity replacing another, but rather as a merging of selves; observing
the cartoonist at work, the narrator states, "Fanny Brandeis, the artist,
and Fanny Brandeis, the salesman, combined shrewdly to omit no telling
detail."[33]

Fanny's metaphorical refashioning of her identity in pluralistic terms
resonates with many of Ferber's autobiographical statements on her Jewish allegiances in *A Peculiar Treasure*. Taken from Exodus 19:5 ("Now
therefore, if ye will obey my voice indeed, and keep my covenant, then ye
shall be a peculiar treasure unto me above all people"), the memoir's title
portrays Jewish identity as an asset (if in somewhat ambivalent terms).

Originally dedicated to Adolf Hitler and intended as a response to the rise of nazism, the memoir repeatedly expresses Ferber's pride in her Jewish identity.[34] Even in the face of persecution, Ferber believed herself "especially privileged" to be a Jew. Rather than erasing Jewishness from her life or her fiction, Ferber weaves together her Jewish and American identities in such a way that her ability to do so comes to stand in for a national ideal. A decade before it would become commonplace for Jewish writers such as Norman Mailer and Saul Bellow to construct the Jew as national allegory, Ferber declared the United States "to be the Jew among the nations."[35] Ferber's use of a passing narrative in *Fanny Herself* similarly counters the notion that Jews erased their ethnic specificity and became white folks through their assimilation into American society. Instead, Ferber proposes that Jews redefined what it meant to be American in the process of inserting themselves into a national narrative.[36]

The challenge that Ferber's work poses to the "Jew-as-white-person model" is heightened by the figure of the working woman who is central to her fiction. Even if Ferber's heroines lost much of their ethnic particularity by the 1920s, there is no question that the characters of Dawn O'Hara, Emma McChesney, and especially Fanny Brandeis continued to inform almost all of her subsequent writing. Ferber's fiction is populated with spirited female protagonists who are typically independent working women, even after they marry. These women display a strength and resilience that allow them to survive when their husbands die or disappear, as so many of Ferber's heroes do. Her female characters, whether figured as ethnic or not, adamantly refuse the codes of white femininity. Like Tucker's music, Ferber's fiction enacts a fantasy of female empowerment that is inseparable from its ethnic, interethnic, interclass, and cross-racial contexts.

The writer's own refusal to abide by gender conventions was even more pronounced than that of many of her heroines. Unable to resolve the conflict between work and marriage, Ferber seems to have made a conscious decision to remain single throughout her life. Near the end of her life, reflecting on the fact that she had never married, she recalled that as a young woman she was faced with two options: "either write or marry-and-live-happily-ever-after—but without the satisfaction of writing."[37] For Ferber, married life was not only incompatible with writing but also with her wanderlust. Although from 1912 onward she called New York City home, she continued to draw on her journalistic training by conducting extensive research for her novels, which, beginning in the 1920s, were set in far regional corners of the United States. From the Oklahoma frontier of *Cimarron* (1930) to New England in *American Beauty* (1931), from the Wisconsin lumberyards of *Come and Get It* (1935) to the Texas ranches and oil fields of *Giant* (1952), from the prairies of the American heartland in *So Big* (1924) to the new territory of Alaska in *Ice Palace* (1958), these novels document a diverse, multiethnic panorama.

Because this expansive documentation can be read as a big-hearted embrace of the nation, Ferber is often viewed as an apologist for America (more so, perhaps, because many of these works were published at a time when the literary trend had turned toward modernist disillusionment). Criticizing Diane Lichtenstein for including Ferber in her study of Jewish American women writers, Joel Porte, for example, describes Ferber's work as embarrassingly "suffused with middlebrow enthusiasm for assimilationist boosterism."[38] But Ferber rarely shied away from balancing her idealism and optimism with her muckraker's determination to expose the darker side of the nation, especially in relation to its treatment of minority groups. Though often misread as a contribution to the romantic genre of the western rather than the satire it was intended to be, *Cimarron* features a pioneer heroine who overcomes initial prejudice against her son's marriage to a Native American woman in order to herself become a champion of the rights of indigenous people.[39] *Giant*, Ferber's epic novel about Texas oil tycoons, similarly addresses racial discrimination, with its heroine accusing her Texan husband-to-be of stealing his land from Mexicans.

While Ferber's commitment to telling a well-rounded story was in part derived from her journalistic beginnings, Harold Bloom also views as it as tied to her Jewishness, which allowed her to "both extol and censure attitudes expressed in the United States."[40] In turn, her willingness to "censure" as well as to "extol" often brought her Jewish identity to the forefront. Despite her conception of herself as a fierce patriot, she was often targeted as an un-American outsider, a fact she also records in her own reminiscences. When she was researching *Cimarron*, a local editorial opined: "This Ferber woman is the most unpleasant personality that has ever come into Oklahoma. . . . Why doesn't she stay in the ghetto where she came from?" *American Beauty*, the story of Polish immigrants who revitalize the deadened landscape of Puritan Connecticut, engendered a similar reaction, with one newspaper demanding, "what right . . . had a Jew to come into New England and write about it!"[41] Later, her critical depiction of Texas history in *Giant* led to an even more vociferous response when she became the recipient of hate mail warning her that she would be lynched or shot if she returned to the state.[42] Based on such vilification, which specifically painted her as a racial outsider, it becomes difficult to see Ferber as someone who staked a claim to whiteness—even at the moments of her greatest triumphs. Despite the many successes of her career, Ferber's vilification as both a woman and a Jew would also come to play a role in the tarnishing of her literary reputation.

"Yiddish Descendants of O. Henry"

Contemporary critics who study Ferber's work inevitably make this observation: the scholarly attention she has received bears an inverse relation to the tremendous popularity she enjoyed for almost fifty years, from the second decade of the twentieth century, when she first seized the national consciousness with the Emma McChesney stories, through the 1950s, when she published *Giant*, another epic family saga, now best remembered on the basis of its film adaptation starring James Dean, Rock Hudson, and Elizabeth Taylor. After she won the Pulitzer Prize for *So Big* in 1925, Ferber's books regularly topped best-seller lists, and *Show Boat* was one of the first novels to be selected for the newly formed Book-of-the-Month Club. Capitalizing on her mass appeal, especially among women, the Hollywood adaptations of her novels (most famously, *Show Boat*, *Cimarron*, and *Giant*) brought her work to even wider audiences.[43] When Ferber died in 1968, her front-page obituary in the *New York Times* declared her "among the best-read novelists in the nation" and stated that "critics of the nineteen-twenties and thirties did not hesitate to call her the greatest American woman novelist of her day."[44]

Yet Ferber's status as a writer was very much in contention during her lifetime as well.[45] It was perhaps F. Scott Fitzgerald who most memorably summed up the literary establishment's view of Ferber. Although not above selling his stories to popular magazines when in need of funds, Fitzgerald would not deign to read writers such as Ferber and her contemporary, Fannie Hurst (subject of the following chapter). In a letter to his editor, Maxwell Perkins, he derisively labeled them "the Yiddish descendants of O. Henry."[46] In *This Side of Paradise* (1920), Fitzgerald, with one of his characters as mouthpiece, offers a further pejorative assessment of Ferber's and Hurst's mass appeal, including them on a list of pulp writers who are disgracing American literature. "Fifty thousand dollars a year," complains poet Tom D'Invilliers to Amory Blaine of the lucrative income such writers took in. "Look at them . . . not producing among 'em one story or novel that will last ten years. . . . Some of them *can* write, but they won't sit down and do one honest novel. Most of them *can't* write."[47] Although aware of her own limitations as a writer, Ferber was pleased to prove Fitzgerald wrong about the longevity of her work. In a 1952 interview, she noted that *So Big, Show Boat,* and *Cimarron* were "a quarter century old" but were "in some curious way . . . still read today, some on college and school lists." In this interview, she hinted at some surprise that her books had staying power despite being "written in the days when it wasn't fashionable to write them, the days of Fitzgerald and the rest."[48] Ferber's assessment of her own career is accurate; although her novels may have appeared on required reading lists in the 1950s, in recent decades her work has been largely ignored by the academy, in part because she does not fit the profile of the alienated (and usually male) writer who has come to dominate the terrain of modern American fiction.

Forty years after *This Side of Paradise*'s portrait of the disillusioned male artist helped to push the course of American fiction in this direction, Ferber and Hurst were to appear on another list, quite similar to Fitzgerald's, when Dwight MacDonald published his 1960 *Partisan Review* essay, "Masscult and Midcult." In this famous denunciation of the "middlebrow," which, according to MacDonald, "really isn't culture at all," but a woeful attempt to ape high art, Ferber's and Hurst's names head the catalog of novelists who "manufacture" their work with the marketplace in mind.[49] In the past two decades, however, scholars such as Janice Radway and Joan Shelley Rubin have turned their attention to literature aimed at the elevation and intellectual edification of educated, middle-class consumers, contesting MacDonald's claim that the middlebrow should not be taken seriously because its mediocrity and commercialism contaminated American culture.[50]

Most recently, critics have begun recuperating the work of early-twentieth-century "middlebrow moderns," to adopt the title of an anthology of literary criticism edited by Lisa Botshon and Meredith Goldsmith. Arguing that middlebrow culture expands our understanding of democratic literary and reading practices by including writers—and reaching readers—of diverse backgrounds, Botshon and Goldsmith show that the pejorative term "middlebrow" was also highly gendered; it signaled the feminization of literature, especially since most of the writers and consumers of this fiction were women. They further point out that middlebrow writers not only came from varied "social, racial, ethnic, and regional backgrounds" but also enacted cross-racial and cross-class identifications in their writing.[51] As an ethnic woman writer who may not have employed "fashionable" literary devices, but who consistently used her fiction to address progressive issues such as women in the labor force and the oppression of minority groups, Ferber exemplifies what makes the middlebrow worthy of study, just as she previously represented all that was wrong with an increasingly commercialized literary marketplace in the critiques of Fitzgerald and MacDonald.[52]

Beyond its latent sexism, there is another, more blatant dimension of Fitzgerald's disdain for the middlebrow that warrants some consideration here. The writer's oft-discussed anti-Semitism is in evidence when he brands Ferber and Hurst "the *Yiddish* descendents of O. Henry," implying that their mediocrity and sentimental excesses derive as much from their Jewishness as from the fact that they were women writers. While the label confirms Botshon and Goldsmith's assertion that middlebrow literature was shaped by the diverse backgrounds of its authors, it also resonates with the work of Jonathan Freedman, who has highlighted the role that Jews have played in the making of middlebrow American culture. Excluded from high cultural venues, including the academy, due to anti-Semitism, Jews took on entrepreneurial roles in new publishing ventures, such as the Book-of-the-Month Club, as a means of forging their assimilation, according to Freedman. The fact that the intellectual elite looked down upon such attempts to bring high culture to the masses further reinforced the modernist metaphor of the Jew as a symbol of social and cultural degeneration. While Freedman focuses largely on Jewish male publishers, his theories of middlebrow culture could be bolstered and expanded by considerations of women and gender. In the context of his argument, it seems more than incidental that the two writers to bear the brunt of scathing critiques of the middlebrow were Jewish women. The fact that the fiction of Ferber and Hurst lost its ethnic specificity as the authors increased in popularity substantiates Freedman's claims that Jewish participation in middlebrow enterprises facilitated assimilation. Yet the novels that Ferber and Hurst wrote, even when they did not deal directly with Jewish characters, depicted ethno-racial identities and relations in often contradictory ways that problematized straightforward assimilationist narratives. The work of Ferber and Hurst "reminds us," in Freedman's words, "that there are progressive as well as regressive dimensions to the making of middlebrow culture, and that these ideals functioned in complex ways across the cultural field."[53]

In addition to her vexed place in American literary history, Ferber has occupied an equally uneasy locus in Jewish American literature. In fact, to most readers today, Fitzgerald's identification of Ferber as a "Yiddish" writer will seem startlingly inaccurate (even if he intended "Yiddish" as a substitute for "Jewish," devoid of linguistic connotations). The study of Jewish American literature in the modern period has typically privileged writers of eastern European descent whose writing does have a distinctly Yiddish sensibility—for example, immigrants such as Anzia Yezierska and Abraham Cahan, who wrote about the experiences of assimilation in Northern urban settings. As an American-born midwestern writer from a German-Jewish background, Ferber fell firmly outside the rubric of Jewish American literature, especially as scholars attempted to position this tradition as part of an emerging multicultural curriculum. While Fitzgerald's disdain for Ferber's work derived in part from her being *too* Jewish, she has since been marginalized from Jewish American literary criticism because she was not viewed as Jewish enough.[54]

Not surprisingly, given ongoing attempts to extend the canon of Jewish American literature to women writers, the task of integrating Ferber into scholarship has fallen to feminist critics. Ann Shapiro, Eileen Watts, and Joyce Antler have identified Ferber as an important Jewish feminist voice whose accessibility allowed her to bring her progressive message to the masses.[55] While Ferber's representations of modern femininity and especially working womanhood make her a largely untapped resource for gender studies, the cross-racial frameworks of her fiction further enhance the richness of the archive she left behind. Ferber wrote about other minority groups in addition to her own, and her fiction features characters who themselves enact cross-racial identifications and performances, with her best-known novels taking up the controversial topics of interracial marriage and miscegenation. As Ferber's first novel to bring all of these motifs together, *Show Boat* may stand accused of perpetuating a tradition of blackface minstrelsy, but it is also a text that, in taking the appropriation of black culture as its subject, openly exposes the ambivalent processes of "love and theft" that underpin white fascination with African American culture.

"A Little Jewish Slave Girl on the Nile"

Although critics understand *Fanny Herself* to be an "exorcism" of Ferber's Jewish identity that allowed her to turn to more universal stories of American life, Ferber's own statements about *Show Boat*'s origins suggest that her Jewish background continued to have a hand in her writing. As with many of her novels that offer panoramic views of the American landscape, Ferber relied on her journalistic training to conduct research for *Show Boat*. In addition to interviewing actors in New York who had begun their careers on showboats, she spent time on the Mississippi aboard the *James Adams Floating Theatre*, the model for Captain Andy Hawks's *Cotton Blossom*. However, according to the author, the true genesis of *Show Boat* can be found in Exodus. In *A Peculiar Treasure*, Ferber explained how a woman born and raised in the Midwest came to write a novel about life on a Mississippi riverboat: "Perhaps, centuries and centuries ago," speculates Ferber, "I was a little Jewish slave girl on the Nile."[56]

Equating the Nile with the Mississippi, Ferber's statement on the Jewish lineage of *Show Boat* addresses the oppositional paradigms that have come to define the study of black-Jewish cultural relations. The fact that she refers to herself as "a little Jewish slave girl" implies that she is justifying her authority to write about the African American experience by postulating an identification based on a shared history of oppression. This reference to Jewish persecution thus supports Howe's claims that minstrelsy is a form of empathetic identification, "with one woe speaking through the voice of another."[57] Yet Ferber's strange and troubling transcendence of time and space underscores the ambivalence of her identification with African American suffering. In conjuring a hypothetical ancestral legacy rather than invoking the modern history of anti-Semitism and diaspora, Ferber simultaneously identifies with and separates herself from the black subjects of *Show Boat* through historical remove, a distancing furthered by age since she imagines herself "a little slave girl," rather than a woman or simply a slave. As an assimilated American Jew who met few impediments to her own career, Ferber finds herself harking back to antiquity for a concrete example of oppression (which is not to say that anti-Semitism was absent in modernity). Because Ferber does not claim to be an outsider in twentieth-century America, her transhistorical analogy suggests the ways in which American Jews were in the process of erasing a less distant history of discrimination, presumably by blending into whiteness.

Displacing white ethnic identity with African American themes (though, notably, not black protagonists), *Show Boat* appears to support Rogin's argument that racist appropriations of blackness aided Jews in assimilating into mainstream white society. At the same time, however, Rogin's thesis fails to account adequately for gender difference and, in particular, the ways in which labor impacts Ferber's female protagonist. By examining Ferber's representations of working womanhood concurrently with her incorporation of plot elements dealing with black culture and characters, including the trope of passing, I demonstrate that *Show*

Boat offers a complex portrait of white femininity in which interracial encounters have the effect of unsettling, rather than reifying, whiteness.

First serialized in the *Woman's Home Companion* in 1926, *Show Boat* went on to sell 320,000 copies in book form by the time Ferber recorded the sales figure in her first memoir in 1939. Upon its initial publication, the *New York Times* reviewer called the novel "a gorgeous thing to read for the reading sake's alone" and even praised its lack of literary inventiveness, assuring readers that this "free-breathing story" is "safe from the careful selectiveness and lacunation of modern schools of writing."[58] Also describing the portion of the book set on the Mississippi as "gorgeous," the reviewer for the *Chicago Daily Tribune* predicted that the novel would "take the fancy of the public even more completely than did *So Big*," which had earned Ferber the Pulitzer Prize the year before.[59] The prophecy was accurate. *Show Boat* became a highly desirable literary property, and Ferber was instantly bombarded with demands for its film and musical rights (some even before the entire novel had been serialized). While the novel's success was due in part to its author's reputation and her recent literary accolades, *Show Boat* had also tapped into the zeitgeist of post–World War I America.

Published in the midst of the Jazz Age and the Harlem Renaissance, *Show Boat* fed into what Langston Hughes termed the "vogue in things Negro" that dominated American culture in the 1920s.[60] What makes *Show Boat* an even more fascinating artifact of this time, however, is the fact that it is not truly a novel about black life, but instead a testament to the long-standing love affair between the American entertainment industry and African American culture, which reached its apex in the mid-1920s. As such, the novel privileges narratives of cultural intermixing and cross-racial performance above the story of its black characters. Although *Show Boat* has received little critical attention in studies of cross-cultural modernism that have proliferated in the past two decades, the novel substantiates conclusions drawn by scholars such as Ann Douglas, George Hutchinson, and Michael North, who have demonstrated that modern American literature and culture were produced through the interplay of black and white influences. "The 1920s was the first decade in which such theft and parody [of black culture] were openly and widely sought and, at moments, celebrated," writes Douglas in *Terrible Honesty: Mongrel Manhattan in the 1920s*. "The Negroization of American culture became something like a recognized phenomenon."[61] Ferber's novel was far from the only white-authored literary work to cash in on the "Negro vogue," initiated, in some accounts, by Eugene O'Neill's radically innovative deployment of black primitivism in *The Emperor Jones*, which premiered at the Provincetown Playhouse in 1920.[62] *Show Boat* was published in the same year as Carl Van Vechten's *Nigger Heaven*, a novel whose incendiary title alone may have well steered controversy away from Ferber. As a further indication of how white producers were mining the creative potential of black culture, *Show Boat*'s musical adaptation debuted in 1927, the year in which Al Jolson declared "you ain't heard nothing yet" in *The Jazz Singer*; Dorothy Heyward and DuBose Heyward premiered their black folk drama *Porgy* (which provided the source for another groundbreaking musical event, Jewish composer George Gershwin's 1935 opera *Porgy and Bess*); and Paul Green's protest play against black oppression, *In Abraham's Bosom*, won a Pulitzer Prize. Verifying Ferber's uncertainty about whether minstrelsy and jazz are "American (or . . . American Negro)," *Show Boat* is the product of that age (aptly named by none other than Fitzgerald) in which it was possible and fashionable to be both at once.

The opening of *Show Boat* establishes the muddying of waters, using the river as its central metaphor, the same river that functions in Ferber's autobiography as metonym for her Jewish identity. In the musical version's most memorable number, "Ol' Man River," Kern and Hammerstein famously transformed the Mississippi into a potent symbol for African American suffering: "Let me go 'way from de Mississippi / Let me go 'way from the white man boss; / Show me dat stream called de river Jordan / Dat's de ol' stream dat I long to cross."[63] In Ferber's hands, however, the Mississippi serves quite a different purpose: it establishes the novel's theme of racial mixing. The novel opens from the point of view of Magnolia's adult daughter, Kim, now a famous actress herself, who is recounting the circumstances of her birth on the Mississippi riverboat during a violent storm. Kim jokes that if her mother had followed through with her plan to name her daughter after the river itself, she would have had to change her name "or give up the stage altogether." Instead, Kim owes her monosyllabic moniker to the specific location of her birth, which took place at the intersection of three states: Kentucky, Illinois, and Missouri. As the novel describes the location that inspired Kim's name, "It was at a point just below Cairo, Illinois; that region known as Little Egypt, where the yellow waters of the Mississippi and the olive-green waters of the Ohio so disdainfully meet and refuse, with bull-necked pride, to mingle."[64] In keeping with Ferber's equation of the Mississippi and the Nile, the novel is styled as an epic of the New World, reconstructing the cradle of civilization on American shores; references

to the ancient world abound from Kim's birthplace to the town of The-
bes, where Magnolia's parents initially settle after their marriage before
taking to life on the river.

Invoking the origins of civilization, the novel opens with its own
foundational myth, but one also infused with images of mixing that ultimately defy definitive origins. Kim's birth not only takes place at a point
of intersection between states but also notably between North and South,
where the colors of the two rivers—the "yellow" of the Mississippi and
the "olive-green" of the Ohio—"meet and refuse, with bull-necked pride,
to mingle." Despite this stated resistance, Ferber's river imagery also implies that such intermingling takes place in defiance of man-made ob-
structions when the novel goes on to compare Magnolia to the "untamed
Mississippi that even now was flouting man-built barriers; laughing at
levees that said so far and no farther; jeering at jetties that said do thus
and so."[65] The comparison turns out to be apt; both Magnolia and Kim
are figures who flout "man-built barriers" due their intimated and actual
crossing of racial lines and their independence as working women. The
novel's initiatory image sets the stage for its theme of interracialism, and
it does so by rather obliquely linking racial mixing to Ferber's own Jewish heritage through thickly veiled references: first, the implication that
Kim, had she borne another name, would have had to change it to pursue
an acting career; second, the symbolic register of "Little Egypt," which
connects the myths of Show Boat's Mississippi to those of the Nile, home
to Ferber's "little Jewish slave girl."

Although the novel opens with a genesis tale, one of the defining aspects of the narrative is its resistance to origins and its continual assertion that identity is a matter of invention and performance, which is
suggested by numerous references to the ways in which the characters'
role-playing extends beyond the proscenium. The practice of name-
changing that Kim refers to in the novel's opening is the norm for the
theatrical crowd of the showboat; many of the characters are introduced
by their birth names and stage names, as well as the roles they impersonate on stage. With surprising subtlety (so subtle, in fact, that it has
been largely overlooked, or overshadowed by its less nuanced adaptation), Show Boat hints at the uncertain origins of both Ravenal women.
This reading may initially seem an unlikely one, given that the opening
of the novel, in describing Magnolia in labor, refers at least seven times
to the whiteness of her appearance; the first of these images, for example,
appears to establish Magnolia as an icon of white femininity by comparing her to her namesake: "So white . . . was she that her face on the

pillow was start[l]ingly like one of the waxen blossoms whose name she bore."[66] However, it is exactly this need for constant reinforcement of the heroine's whiteness that begins to shadow her in uncertainty since white identity typically derives its power from its invisibility, from the very fact that it does not need to be named but can rather be assumed.

The novel goes even further in constructing ambiguity about the racial backgrounds of Magnolia and her daughter by depicting both of their fathers, Captain Andy Hawks and Gaylord Ravenal, respectively, as self-invented men with enigmatic pasts. In fact, the only uncontested origins in *Show Boat*'s backstory are those of Magnolia's mother, Parthenia Ann (Parthy), whose name and bearing ascertain her Puritan upbringing. Characterized by an extremity of differences that at least metaphorically implies miscegenation, the marriage between Parthy and Captain Andy incongruously unites the prim and proper New Englander with the roving riverboat pilot who "drift[ed] up into Massachusetts," presumably from the South. While the novel supplies the details of Parthy's past, it remains comparatively silent on the subject of Andy's, other than to relate the story he uses to woos his wife: "Andy told her that his real name was André and that he was descended, through his mother, from a long line of Basque fisher folk. . . . It probably was true, and certainly accounted for his swarthy skin, his bright brown eyes, his impulsiveness, his vivacious manner."[67] The stated "probability" of the tale suggests it is more likely a fiction, and the fact that Captain Andy needs to account for his "swarthy" complexion and "vivacious" (read: non-Puritan) demeanor also raises the specter of passing. Although readers remain in the dark about much of Andy's past, the captain does have a "coming out" scene in the novel. Upon purchasing the *Cotton Blossom* without Parthy's consent, he reveals to his scandalized wife and enchanted daughter an aspect of his past that he had kept secret up until then: Captain Andy had himself been a showboat actor. In his brief summary of his acting career, Andy mentions only one role; in the afterpiece, he "played the nigger." Appropriately for a text that constantly draws attention to the performativity of identity, Andy does not reveal black roots, but rather comes out as an actor who has performed in blackface. This pronouncement provokes a horrified response from Parthy that again alludes to the metaphorical miscegenation of their marriage: "And let me tell you it's a good thing for you that you kept it from me all these years. I'd never have married you if I'd known. A show-boat actor!"[68]

In contrast to her mother, Magnolia is charmed by the revelation of her father's past. Resembling her father in "manner, temperament, colouring," the daughter also inherits his love of the theater and, of course, his ambiguous origins. In *Show Boat*, theatricality and racial mixing are consistently linked. Growing up on the showboat, Magnolia receives her most sustained course of education in black performance, learning "to strut and shuffle and buck-and-wing from the Negroes whose black faces dotted the boards of the Southern wharves as thickly as grace notes sprinkle a bar of lively music."[69] Such overblown similes allude to the amalgamation of black and white that comes to define American music and performance. While Magnolia is figured as a cultural mulatto, or white negress, through her appropriation of blackness, the text also insinuates that her mixed identity has to do with more than her style of performance. The opening of the novel may have persisted in describing her as "white," but, as it turns out, the faintness of her appearance had more to do with the trials of childbirth, since, later in the text, she repeatedly is described as "dark-complected." The novel comes closest to confronting the issue directly when Magnolia is preparing for an excursion with Julie (whose own mixed-race background has yet to be revealed), and Parthy instructs her rebellious daughter to wear a hat with the admonition, "Black enough as 'tis."[70]

Although favoring her father in most respects, Magnolia, like her mother, ends up marrying a man with a mysterious family history and a tendency to roam, the gambler Gaylord Ravenal. While Parthy wisely doubts whether he is indeed "a Ravenal of Tennessee, or whatever rascally highfalutin story he's made up for himself," Captain Andy takes an immediate liking to his daughter's beau, recognizing that Gaylord's proficiency in self-invention has trained him well for the showboat stage.[71] Having learned a lesson from her own experience of marriage, Parthy is quick to recognize the ease with which one can fabricate a personal history. When Parthy hears that Gaylord has verified his lineage as a "Ravenal of Tennessee" by taking Andy and Magnolia on a visit to his family plot, she protests their foolhardy readiness to trust him: "I could show you gravestones. I could say my name was Bonaparte and show you Napoleon's tomb, but that wouldn't make him my grandfather, would it!"[72] During this graveyard visit, the novel intimates that Gaylord's reinvention may be an attempt to obscure his racial background. Showing Andy and Magnolia the last will and testament documenting the history of the Ravenals, the gambler-turned-actor claims to descend from a long line of Gaylords, who were the "black sheep" of the family. This explanation for his lack of current family connections prompts a knowing exchange between father and future son-in-law:

"Black too, are you?" said Andy then, drily.

"As pitch."[73]

Ferber employs multiple meanings of "black" to cast doubt on the racial identities of four of the novel's central white figures: Captain Andy, Gaylord, Magnolia, and Kim. Generations of *Show Boat*'s stage and screen audiences have understood the narrative's main characters to be white, but it is through implications such as this one that the novel renders ambiguous the identities of most of the family at the center of its saga. As the initial image of the river forewarned, *Show Boat*'s characters exist at the convergence of borders that may or may not mingle.

Black Like She; or, The Girls Who Went White

The tendency to overlook the vague biological roots of *Show Boat*'s main characters may, in part, be the result of the better-known musical adaptations, which eliminate this element of ambiguity. Yet for *Show Boat*'s theatrical audiences, the most memorable, nonmusical moment remains the so-called miscegenation scene. In the novel, this scene temporarily deflects attention toward a secondary character, the showboat's star, Julie Dozier. Dramatically "outed" by a spurned lover who reveals the secret of her mixed-race ancestry, Julie is found guilty of passing for white and of an illegal marriage to a white man, her fellow actor Steve Baker. Upon receiving the warning that the sheriff has been notified of their illegal union, Steve—well prepared for the inevitability of the disclosure—promptly cuts Julie's hand and sucks her blood. Because the others on the showboat can then truthfully testify that Steve, too, has black blood in him, the couple is able to outwit the sheriff, who threatens to arrest them for violating Mississippi's law against miscegenation.[74] Most of the showboat's cast and crew are sympathetic to Julie and come to her defense. Nonetheless, under the threat of violence to the entire troupe if the show were to go on with "mixed blood," Julie and Steve are forced to leave the company after her identity is revealed.

Although the musical adaptation of Ferber's novel takes major and minor liberties with her text, this scene is transcribed almost word for word—in part because Ferber took great pains to stage it as melodrama with numerous references to its own theatricality. For example, the scene in its entirety is compared to "a rehearsal of a *Cotton Blossom* thriller."[75] This interlude appears to recontain the threat of racial ambiguity by expelling Julie from the showboat, but it also dismantles racial classifications and flouts the absurdity of the one-drop rule, just as the Mississippi was earlier described as flouting its "man-built barriers." Whether set on stage during a rehearsal (as it is in the musical and James Whale's 1936 film version) or behind the scenes, more scandalously, in the couple's bedroom (as it is in Ferber's novel), this episode, in taking place among actors on a showboat, derives further meaning from its metatheatrical context. The fact that the scene's key players *are* players works to expose race as a social performance and a legal construction subject to loopholes.

Taking note of Julie's story and a similar subplot in Hurst's *Imitation of Life*, scholars such as Susan Gubar have remarked on the unusual occurrence that Jewish women writers produced two popular texts in the genre of the passing novel.[76] Commonly associated with African American literature, the novel of passing, in which a mixed-race character crosses to the white side of the color line, reached its heyday during the Harlem Renaissance with the publication of Walter White's *Flight* (1926), Nella Larsen's *Passing* (1929), Jessie Fauset's *Plum Bun* (1929), and the republication of James Weldon Johnson's *The Autobiography of an Ex-Colored Man* (1912, 1927)—to cite just the most famous examples. The topic of passing has produced a voluminous body of scholarship, with recent literary and cultural studies extending definitions of passing to include categories of identity other than race, such as ethnicity, class, gender, sexuality, and religion.[77] The literature of passing has also become an important site for examining intersections between African American and Jewish identity in American culture, in particular by allowing critics to compare the groups' proximities to whiteness.

Such inquiries have been propelled, in part, by the publication of contemporary passing novels such as Philip Roth's *The Human Stain* and Danzy Senna's *Caucasia* in which black protagonists pass for Jewish.[78] Roth and Senna, however, draw on a rich interethnic tradition; Jewish and African American writers have been using passing to mediate between the experiences of Jews and blacks in the United States since the early twentieth century. In addition to the phenomenon of passing novels authored by Jewish women (which might include lesser-known examples like Vera Caspary's 1929 *The White Girl* in addition to *Show Boat* and *Imitation of Life*), the figure of the chameleonic Jew appears in a surprising number of African American–authored passing narratives, including those by White, Johnson, Fauset, and Larsen cited above. Surveying such cases, Daniel Itzkovitz demonstrates that the "movements" of Jews into the mainstream "resonate[d] with the struggles of . . . passing African

American characters"; he argues that instead of confirming Jews' whiteness, as Rogin would have it, such examples expose "the unsettled place
of *Jewishness* in early twentieth-century American culture."[79] Drawing
on Lauren Berlant and Elizabeth Freeman's formulation of "queer nationality," Itzkovitz further demonstrates that "the unsettled place of
Jewishness" (as simultaneously representative of the nation and racially
other) creates a "fantasied space" in which difference is subsumed under sameness and definitions of whiteness are destabilized rather than
fixed.[80]

The rubric of passing has also provided several critics with an occasion to reevaluate Jewish assimilation narratives.[81] In *Performing Americanness*, a recent study pairing modern Jewish and African American
fiction, Catherine Rottenberg argues against interpreting novels by Jewish writers through the framework of assimilation because "the concept
retains an essentialist notion of the self as well as a static and monolithic
notion of U.S. and Jewish culture." Highlighting the motif of theatricality in works by Yezierska and Cahan, she suggests that these texts are
better categorized as "passing narratives of sorts" because "passing is not
understood to be either necessarily subversive" or "recuperative" of he-
gemonic norms. Instead, argues Rottenberg, "passing becomes the point
of entry into a discussion of race as performative reiteration."[82]

In light of Itzkovitz's and Rottenberg's comparative analyses of Jewish
and African American identity through the lens of passing, we might
reconsider the notion that *Show Boat* represents a drastic departure from
Ferber's prior fiction. In fact, illustrative of Rottenberg's claims, Ferber's
early fiction provides some of the best literary examples we have of assimilation rendered as passing. In most Jewish American literature, assimilation is depicted as a gradual process in which ties to the past are
shed slowly, rather than severed radically, as characters become more
American. In both Ferber's *Fanny Herself* and her 1918 short story "The
Girl Who Went Right," female protagonists actively—and quite suddenly—make opportunistic decisions to hide their Jewish identities for
the sake of employment. While the character of Julie is, in a sense, borrowed from nineteenth-century sentimentalism and the African American literary tradition, she is more than a stock mulatto figure. Crossing
the color line in order to find work as an actress in the segregated theater,
she is also an extension of Ferber's concern with female characters who
must obscure their heritage when it becomes an obstacle in their careers.
The troubling of whiteness that Ferber began with the fashioning of pluralistic identity in *Fanny Herself* is thus continued in *Show Boat*, with

Jewishness providing both backstory and subtext for Ferber's formulation of an interracial American ideal.

When critics categorize *Show Boat* as a novel in the passing genre, they are typically referring to the miscegenation subplot alone and not to the fact that Ferber also creates some mystery as to the racial origins of her primary characters. Julie's story is read as a fairly conventional passing plot in which racial boundaries are upset temporarily only to be restored. Because Julie exits the narrative at the point that her passing is exposed, it is tempting to view her character as a reiteration of the trope of the tragic mulatto; the trope was often used to express white anxiety about racially ambiguous bodies, as well as their corresponding recontainment, which typically took place through death—hence the adjective "tragic." Despite her recontainment, Julie remains significant for the ways that her racial crossing bears consequences for at least two of the presumably white characters in the novel. To focus solely on the more conventional story of Julie's passing neglects the fact that Steve also crosses the color line by passing for black. Furthermore, a close reading of the miscegenation scene suggests that the marriage of Julie and Steve is not the only case of miscegenation on board the *Cotton Blossom*. Rather than reinforcing boundaries between black and white, Julie's narrative sets into motion an uncertainty about race that opens a space in which assumptions about characters' white identities are continually undermined.

Prior to the revelation of Julie's identity, the novel drops several clues, which are not that different from those used to call into question the identities of its main characters. In part, doubt is cast on Julie because she is an actress in a time when the theater was associated with the taint of immorality that metaphorically darkens her, a trope that could later be applied to Magnolia as well. While Parthy reserves suspicion and disdain for Julie as a woman who makes her living in the theater, Magnolia takes quite a different view, idealizing her older friend, as in this description: "Julie's eyes were deep-set and really black, and there was about them a curious indefinable quality. Magnolia liked to look into their soft and mournful depths. Her own eyes were dark, but not like Julie's. Perhaps it was the whites of Julie's eyes that were different."[83] The passage plays with the idea that one's "true" race is detectable in certain body parts, a common motif in interracial literature.[84] Julie's eyes may be "really black," just as she is revealed to be, but the "curious indefinable quality" renders her identity ambiguous. The comparison between Julie's and Magnolia's eyes can be read in competing ways—as reinforcing the identification between the two characters, or establishing Magnolia as white in relation to Julie (in other words, Magnolia may be "dark," but she is not "really black" in the same way that Julie is). The description goes on to suggest that the "indefinable quality" of Julie's eyes lies not in their blackness, but in their whiteness. Intimating that there are different shades of white, the passage contributes to the text's destabilization of white identity, its inability to be defined, while the hypothetical "perhaps" holds out the possibility that Julie's whiteness may not be different from Magnolia's after all.

Like her fellow chronicler of life on the Mississippi, Mark Twain (a literary influence explicitly acknowledged in the first chapter of *Show Boat*), Ferber proves race to be "a fiction of law and custom."[85] Twain coined the famous phrase in *Pudd'nhead Wilson*, a "Prince and Pauper" tale that begins when babies of different races are switched at birth; the fable allowed Twain to explore the fictions of race by placing the tale of a black man who passes for white alongside that of a white man who passes for black. Ferber employs multiple passing narratives to similar effect. In the "miscegenation scene," not only is Julie's passing exposed, but the scene turns on the ability of a white character, Steve, to pass for black. The metaphorical mixing of blood is described in eroticized, vampiric tones; after cutting Julie's hand, Steve "bent his blond head, pressed his lips to the wound, sucked it greedily." Steve's desire for blackness can be understood as a rejection, rather than substantiation, of his whiteness. The following dialogue ensues between Steve and the sheriff who arrives to arrest him and Julie:

> "You wouldn't call a man a white man that's got Negro blood in him, would you?"
>
> "No, I wouldn't; not in Mississippi. One drop of nigger blood makes you a nigger in these parts."
>
> "Well, I got more than a drop of—nigger blood in me, and that's a fact. You can't make miscegenation out of that."
>
> "You ready to swear to that in a court of law?"
>
> "I'll swear to it any place. I'll swear it now. . . . I'll do more than that. Look at all these folks here. There ain't one of them but can swear I got Negro blood in me this minute. That's how white I am."
>
> Sheriff Ike Keener swept the crowd with his eye. Perhaps what he saw in their faces failed to convince him. "Well, I seen fairer men than you was niggers."[86]

The critique of race offered in Ferber's dialogue is fascinating in its use of semantics. Note, for example, that Steve does not lie and pronounce himself black, but rather declares, "That's how white I am." We also see his reluctance to assume the racist language proffered by the law; Steve's initial reference to "Negro blood" becomes "nigger blood" in the sheriff's response. Steve hesitates—indicated by the dash—before repeating the offensive word, only to return to his original term, "Negro blood." In contrast to the musical's controversial use of the term "nigger" (which Hammerstein often put into the mouths of blacks themselves), Ferber tends to reserve the word for use by overtly racist characters, whose boorishness is on full display. The dialogue's distinction between "nigger" and "Negro" addresses the ways in which race is constituted linguistically, despite attempts to pass it off as scientific fact through the discourse of blood.[87] Even the sheriff's words concede that race is a legal construction, since he stipulates "not in Mississippi" and "in these parts," thus indicating that definitions of blackness varied from state to state.

In her analysis of the "miscegenation scene" in the musical, Linda Williams finds "Steve's negrophilic 'posing'" to be "the most disruptive of the boundaries of the color line that *Show Boat* simultaneously challenges and upholds," especially because he performs blackness without recourse to "the exaggerated blackface tradition."[88] As Williams goes on to note, the musical restores racial order by eliminating Steve and Julie following this scene (in fact, while Julie makes an appearance later, it is Steve, the character who is more disruptive to the color line, who disappears completely). In the novel, however, Magnolia turns out to be the character who is most disruptive to the color line. The fact that the text continually sidesteps confirmation of Magnolia's origins asserts the fluidity of racial boundaries through performative enactments that resist stabilization or narrative containment. Because she remains a racially ambiguous character throughout, Magnolia simultaneously passes for white and passes for black; her dual passing is highlighted in scenes that ally her with Julie (as a character who passes for white) and with Steve (as a character who passes for black). The "miscegenation scene," for example, culminates in the conjoining of Magnolia and Julie, leaving us with a visual image that defines the protagonist as an emblem of race mixing. Julie, dressed in black, and Magnolia, dressed in white, run toward each other on the verge of their teary farewells; the chapter concludes thus: "And when finally they came together, the woman dropped on her knees in the dust of the road and gathered the weeping child to her and held her close, so that as you saw them sharply outlined against the sunset the black of the woman's dress and the white of the child's frock were as one."[89] Like Ferber's earlier fiction, in which essentialist notions of identity were challenged through material metaphors, this scene figures racial difference as the contrast between colors of clothes, rather than as biological or bodily distinction. The differences can be overcome and interwoven to create a new entity: black and white become "one."

Solidifying the merging of Magnolia's and Julie's identities, the younger woman grows up to assume the older one's role in the showboat troupe. Race seems to temporarily take a backseat as the novel follows the vicissitudes of Magnolia's adulthood, from her courtship, marriage, and pregnancy to her attempts to support herself and her young daughter after she is abandoned by Gaylord. Race reenters the narrative when Magnolia, having traded her itinerant existence on the showboat for the equally unstable fast life of early-twentieth-century Chicago, becomes a "coon singer" on the variety stage. Applying Morrison's theory of the Africanist presence to the text, critics have observed that her upward mobility occurs "on the backs of blacks." Characters such as Julie, Jo, and Queenie played formative roles in Magnolia's musical and theatrical training on the showboat, but their positions, in direct contrast to their protégé's, remain fixed. In *Showing Grit*, for example, M. Nourbese Philip describes Julie as "the Other to Magnolia's whiteness," explaining that "Julie is what Magnolia's existence as a white person is developed against—the lack of freedom and agency of Black people."[90]

Show Boat may function as an apt test case for Morrison's theory of the Africanist presence, but the majority of the evidence for such a reading hinges on the adaptation rather than the novel. In addition to bringing the motif of black suffering to the forefront through its theme song, "Ol' Man River," the musical also inserts a complementary motif of black sacrifice; the notion that black virtue is obtained by doing good for whites can be traced from the sentimental tradition, where it is epitomized in *Uncle Tom's Cabin*, through contemporary popular culture manifestations in films like *The Green Mile*. To audiences of the adaptation, it would appear that Magnolia's career is facilitated by Julie's continual sacrifice. In Hammerstein's revision, Magnolia's distress at Julie's banishment from the showboat is quickly assuaged when she learns that she will have the opportunity to take over Julie's role and fulfill her dream of becoming an actress. In the novel, Magnolia is still a child when Julie leaves, and many years pass before she assumes the older woman's place in the troupe. Magnolia's following in Julie's footsteps does not read as white replacing black, but rather as a fulfillment of the promise that "the black of the woman's dress and the white of the child's frock" would become "one." Nor, in the novel, does Julie definitively reappear following her expulsion from the showboat; in a brief moment, Magnolia suspects she that sees her former friend working as a secretary in a brothel, only to have the older woman just as quickly "vanish . . . up the stairs like a black ghost."[91] In contrast, Hammerstein created an additional scene for Julie that is intended to echo directly the consequences of her banishment. In this scene, Magnolia, after being abandoned by Gaylord, arrives for an audition at a Chicago variety theater. Julie, now an alcoholic and apparently abandoned by Steve, is the theater's torch singer. Unbeknownst to Magnolia, Julie recognizes her, realizes she must badly need a job, and announces that she intends to run off on a drinking spree, thus forcing the management to hire Magnolia in her place. Julie's good deed goes unrewarded, for Magnolia remains wholly unaware of the other woman's sacrifice on her behalf. In the spirit of Uncle Tom, Julie is the virtuous black figure who sacrifices herself in order to launch the career of her white friend.

Sans Julie, Ferber's rendition of the audition scene reads quite differently. Instead of reinforcing the argument that white success occurs "on the backs of blacks," the scene is another instance of the novel's tendency to complicate white identity. Accompanying herself on a banjo, Magnolia performs "Negro songs," mimicking "that soft and husky Negro quality which for years she had heard on river boats, bayous, landings." So convincing is Magnolia's performance that she (much like Sophie Tucker) is taken to be a black woman—or, more precisely, the director asks, "You a nigger?" In response, "the unaccustomed red surged into Magnolia's cheeks, dyed her forehead, her throat, painfully. 'No, I'm not a—nigger.'" In the context of Ferber's previous passing texts, it is difficult to read this scene without recalling that Fanny Brandeis, interviewed by her new boss, replied "No" when he asked if she was a Jew. In the context of *Show Boat* itself, the audition scene is a textual echo of the miscegenation scene, seeming to align Magnolia with Steve in their abilities to pass for black. For example, the sheriff's declaration to Steve, "I seen fairer men than you was niggers," is echoed in the director's half-hearted apology to Magnolia: "No offense. I've seen 'em lighter'n you."[92] But the scene provides little confirmation of Magnolia's whiteness, beginning with the fact that she actually changes color in response to the director's question. Magnolia's pause before pronouncing the word "nigger" echoes Steve's hesitant uttering of the word in the miscegenation scene, but it is also important to keep in mind what Magnolia is refusing here. She is denying the racist interpellation, "nigger," *not* the possibility that she is of mixed race. This attempt to refuse racist language is similarly evident when the director asks her, "What kind of a coon song do you call that?" and she replies, "It's a Negro melody."[93]

In fact, the melodies Magnolia performs at her audition are not "coon songs," but spirituals, and they do not seem to have been chosen at random. For *Show Boat*'s original readers, Magnolia's first song, "All God's Chillun Got Wings," would undoubtedly evoke the title of Eugene O'Neill's play about interracial marriage, produced to great controversy just two years earlier; as such, it provides a bridge back to the novel's miscegenation scene. Magnolia goes on to sing her favorite spiritual, from which the text quotes the chorus in full: "Go down, Moses / 'Way down in Egypt land, / Tell ole Pharaoh, / To let my people go."[94] Banned on plantations because of its blatant protest, "Go Down, Moses" is a prototype of the African American spiritual that took its inspiration from the Old Testament and, in particular, from the book of Exodus. The spiritual draws analogies between African Americans and Israelites, the South and Egypt, white slave-masters and Pharaoh, freedom and the promised land of Canaan. This spiritual appears in the novel at the exact point that Magnolia embarks on her new career as an imitator of black art. The question of ontology that Ferber never resolves in relation to Magnolia's racial background is also central to the controversy over the appropriation of black material by whites, since the accusation of "theft" implies the right of authenticity. Magnolia's theatrical comeback as a "coon singer" complicates the logic of appropriation—first, because we do not know whether she herself has a legitimate claim to blackness and, second, because her favorite spiritual itself exemplifies the complexities of cross-cultural exchange. Ferber, we should recall, justified her own writing of *Show Boat* with the speculation that she was once a "a little Jewish slave girl on the Nile." While at first glance this statement draws a problematic analogy between black and Jewish oppression, "Go Down, Moses" reminds us that the parallel is suggested by African American religion and folklore and, as the last chapter of this book demonstrates, was enlisted in the service of black writers such as Zora Neale Hurston as well. While critics have argued that mediations between black culture and white audiences enabled Jews to achieve whiteness, *Show Boat*'s audition scene suggests a more complex interpretation of black-Jewish relations, reframing them in terms of mutual exchange rather than simply unidirectional appropriation.

In alluding to the misrecognition that can accompany racial appropriations, the audition scene suggests that the performance of blackness calls into question, rather than substantiates, Magnolia's whiteness. Magnolia is not the ideal of white femininity that her name implies. This is confirmed by the ending of the novel, which—like many narratives of passing—is figured as a homecoming.[95] Sacrificing her international celebrity, Magnolia returns to the showboat to become its proprietor. Appalled by her mother's decision, Magnolia's daughter, Kim, ventures South to retrieve her, announcing her plans to "establish a real American theatre in New York," where she will perform "Ibsen and Hauptmann, and Werfel, and Schnitzler, and Molnar, and Chekhov, and Shakespeare." But Magnolia ignores her daughter's complaints about "[f]lies and Negroes and mud and all this yellow terrible river that you love more than me," as well as Kim's desire to appropriate European high culture as "real American theatre." Magnolia rejects the stability of whiteness and of a more traditional gender role—here, represented by motherhood—for a stormier life on the yellow river.[96] Magnolia's return to the river may be a return to her origins, but the river in *Show Boat* is also the origin of ontological uncertainty. Having made her home on a showboat, Magnolia is permanently unmoored; lacking solid ties to the land, she is not only uprooted, but without roots, her identity a matter of performative invention.

It was the river, too, that provided a link between Ferber's Jewish past and her authorship of *Show Boat*. My reading of *Show Boat* suggests that the interracial themes that pervade her fiction remained tied to her Jewish identity. The conflict between assimilation and pluralism that Ferber explored through the character of Fanny Brandeis becomes one episode in Ferber's vaster narrative of a transnational America, defined by interracial and interethnic encounters resulting from the forces of colonization and imperialism, migration and immigration. From the Oklahoma frontier of *Cimarron* to the Texas border of *Giant*, Ferber's fiction documents a multiethnic American landscape that resists all attempts to impose "man-built" borders. Her novels continually take up the controversial topics of miscegenation and interracial romance—between blacks and whites, Mexicans and whites, and Native Americans and whites—in order to argue against attempts to maintain white purity by restricting contact between the races. The concerns of *Show Boat* were not a temporary fascination for Ferber, motivated only by the "Negro vogue" that swept the nation in the 1920s. Her 1941 novel, *Saratoga Trunk*, for example, returns to many of the themes underlying *Show Boat*. *Saratoga Trunk* bears special consideration here because of the ways it complicates narratives of passing and blackface through a racially ambiguous heroine who supersedes binary oppositions and defies definition.

"Both at Once"

In *Saratoga Trunk*, a mixed-race protagonist again becomes central to Ferber's investigation of racial performance. Her father a Creole aristocrat and her mother a beautiful *placée*, "queen of that half-world peopled by women of doubtful blood," the novel's protagonist, Clio Dulaine, is not an actress by profession, but rather makes a life out of "play-acting," assuming various roles as she takes on high society, first in New Orleans and then in Saratoga.[97] Born in New Orleans (a location that contributes to the ambiguity of her background), but raised partially in France, Clio is depicted as a mixture of languages and cultures, her identity nearly impossible to pin down. Although the novel strongly intimates that she carries some combination of mixed blood, it repeatedly refrains from clarifying her racial heritage. While Clio may at first cling to her Creole roots, her "true" identity is irrelevant, for she comes to live by the dictum, "No matter what I say I am—that I am. I shall be what it suits me to be."[98] After the deaths of her family members, Clio is assisted in this endeavor by the attendance of two faithful servants, the Negress Angélique Pluton, who goes by Kaka, and the dwarf coachman Cupide, who looked white but was thought to be Kaka's son. Clio vows not to follow in the path of her mother by becoming a kept woman, but instead intends to use her beauty and her talent as a "natural mimic" to win herself a wealthy husband.[99] Teaming up with a fellow schemer, the similarly self-invented Clint Maroon, Clio travels to Saratoga where she passes as Madame de Chanfret, American widow of a French marquis. So persuasive is Clio's performance that it erases any prior identity: "Sometimes even she found it difficult to tell when she was herself and when she was the mysterious Mrs. De Chanfret. Perhaps no one enjoyed her performance more than she. Frequently she actually convinced herself of her own assumed role."[100] Although she captivates Saratoga society and almost succeeds in her plot of winning over the unwitting millionaire Bart Van Steed, Clio stops just short of achieving her goal, in danger of being exposed as "an adventuress" with "a touch of the tarbrush."[101] Realizing that she is in love with Maroon, the man she earlier insisted was no more than her business "partner," Clio sabotages her own scheme, and the novel ends with the happy union of the two self-invented lovers.[102]

Although Ferber is known as a chronicler of the American success story, Clio, like Magnolia, ultimately chooses *against* obtaining upward mobility by marrying into whiteness. In the novel's climactic scene, which takes place at a masquerade ball in Saratoga, Clio thwarts her own plans to ascend the social ladder when she appears in a dual spectacle that sends up her ambiguous racial heritage. Although she initially intended to attend the ball as a marquise—itself a perilous statement about the role she has taken on—she changes her mind at the last minute. With clothes borrowed from Kaka, Clio appears as "a black mammy in voluminous calico and a vast white apron, a kerchief crossed on her bosom, her head swathed in a brilliant orange tignon [with] [g]old and diamond hoop earrings dangl[ing] from beneath the turban's folds." With a "rolling eye" and a "grin" that was a "scarlet and white gash in the blackened face," Clio performs for the crowd, breaking into a shuffle in "defiance against every convention she so hated." But Clio's performance does not end there. She returns to her room only to make a second appearance. She removes her makeup, applies white powder to her face, and transforms herself into a marquise, draped in satin. This time, instead of embodying blackness herself, she brings Kaka along as her "attendant, all very proper."[103] Even though Clio appears first in blackface and then in whiteface, blacking up does not lead to Clio's reinvention as white, for it is at this moment that she forsakes her proposed plot to marry into upper-class society, choosing instead to align herself with the equally mysterious Clint Maroon, whose last name refers to fugitive slaves and to the state of being stranded between places. Clio's double masquerade can be read as a revision of *Show Boat*'s "miscegenation scene." Just as that famous scene involved a double passing narrative (in which a black character passes for white and a white character passes for black), this scene similarly exposes both blackness and whiteness as social performances. The destabilizing effect is very much the same, as Clio defies the convention of racial classification. Initially confused over whether she is "Mama's family" or "Papa's family," Clio has resolved to be "both at once."[104] This idea of *choosing* to be "both at once" resonates with the model of cultural pluralism earlier embodied in *Fanny Herself*. It is an echo of the tableau in *Show Boat* in which "the black of the woman's dress and the white of the child's frock were as one." And it accounts for Ferber's inability to distinguish between cultural forms that are "American" and those that are "American Negro."

* * *

While Kern and Hammerstein's *Show Boat* holds an honored place in the annals of American musical theater, its appropriation of African American suffering for the purposes of white entertainment offers a porthole through which to view the fraught terrain of the black-Jewish cultural imaginary. Given all the attention garnered by the landmark musical, which premiered just one year after Ferber published her 1926 novel, it became nearly impossible for critics to separate the source from its adaptations. As a result, Ferber's articulation of an interracial ideal, suffused with its own share of "idealistic chutzpah," was lost in the shuffle. Ferber may be guilty of perpetuating the black-white binary in some of her minstrel-like characterizations, but her novel, when read closely, also complicates such dichotomies. *Show Boat* is a paradoxical concoction, a strange mixture of crude contrasts between black and white and subtler nuances that have the potential to explode the myths of whiteness that the novel and its adaptation are more often censured for upholding.

In a 1950 interview, Langston Hughes suggested that African American writers might find a model in the career trajectory of Ferber, a writer he listed among his own earliest influences. Noting that Ferber "originally wrote stories of Jewish life, but she broadened her perspective and went on to write *So Big*, *Show Boat*, and *Cimarron*," Hughes predicted that African American letters was "headed in the direction of similar and perhaps superior achievement."[105] This statement may at first seem odd coming from Hughes, an ardent proponent of the black aesthetic in literature. Hughes is not advocating that African American writers should forsake their black outlook and consciousness, however. Instead, in invoking Ferber as a model, he suggests that one's minority position can operate as the basis for a broadened perspective in which the notion of what is universal—and American—will be redefined.

3 / Limitations of White: Fannie Hurst and the Consumption of Blackness

Published in 1926, Edna Ferber's *Show Boat* was quickly overshadowed by its groundbreaking musical adaptation. At the beginning of the following decade, Fannie Hurst's racially themed novel, *Imitation of Life*, similarly became a casualty of its author's tremendous popularity when it was snapped up by Hollywood filmmakers. First serialized in *Pictorial Review* in 1932 under the title "Sugar House," Hurst's narrative was published in novel form in 1933 and renamed, in accordance with its author's wishes, *Imitation of Life*—a title that has come to bear enormous weight in cultural and critical responses.[1] Ferber's induction of the businesswoman as a new literary type in the Emma McChesney stories and *Fanny Herself* helped pave the way for *Imitation of Life*, which follows a white woman's rise from door-to-door peddler of maple syrup to chief executive of a waffle-and-coffee-shop empire. Hurst's female variation on the theme of American success incorporates a racial angle when her protagonist, a widowed mother, hires a black maid to run her home and care for her child. The lives of white Bea Pullman and her daughter, Jessie, become intertwined with those of black Delilah and her light-skinned daughter, Peola, who grows up to renounce her mother in order to cross the color line and pass for white.

As soon as *Pictorial Review* announced the serialization of Hurst's novel, the major Hollywood studios began vying for rights to the material. *Show Boat* captured Kern and Hammerstein's interest largely because its racial themes tapped into the zeitgeist of the Jazz Age. The racial plotline of *Imitation of Life*, in contrast, would yield considerable anxiety on the part of the studios due to the Production Code, which prohibited representations of miscegenation, but the story's appeal for modern women made it an irresistible literary property that promised to draw large audiences. Thanking Hurst for sending her a copy of the manuscript to review, the story editor at Fox Film Corporation wrote that Bea Pullman's plight touched her "personally, being a mother of a grown daughter and knowing 'the price of a career'!"[2]

Universal Pictures was to win the film rights, and the first cinematic adaptation of *Imitation of Life* premiered in 1934, directed by John Stahl. In 1959, the life of Hurst's fiction was extended once again when Universal remade *Imitation of Life* into a lavish melodrama with Douglas Sirk at the helm. The cinematic adaptations of *Imitation of Life* have produced a voluminous body of film scholarship, contributing to investigations into the genres of melodrama and the woman's film and to cultural criticism on the intersections of gender, race, and class. Although many critics acknowledge the 1933 text as a source, analyses of the novel continue to be mediated through the films to the extent that scholars often mistakenly attribute plot elements to Hurst that were altered in the process of adaptation; at the same time, the revisions themselves have been a common topic of analysis because they shed light on the kinds of sexual and racial representations that were permissible on screen.[3]

Even in its own time, however, responses to Hurst's novel, especially in relation to its treatment of race, were refracted through the lens of its cinematic adaptation. Upon its publication, *Imitation of Life* was reviewed extensively in the mainstream press, but it was not until the release of Stahl's film one year later that the novel became a subject of debate among African Americans. Although responses to the film and novel were decidedly mixed, *Imitation of Life* lends itself to be read as a problematic appropriation of black themes that follows in the footsteps of the minstrel tradition. African American writer Claude McKay, for one, dismissed the novel as a "syrup-and-pancake hash."[4] Most famously, the novel met with opprobrium from black intellectual Sterling Brown. Reviewing the 1934 film adaptation for *Opportunity*, the organ of the National Urban League, Brown accused the novel's author of perpetuating Southern plantation myths. Hurst's Delilah, in Brown's view, is "the old stereotype of the contented Mammy," and Peola is "the tragic mulatto," reflecting "ancient ideas about the mixture of the races."[5]

Hurst was well aware that the film adaptation overshadowed and strongly shaped opinion of her novel. In a public response to Brown, also published in *Opportunity*, and in private letters to several African

American correspondents, Hurst admitted that "there are many aspects" of the film that "fall short or deviate or even malign my original theme." However, she also took issue with the "carping, petty angles of criticism" that ranged from "the superficialities of idiom" to "the shape of the cook's cap," claiming that they distracted from the "larger social values" of the film. Whatever gripes Hurst might have had with Stahl's transformation of her material, she held firm to her conviction that the adaptation of her novel was a breakthrough in the genre of the social problem film, writing that "it practically inaugurates into the important medium of the motion-picture, a consideration of the Negro as part of the social pattern of American life."[6] This view has been endorsed by film historians such as Donald Bogle and Anna Everett, who have shown that the film was, if not a giant leap, then a good-size step forward in its attempt to address seriously racial injustice and to portray African American characters in a dignified manner rather than as the comic buffoons or violent marauders seen in earlier cinema.[7]

While *Show Boat*'s adaptation by Jewish men opened additional space for considerations of the text as a product of the black-Jewish cultural imaginary, the eclipse of Hurst's novel by its adaptations has largely obscured the role that Jewishness plays in her narrative. The lack of attention to Jewishness has been furthered by Hurst's erasure from most accounts of American Jewish literary history—an excision due to many factors, including her secular, midwestern, and middle-class background; her own stated ambivalence about her Jewish heritage; the fact that most of her novels do not feature obvious Jewish themes and characters; and her consistent categorization as a middlebrow writer. The 2004 Duke University Press reissue of *Imitation of Life*, the only novel by Hurst now in print, is indicative of renewed interest in the author and in what is considered to be her best-known work. The introduction to the reprint by its editor, Jewish cultural studies scholar Daniel Itzkovitz, further suggests that the novel deserves consideration as part of a Jewish literary and cultural tradition.[8]

Contributing to such recent reevaluations, this chapter asks what it means for Hurst as a Jewish woman writer to take up "the race question" and how her portrayal of African American characters and themes complicates existing paradigms of black-Jewish cultural relations. Instead of viewing this text as yet another example of "theft" that made its author "white and assimilable" (in Batker's words), I argue that Hurst's engagement with black culture needs to be understood in dialectical relation to her Jewish identity, her previous representations of Jewish life in fiction, and the various challenges to gender conventions posed by her life and her work. Despite recent recovery attempts, including Brooke Kroeger's in-depth 1999 literary biography, Hurst remains a little-known figure within the academy and virtually unknown outside of it. Classifications of Hurst as either a mass-market sentimentalist or, more narrowly, as an author whose entire reputation rests on *Imitation of Life* have overridden the complexities of a prolific and fascinating career that bridged fiction writing and social activism. As a corrective to historical erasure as well as to the many misconceptions circulating about the author and the text that has come to represent her, the first half of this chapter is devoted to substantial background on Hurst as a public figure who was committed to women's, Jewish, and civil rights issues. My intent is not to offer a strictly biographical reading of *Imitation of Life*; rather, in situating this midcareer novel within the broader context of Hurst's life and work, I arrive at a more nuanced interpretation of the original text and the various controversies it engendered. As I show, Hurst's multifaceted involvement with black life and culture extended well beyond *Imitation of Life* to her role as a social reformer and a white participant in the literary and artistic activities of the Harlem Renaissance. Through her participation in various venues of racial uplift, Hurst formed professional and personal relationships with African American artists, intellectuals, and activists that predated and postdated *Imitation of Life*—most famous among them, her much-discussed friendship with Zora Neale Hurston, which began when Hurst employed the black writer as her secretary. In this chapter and the next, I examine this interracial relationship and place Hurst's and Hurston's fiction side by side; in considering the exchange between two early-twentieth-century ethnic women writers, I further challenge the view that black-Jewish cultural relations consist of a unidirectional appropriation of blackness by Jewish producers.

Hurst's extensive advocacy on behalf of black causes did not shield *Imitation of Life* from charges of racism similar to the ones directed at *Show Boat*. Like Ferber's novel, however, *Imitation of Life* not only participates in a blackface literary tradition but is also *about* the commodification of black culture, a topic Hurst similarly addressed in "The Smudge," her 1922 story about a female blackface performer. While Ferber published *Show Boat* amid the "Negro vogue," Hurst composed *Imitation of Life* after the onset of the Great Depression that signaled the end of the Harlem Renaissance. Although the popularity of racially themed works persisted into the 1930s, Hurst's novel does more than cash in on a fad; it is well positioned to comment on it as well. It does so through the tale of the unequal partnership formed between white Bea and black Delilah, in which Bea mass-produces Delilah's maple-sugar hearts and waffles, eventually transforming her business into a lucrative chain of coffee shops and using the image of "Aunt Delilah," an obvious reference to "Aunt Jemima," to sell her products. Narrated from the third-person limited point of view of Bea, *Imitation of Life* continually draws attention to the inauthenticity of the black image in the white mind and thus critiques the limits of white subjectivity.

Nor does Bea's appropriation of Delilah's recipes and image, as exploitative as it may be, simply bring a stabilized white identity into being. Instead, *Imitation of Life* offers a complex portrait of white femininity, whose instability can be attributed to the protagonist's participation in the workforce. The white woman's labor and resulting success remain tied to and dependent on her association with blackness and black labor, but the effect of this cross-racial contact is double-edged; the juxtaposition with blackness simultaneously grants Bea access to a white power structure and "queers" her as a woman who refuses to conform to ideals of motherhood, domesticity, and heterosexuality. Delilah may function at times as an "Africanist presence" and thus a point of contrast for Bea, but Delilah's mixed-race daughter, Peola, is a source of identification, rather than differentiation, for the text's white heroine. Peola's passing highlights the instability of Bea's own position and the limitations she faces as a woman in big business. Peola's subplot also serves as a strong link to Hurst's earlier treatments of Jewish identity in her fiction. Hurst's representation of passing in *Imitation of Life* can be traced to the complication of whiteness she explored in her assimilation narratives in which Jewishness represented the ambivalence of being "almost white but not quite."[9] *Imitation of Life* features a gentile protagonist who is not marked explicitly as ethnic, but the ghost of Jewishness appears in the text, especially in the form of the secondary character of Bea's fellow businesswoman, Virginia Eden (née Sadie Kress). Although her background remains shrouded in ambiguity, Virginia Eden can be read as a representation of a passing Jew, a figure who consolidates the various threads of my analysis.

Fannie Hurst: Author, Feminist, and Jewess

Born in 1885 (though for some time she claimed 1889 as her birth year), Hurst was raised in St. Louis, Missouri, by well-off, assimilated German-Jewish parents, who fostered in their daughter a deep ambivalence about a heritage that, for them, was rooted more in racialism than religion.[10] Hurst's ambivalence toward her Jewish background is apparent throughout her autobiography, *Anatomy of Me*, where she acknowledges the destructive forces of Jewish self-hatred and describes being simultaneously subjected to anti-Semitism and to her parents' racist attitudes toward eastern European Jews and African Americans. Hurst went on live her life in defiance of her parents' conservative views, middle-American values, and nouveau riche ambitions. Rather than conform to their expectations that she marry well, for example, she insisted on attending college at Washington University in St. Louis and then went on to pursue a career as a writer. Her career began in earnest when, against her parents' wishes, she moved to New York City in 1910. There, she often immersed herself in working-class Jewish environments that captivated her imagination and inspired her early fiction. Hurst's marriage to pianist Jacques Danielson in 1915 further came as a shock to her parents; not only did they consider Danielson, a Russian Jewish immigrant, to be an inappropriate mate for their daughter, but the modern couple had made the most untraditional of matrimonial arrangements, maintaining separate residences so as to prioritize their work and keeping their union a secret from the public. (They managed to maintain this secrecy until 1920, when their marriage was discovered by a reporter who broke the story in the *New York Times*.) Aside from her writing, Hurst was a social activist and philanthropist who took up an extraordinary array of liberal causes, including women's rights (as a Lucy Stoner, for example, she advocated women's right to retain their maiden names after marriage), treatment of gays and lesbians, tenement reform, workers' compensation, and civil rights. Although she did not observe religious rituals, she also devoted her time to various Jewish activities, charities, and organizations; was active in aiding European refugees following Hitler's rise to power in the 1930s; and visited Israel in the 1950s.

When Hurst died in 1968, her obituary ran on the front page of the *New York Times*, a testament to her tremendous public appeal, but the *Times*'s summary of her career simultaneously condemned her to oblivion as a hack writer and "sob sister," the sobriquet often attached to her name. Its headline identifying her as a "popular author of romantic stories," the obituary noted that in the six decades of her prolific career she produced over one hundred stories and thirty books, which were "read under every hairdryer in America." Further dismissing the many film adaptations of her novels as "shameless tearjerkers," the obituary neatly summed up the critical consensus on her fiction by citing a literary critic who described her prose style as "flow[ing] like the Mississippi—wide, deep and rather muddy."[11] Despite the opinion of the literary establishment, Hurst's popularity was measurable in the astounding financial rewards she took in for her writing. She regularly earned over $5,000 for a single story in *Cosmopolitan*, and *Pictorial Review* paid her $45,000 for the first serial rights to the novel that became *Imitation of Life*.[12] There was accuracy to the phrase that frequently accompanied her byline, touting her as "the highest paid short story writer in America."

Like Ferber's, the fame Hurst enjoyed in her lifetime bears an inverse relation to the scholarly attention she has received since. The tides may be changing, but slowly. Since the early 1990s, literary critics such as Susan Koppelman, Ann Douglas, and Stephanie Thompson have called attention to the sociological richness and stylistic innovation of Hurst's fiction.[13] Indeed, to reduce Hurst to a sentimental purveyor of love stories is to note a single and scarcely dominant dimension of a vast and varied body of work. Her early fiction, for example, appealed to a Progressive-era market for its realism and social protest qualities. Although Hurst did not exactly forsake her bourgeois upbringing, her desire to be among the masses fueled the methods and materials of her fiction, which featured ordinary people, often the poor and downtrodden. Promotions for her fiction made much of the discrepancy between the writer's background and her subject matter, playing up her willingness to "slum" in order to conduct research. "Fannie Hurst chose to suffer!" screamed one advertisement, going on to explain that Hurst, "born to comfortable surroundings . . . didn't have to work, to know the fierce emotions of the poor, to understand the problems of girls less fortunate than she. But Fannie Hurst wanted to know their hopes—to probe their warm secret selves."[14] Other reports, exaggerated for purposes of publicity, detailed how Hurst "worked as waitress and factory hand to get in touch with life" or opted to cross the Atlantic in steerage rather than first class to gather material for her latest novel.[15] While Hurst's fiction does at times show the effects of mass production, what one reviewer of *Imitation of Life* called "the wear and tear of her determination to become the story-teller of the millions," her ability to meld the reformist sensibility of naturalism with modernist experimentation is especially evident in her second full-length work, *Lummox* (1923). Likely influenced by Gertrude Stein's *Three Lives* in both subject matter and style, *Lummox* uses stream-of-consciousness narration to tell the story of an inarticulate domestic servant as she struggles with poverty, violence, rape, and an out-of-wedlock pregnancy.[16]

Hurst's dual identity as fiction writer and spokesperson on women's issues was suggested by the fact that the press often referred to her as an "author-feminist." Adamant in her belief that women should pursue careers and be active in politics, she advocated a reformation of gender roles. As a 1926 headline summed it up, "Fannie Hurst Says Careers Aid Women; Authoress Declares Feminine Workers Not 'Masculine'; Made Sweeter, She Avers."[17] Most famously, Hurst advocated for a more progressive stance toward feminine and domestic ideals by calling for marriage reform. Her reputation may have been built on the escapist romance, but she held pragmatic views of relations between men and women and used her public fame as a platform for exposing the shibboleth of wedded bliss. Evocatively critiquing the institution of marriage as "a leaky, old ramshackle building in which we are living without modern sanitation," Hurst initially shared Ferber's determination not to marry in order to devote herself to her writing, but she ultimately decided to use her union with Danielson as an experiment in gender equality.[18] Their practice of keeping separate residences and meeting by appointment in order to maintain "personal liberty" was replicated by other couples of the era and became known as a "Fannie Hurst marriage."[19]

Hurst's fiction similarly addresses the rapidly shifting gender norms of the period, and the recent wave of critical interest in her work rightly identifies her as a "neglected source on the emergence of modern feminine sexuality."[20] Her treatment of working womanhood and critique of compulsory heterosexuality remain surprisingly relevant one hundred years after she began exploring these new gender ideologies in her fiction. As New Women were carving out paths for themselves, Hurst used the narrative arcs of her protagonists to test the waters, exploring the balance between the time-honored themes of love and marriage and the relatively new concerns of work and independence. In contradistinction to her own life choices, some critics have read Hurst's stories as expressions of the fear that eschewing the domestic life would lead to unhappiness. The title *Imitation of Life*, for example, has been understood to signify Bea's regret at devoting herself to her career and thus giving up opportunities for romantic love. But this ambivalence about women's entrance into the public sphere was not always present in her fiction. One of her best short stories, "Summer Resources," for example, sends quite a different message. Constructing a Jewish female protagonist as an icon of New Womanhood, it tells the story of Myra Sternberger, a dress designer who poses as a player on the marriage market, flirtatiously cajoling garment industry bachelors into showing her their latest designs and then outwitting them by re-creating their styles at lower prices. It is one of many stories in which we can find the seeds of *Imitation of Life*.

Among the aspects of Hurst's critical neglect, the most surprising is her exclusion from the canon of Jewish American literature.[21] *Jewish American Literature: A Norton Anthology*, published in 2001, includes no entry for Hurst (although it does for Ferber). While expressly Jewish protagonists and themes may be absent from most of Hurst's novels, her short fiction is another story altogether.[22] For well over a decade, Hurst laid the foundation for her career as a novelist by telling the stories of the Jewish immigrant families she encountered while visiting New York's East Side to collect material for her writing. Published in popular periodicals such as the *Saturday Evening Post* and *Cosmopolitan*, Hurst's stories portray an urban milieu populated by Meyerburgs, Ginsbergs, Cohns, and Shapiros. Dialogue driven, they capture the sounds of an immigrant-accented vernacular spoken by "working goils" and their "fellows."[23] Focusing on the drama of assimilation and expressing deep regret about forsaking the past, many of these stories represent the generational divide between sentimentalized "Yiddishe Mamas," who nostalgically cling to their ghetto roots, and their Americanized sons and daughters, who have remorselessly climbed their way uptown. Throughout her career, Hurst returned again and again to one of the most common themes of American Jewish fiction: intermarriage between Jews and gentiles. First exploring the topic in her 1923 *Cosmopolitan* short story "Seven Candles," she carried the theme over to subplots of several novels, including *Lummox, Back Street* (1931), and *Family!* (1960). In both her treatment of intermarriage and her outspoken critique of the American dream, Hurst's short stories share much in common with the writing of Anzia Yezierska, an immigrant of eastern European descent who is unequivocally claimed as a Jewish American writer.[24]

In the 1920s, as Hurst added novels to her repertoire, she, much like Ferber, began moving away from a primary focus on Jewish themes. At the beginning of her career, she seemed to be caught between competing demands of the marketplace when it came to the publication of ethnic fiction. On the one hand, she found a rapt audience *because* of her Jewish themes, which appealed to immigrant readers as well as those interested in vicariously experiencing the exotic East Side. On the other hand, some editors were wary that her ethnic characters and settings would limit her readership, even as they recognized that her working women protagonists were an undeniable attraction for their magazines' female subscribers in the era of the New Woman. For example, as early as 1912 Hurst was advised by Ray Long, editor of *Red Book* and later *Cosmopolitan*, to abandon ethnic specificity when he requested some "shop girl stories (preferably those which do not deal with Jewish characters)."[25] Over time, Hurst appears to have taken Long's advice; as her fan base grew to national and then international proportions, her Jewish heritage became less pronounced in her writing, even if it always seemed to lurk beneath the surface.

Hurst's turn away from Jewish themes in her fiction did not translate into an abandonment of her public identity as a Jew, despite the fact that many scholars claim she passed for gentile.[26] Throughout her life, she allied herself with Jewish charities and causes, was a sought-after lecturer for many Jewish organizations, and acted as spokesperson for the nation's immigrant population. So extensive were her activities in this arena that she maintained several files on "Jewish Matters" in her office. In 1929, she risked vilification by denouncing the national celebration of Christmas, publicly attacking the holiday as a materialist sham. In 1946, she hosted "A Tribute to the Contributions of the Foreign Born to America" in honor of the sixtieth anniversary of the Statue of Liberty. In 1961, she was inducted into the Jewish Academy of Arts and Sciences, an honor bestowed on "men and women of Jewish extraction who distinguish themselves in the arts and professions." While Hurst's role as judge for writing contests of African American fiction during the Harlem Renaissance has received ample attention, she similarly devoted herself to the promotion of Jewish literature, judging short story and novel competitions for *Jewish Survey* and the Jewish Publication Society of America.[27] Hurst herself was a contributor to Jewish periodicals such as the *Jewish Tribune* and the *American Hebrew*, and the Jewish press profiled her on a regular basis. Requesting an interview with Hurst in 1949, a reporter for the Yiddish socialist paper the *Jewish Daily Forward* wrote, "Your short stories and novels have been read and admired by all of us on this newspaper for many many years. In fact, our editor-in-chief, Abraham Cahan, never tires of praising your books. Unless I am much mistaken, he has read about twenty of them and enjoyed them all hugely."[28]

In reassuring Hurst of the *Forward*'s interest in her work, the reporter's words simultaneously hint at her tentative relationship to a Jewish literary establishment that seemed uncertain about whether the celebrity author ought to be embraced as a Jewish writer as well as whether she would want to be claimed as such. Hurst is traditionally separated from contemporaries such as Cahan and Yezierska because she had little personal experience with immigrant culture. With her secular, fashionable, and even glamorous lifestyle, Hurst stood for the success of the assimilationist project, but even as she became a darling of the melting pot, she kept at least a tenuous hold on her membership in the Jewish "race." Seemingly "outing" Hurst, a Canadian weekly, the *Jewish Standard*, titled its 1931 interview with the author, "Fannie Hurst—The Jewess," and promoted the piece by claiming that Hurst would talk "more freely and intimately" about herself "and things Jewish than she has ever done before." The title of the article implies that "Jewess" was not an aspect of identity commonly associated with Hurst. In a 1925 profile that appeared in the *Jewish Tribune*, Hurst was asked for her opinion on whether Zangwill's "melting pot" was achievable. "If by the 'Melting Pot' you mean assimilation, then I should say 'Yes' emphatically," she replied. "Can the Jew be assimilated? America is the answer. The Jew need not lose his racial characteristics. True, he is breaking away from the old traditions, beautiful in themselves. But he still has to be reckoned with as a Jew."[29]

Hurst embodied—and continues to embody—the contradictions of her response. In the *Jewish Standard* profile, for instance, the author, regally seated on her red satin sofa, provided an opportunity for the interviewer to reflect on "the adaptability and variety of the Jewish race." Identifying herself as "intellectually . . . a cosmopolitan" and insisting that "rituals, ceremonials, dogmas" have no hold on her, Hurst noted the weakening of "Jewish racialism" and declared her generation to be "the last carbon copy of that Jewishness."[30] Hurst (who, in fact, methodically retained carbon copies of almost everything she wrote) employed a fitting metaphor, one that could be applied to her writing as well. Though the Jewishness of her fiction may have weakened with the passage of time, it did not fade altogether, and we can continue to read the faintest imprint of that carbon copy in her work. As I explore in the following section, this imprint is especially evident in her writing on African American racial identity, for just as Hurst initially found a wellspring in her ghetto wanderings, she was swept up in the white vogue for black culture that took place in the 1920s.

The Negrotarian

Whatever effort scholars have made to reclaim Hurst in her own right, she is best remembered today for her relationship with one of the most famous women writers, black or white, of this period, Zora Neale Hurston.[31] As a "Negrotarian," in Hurston's clever nomenclature, Hurst was a dedicated white participant in the Harlem Renaissance, regularly attending her close friend Carl Van Vechten's mixed parties and providing patronage for African American artists. Hurst's involvement with racial uplift was more than a passing interest, however. In addition to her files on "Jewish Matters," she maintained several files on "Negro Matters," which were bursting with requests for aid from various civil rights organizations. These files reveal that from the 1920s through the 1950s, she gave time, money, and her name to numerous black causes and associations, including the National Urban League, the National Health Circle for Colored People, the City-wide Citizen's Committee on Harlem, and the NAACP. Serving on executive boards, making donations to black colleges, authoring fund-raising appeals and antilynching statements, lecturing on race relations, and judging artistic and oratorical competitions, Hurst ran the gamut from activities that fostered African American art to civic reform, social activism, and philanthropy. Even though some would come to view her depiction of African Americans in *Imitation of Life* as a betrayal of her progressive racial ideologies, Hurst—like most of the black intellectuals of the Harlem Renaissance—did not firmly separate literary endeavors from political ones.

Hurst's commitment to racial uplift and civil rights needs to be understood in the context of broader cultural forces that drew whites to Harlem, spurred fascination with black art, and created interracial political coalitions in the early-twentieth-century United States. In the post–World War I period, many whites, disillusioned with modern civilization, sought refuge in African American culture, viewing blacks as primitivist symbols that countered the alienation of an increasingly mechanized and industrialized society. In his autobiography, *The Big Sea*, Langston Hughes captured the cultural dynamics of the time when he wrote of the whites who flocked to the cabarets and bars of Harlem. "The strangers," observed Hughes of Harlem's newest patrons, "were given the best ringside tables to sit and stare at the Negro customers—like amusing animals in a zoo." Though many black artists, including Hughes himself, enjoyed the attentions and patronage of whites, inequality and hypocrisy did not go unnoted, even when masked by benevolence. Hughes is quick to expose the limitations of this willingness to cross racial lines; not only, as he points out, were African Americans still prevented from entering white spaces, but the whites who came to Harlem had the misconception "that all Harlemites left their houses at sundown to sing and dance in cabarets, because most of the whites saw nothing but the cabarets, not the houses."[32] Hurston addressed a similar racial dynamic in her 1926 essay "How It Feels to Be Colored Me," stating, "I feel most colored when I am thrown against a sharp white background." Relaying the experience of sitting beside a white customer at a Harlem jazz club, she described how the juxtaposition results in the white person becoming "so pale with . . . whiteness" and the African American author "so colored."[33] Rather than disrupting the rigidity of racial binaries, the cross-racial contact engendered by the "Negro vogue" often had the effect of heightening—and even producing—the difference between black and white.

As the vogue expanded the market for African American literature, both black and white writers came under fire for perpetuating stereotypes, and black intellectuals became embroiled in debates about propagandistic and aesthetic criteria. Hurst was a reader of black literature (her personal library contained works such as James Weldon Johnson's *Book of American Negro Spirituals* and Hurston's first novel, *Jonah's Gourd Vine*, for which Hurst herself had written the introduction), and she was thus undoubtedly privy to the controversies surrounding the production of African American art.[34] It would have been difficult, for example, for her not to have heard the death knells to the "Old Negro" sounded by black intellectuals. In his 1925 essay ushering in the era of "The New Negro," Alain Locke described the "Old Negro" as "more of a myth than a man . . . a stock figure perpetuated as an historical fiction partly in innocent sentimentalism, partly in deliberate reactionism." Locke followed this declaration of the end of the "Old Negro" with a catalog of demeaning stereotypes: "The day of 'aunties,' 'uncles' and 'mammies' is . . . gone. Uncle Tom and Sambo have passed on."[35] While some, like Hurston and Hughes, responded to the call for the "New Negro" by reclaiming the folk, other black writers countered stereotypes by depicting an elite world of genteel, light-skinned African Americans, characters so close to bourgeois whites in manner and looks that they are able to blend easily into the white world. Hurst must have been familiar with such treatments of mixed-race identity and passing in the works of Nella Larsen, Jessie Fauset, and Walter White. She was also most certainly aware of the controversy over white usurpation of black material sparked by the publication of Van Vechten's scandalously titled novel *Nigger Heaven* in 1926.[36]

It was Van Vechten who introduced Hurst to Harlem, folding her into his social and literary circle, and it was Van Vechten, avid Negrophile that he was, whose advice Hurst often sought on "Negro Matters." She once wrote asking him to recommend books on race relations, confessing that she "missed some of these along the way" and found herself unable "to answer questions, which I put to myself, as intelligently as I should like."[37] Yet historian David Levering Lewis distinguished Hurst from Van Vechten in discussing the forces that attracted the Negrotarians to Harlem. While Hurst fell into the category of those who were "sincere," the more mercurial Van Vechten—who once admitted that he found "jazz, the blues, Negro spirituals" stimulating "for the moment," but would "doubtless . . . discard them too in time"—represented those who were "merely fascinated."[38] We might account for this difference by considering an additional set of motivations underlying Hurst's engagement with racial uplift; grounded in her political beliefs, these motivations were at least tangentially linked to her Jewish identity.

In the early twentieth century, white liberalism and civil rights activism seemed bound to become the special provenance of Jews. In 1909, the NAACP was formed with substantial assistance from Jewish social workers, lawyers, and philanthropists. In 1915, the lynching of Jewish factory owner Leo Frank in Georgia intensified the political coalition between African Americans and Jews. By the 1920s, "being of use to the Negro" had become "a specialty of the second most abused Americans of the early twentieth century," as Lewis wrote in *When Harlem Was in Vogue*. Lewis's explanation and the example of the Leo Frank case suggest that blacks and Jews were drawn together by shared experiences of mistreatment and the fear of a common enemy.[39] However, historians have also uncovered a more complex set of factors undergirding this alliance. Jewish commitment to African American causes may have arisen from a common sense of marginality, but, as Cheryl Greenberg points out, the black and Jewish experiences of discrimination were in no way equivalent; differences in experience and in status created tensions between the two groups, leading to paternalistic attitudes on the part of Jews and the reproduction of hierarchies within the very organizations that brought them together as allies.[40] Some degree of self-interest buttressed Jewish participation in this early phase of the civil rights movement. According to Hasia Diner, combating antiblack racism would "bring in its wake certain benefits for American Jews," leading to the elimination of anti-Semitism while also proving them to be true Americans, dedicated to the democratic cause of freedom, which would further secure their "social and political lot." Although this self-interest was later understood, in the context of the Black Power movement, as an exploitative desire to wield control over those at the bottom of the social ladder, Diner also reminds us that "there was little direct political prestige for the elite of American Jewry as a result of its championship of black causes."[41] Observing that many of the Jews involved in the early civil rights movement were highly assimilated (Hurst, then, is hardly an exception), Eric Goldstein concludes that their connection to African Americans "could serve as a potent means of mitigating the emotional trauma of the assimilation process." For Goldstein, Jewish civil rights advocacy sheds light on the ways that Jews were in the process of negotiating their whiteness in the first half of the twentieth century: "Jews' highly ambivalent approach to African Americans . . . reflected their inability to either reject or embrace the racial conventions of white America."[42]

Hurst's immersion in "Negro Matters" illuminated her own ambivalent relationship to her Jewish identity and to the white mainstream. As she admitted in *Anatomy of Me*, although she spent a lifetime "lifting pen and voice against the second-class status of the American Negro," she only belatedly came to recognize "the long body-and-soul flagellation of another race—my own."[43] Hurst's role as civil rights advocate and her public friendships with African Americans, especially Hurston, at once deflected attention away from her own status as a minority and allowed her to keep a toehold on her sense of racialism, that "last carbon copy" of her Jewishness. Her outspokenness on issues of racial inequality led one of New York's leading black papers, the *Amsterdam News*, to label her a "brilliant author and militant defender of the rights of all minority groups."[44] Interestingly, however, the article does not mention that Hurst herself belonged to a minority group, indicative of the ways that her passionate support of African American causes had the potential to overshadow her Jewish identity. Hurst's own reluctance to draw attention to her Jewish heritage was in part a recognition of the fact that there was little correspondence, in extent and kind, between the marginalization experienced by Jews and blacks in the United States. She was well aware that the nation offered opportunities for Jews that it did not for African Americans. Although she acknowledged that American Jews had "not escaped discriminatory practices," she also noted that they had "enjoyed [their] longest period of comparative peace and security and [have] had opportunity and wherewithal to indulge [their] aesthetics."[45] Viewing herself as the beneficiary of these privileges, she was uncomfortable claiming a minority status, but her sense of Jewish difference did lead to an empathetic identification with African American victims of racism.

Allusions to the persecution experienced by Jews were more likely to surface when Hurst addressed racial violence rather than social discrimination, and the parallel she most often drew was between American racism and European anti-Semitism. In a 1935 issue of the *Crisis* featuring articles by members of The Writers League Against Lynching, for example, she issued the following statement: "It becomes grotesque to contemplate our country rising in righteous indignation against the atrocities tolerated by a Hitler, when hundreds of our own wayside trees are gibbets from which have dangled the broken necks of men who have been strung up there by the bestiality of unpunishable mobs."[46] While the statement is notable for its prioritizing of domestic concerns about violence aimed at African Americans over the international issue of Jewish persecution under Nazi rule, it also suggests her awareness of the analogies linking blacks and Jews. Indeed, as the situation in Europe worsened, Hurst's stand against racism at home became a vehicle for confronting anti-Semitism abroad. In a well-received speech at the National Urban League dinner in 1937, she declared that "the problems of race . . . have never been more provocative, more disturbing, and more imperatively in need of various solutions." Noting that "racism and race thinking" have been brought "to the front of modern psychology these war-bitten days," she momentarily digresses from the "Negro problem" to offer "Hitlerism" as "one classic example of national racism."[47] In this speech, Hurst had no difficulty redirecting attention to racial injustice at home, but by the following year she found herself in the position of having to withdraw from some of her commitments to black causes in order to devote her energy more fully to the relief of Jewish refugees. In a 1938 letter to the executive secretary of the National Health Circle for Colored People, she expressed regret that she could no longer give of her time, explaining that the "enormous burdens which have been shifted to American shoulders with the influx of émigrés from Germany and Austria" have made it "impossible for me to lift a finger in any other direction at the moment."[48]

Although little of what we know about Hurst's racial attitudes adds up to the kind of backward depictions of African Americans some readers saw in *Imitation of Life*, Hurst's views can seem patronizing at times, especially in light of today's more enlightened consciousness about race. Gay Wilentz and Virginia Burke have drawn attention to the problematic figurative language Hurst used in discussing Hurston and her work; the introduction to *Jonah's Gourd Vine*, for example, praises Hurston's authenticity and literary achievement, but it also states, "A brilliantly facile spade has turned over rich new earth. Worms lift up, the hottish smells of soil rise, negro toes dredge into that soil, smells of racial fecundity are about."[49] Clearly, even the most well-intentioned statements can go awry, and white liberalism can never quite shake free of the white man's burden and its implied belief in black inferiority. Although guilty at times of unfortunate phrasing, Hurst also appears to be one of few white participants in the Harlem Renaissance conscious of the deleterious effects of patronage. Even as she took the podium at the National Urban League dinner, she expressed her unwillingness to condescend to her black audience, refusing to pose as someone who was "better informed" on matters of race than they were.[50] She was astute enough to note that "Negroes nowadays resent being studied by whites and the whites are a bit too patronizing in their manner" and, on another occasion, apologized if she was guilty of "well-meaning patronage toward the Negro, an attitude I abhor."[51] In introducing Hurst's speech at the National Urban League dinner, Hurston also differentiated her fellow writer from white speakers who "patronize us." In contrast, Hurst "really has something to say," Hurston insisted. "She meets us in a way that I like" and "is very frank in whatever she does."[52]

Friend or Patron?

Despite the fact that Hurston publicly characterized Hurst as one of the more forthright and egalitarian of the Negrotarians, scholars have drawn attention to the inequalities that shaped the relationship between the two writers.[53] In public statements, Hurston classified their relationship as a friendship, but privately she harbored concerns about the sincerity of Hurst's intentions and viewed their companionship as paternalistic on the white woman's part. In a chapter of her autobiography titled "Two Women in Particular," Hurston paired Hurst with African American blues singer and actress Ethel Waters, describing both women as "rare talents" who "have meant a great deal to me in friendship and inward experience."[54] Although Hurston went on to write that "Hurst has picked on me to my profit," she was also aware of the ways that Hurst herself profited from the association and that the "friendship" should be treated with skepticism. In a letter to her future sister-in-law, a Hurst fan, Hurston contradicted her defense of Hurst's frankness at the Urban League dinner when she wrote, "A kind letter from you gives me just as much or more pleasure as one from *any* celebrity. They are OFTEN insincere. Their show of friendship mere patronage."[55]

A slippery, double-voiced autobiographical narrator, Hurston has been known to construct and reconstruct the "facts" of her life, often presenting herself differently to white and black audiences. As a result, her views on Hurst appear contradictory. I would argue further, however, that this interracial relationship is difficult to define because its circumstances *were* rife with contradictions. One of the challenges of characterizing Hurst and Hurston's relationship is that it does not fit neatly into any single conventional category of personal or professional association. It is worth keeping in mind that the two women negotiated the conditions of their relationship at a time when interracial friendships among women of their education and social standing were rare and not readily accepted. On the one hand, their relationship might be described in the hierarchical and paternalistic terms of employer-employee, patron-artist, and mentor-protégé. On the other hand, the association might be described as one between peers who were friends, kindred spirits, fellow writers, artistic colleagues, and travel companions. As the two women worked, lived, and traveled together, their relationship transgressed certain social boundaries, while also being circumscribed by them. Hurston's employment by Hurst provided grounds to justify an interaction that would have more easily occurred between women of the same race; it thus operated as a public guise for an interracial friendship that would not have been sanctioned by others.

The story of this friendship contains many of the elements that defined encounters between blacks and white during the Harlem Renaissance, with both Hurst's and Hurston's renditions hinting in only the most covert ways at the role that Hurst's Jewish background played in their interactions. In Hurston's recollections of Hurst, she reveals that at times she was made to feel like an exotic object. Hurst tends to focus on more overtly politicized aspects of their encounters, describing how the women were forced to confront racism. In providing an opportunity to explore a close interracial relationship between women, their accounts also allow for a consideration of a gendered dimension of black-Jewish relations that has received relatively little attention. The fact that Hurst was drawn, in particular, to the persons and work of Hurston, Dorothy West, and Marita Bonner indicates that her feminist sensibility influenced her championship of black women writers.[56] Hurst and Hurston did not necessarily find common ground because of their shared status as ethnic minorities, but they did view themselves as kindred spirits in many ways, and their affinity for each other had much to do with the unconventional lives they led as women. As women writers, they both privileged work over marriage. Hurston herself had a number of "Fannie Hurst marriages," rarely living in the same place as any of her several husbands. Attentive to self-presentation, both women carefully fashioned their public personae and became celebrities based on the vibrancy of their personalities as well as their writing. Their relationship, as documented in their correspondence and written reminiscences about each other, remains an enduring example of the potential and the limitations of exchange between black and Jewish women in the early twentieth century.

The two women met when Hurst served as a judge for the 1925 *Opportunity* literary contest that awarded Hurston second prize in the short story category for "Spunk." At the same event, Hurston was introduced to Barnard founder Annie Nathan Meyer, another Jewish advocate for African American uplift, who was set on desegregating the college and quickly arranged for Hurston's admission to Barnard. Advised by Meyer to appeal to Hurst for assistance with tuition funds, Hurston accepted Hurst's offer to hire her as a live-in secretary. Providing the new Barnard student with income and room and board, the arrangement was not prompted by Hurst's need for secretarial assistance, nor was it strictly clerical; the element of artistic exchange was also present, as the women began sharing their work. Although the arrangement was short-lived (likely due to Hurston's poor typing skills), the two maintained a friendship and correspondence throughout their lives. They exchanged ideas, discussing and reading each other's writing, including in manuscript form. They also traveled together, often with the intention of collecting material for their respective work.

When Hurst initially terminated Hurston's employment, she noted that Hurston was ill-equipped for clerical work and teased, "I think I should be your secretary," thus unwittingly exposing the power relations of the partnership.[57] The joke is akin to Langston Hughes's short play "Limitations of Life" in which he parodied Hurst's *Imitation of Life* by reversing the roles of the black and white characters so that a black society matron, "Mammy Weavers," is served by a "pretty blond maid."[58] After relieving Hurston of her secretarial duties, Hurst offered for the other woman to continue living in her home; apparently, however, she needed the guise of an employer-employee relationship, since she decided that she would rehire Hurston as her "chauffeur."[59] In Hurst's version of events, the impetus for this new assignment comes from Hurston herself, who allegedly used driving as an excuse to get out of tedious secretarial tasks, proposing, for example, that she drive Hurst "up to the Harlem bad-lands or down to the wharves where men go down to the sea in ships."[60] While slumming was an admitted vocation of Hurst's, here she depicts Hurston as the instigator. Hurston, in contrast, attributes the idea to Hurst, who "likes for me to drive her" and "on the spur of the moment . . . has taken me galloping over thousands of miles of this North American continent in my Chevrolet for a lark."[61] Although Hurston is the one in the driver's seat, she makes it clear that it is Hurst who is in control, dictating the terms of their encounters.

As the relationship began as one of both patronage and employer-employee, the signs of these hierarchies persisted throughout their lives and simultaneously colored their different views of their engagement with one another. Although Hurston did not refer to herself as a "pickaninny" as she did in correspondence with other patrons, the letters between Hurst and Hurston bear evidence of their unequal relationship. Hurston's letters were typically addressed to "Dear Fannie Hurst," while Hurst more familiarly addressed Hurston as "Dear Zora." Hurston also engaged in some obsequious ego-polishing with Hurst, addressing her in one letter as "Genius Fannie Hurst" and signing off "Your devoted disciple."[62] Hurst had a great deal of affection and respect for Hurston, but she tended to see her as a literary protégée (even though Hurston was only five years younger). For example, even in 1943, when both women were established authors, her letters to Hurston bear a maternal tone, as she writes about "burst[ing] with pride" over the other woman's achievements.[63]

Hurst's and Hurston's reminiscences of each other reveal that they had different views of the ways that race shaped their interactions. Hurston, who called attention to the Jewishness of benefactors such as Meyer and Franz Boas, showed surprisingly little awareness of Hurst's Jewish identity. While Hurston may have seen Hurst as simply another white benefactor, a privileged society woman who was "born to wealth," more subtle evidence also suggests that Hurston believed that their cross-racial companionship served to downplay Hurst's Jewishness and play up her whiteness.[64] Hurston's biographer, Robert Hemenway, wrote that "privately [Hurston] expressed doubts about why Hurst was so interested in their appearing in public together; she told at least one friend that she thought it was because Hurst liked the way Zora's dark skin highlighted her own lily-like complexion."[65] Color comes up repeatedly in Hurst's recollections of Hurston, whom she calls a "woman half in shadow" and "an iridescent personality of many colors."[66] The contrast between Hurst's and Hurston's descriptions of each other is telling. While Hurst tends to attribute Hurston's colorfulness to her personality, Hurston notes how the effects of Hurst's identity and coloring are derived from and highlighted by her strategic mode of dress. In *Dust Tracks on a Road*, for example, she stated that the always fashionable Hurst "knows exactly what goes with her very white skin, black hair and sloe eyes, and she wears it. I doubt if any woman on earth has gotten better effects than she has with black, white and red. Not only that, she knows how to parade it when she gets it on. She will never be jailed for uglying up a town."[67]

A chapter excised from the original publication of *Dust Tracks on a Road* expounds upon Hurst's keen fashion sense and addresses the role that Hurston—herself known for flaunting a flamboyant style—occasionally played as an accessory in Hurst's modish ensemble: "Behold her phoning to a swanky hotel for reservations for herself and the Princess Zora, *and* parading me in there all dressed up as an Asiatic person of royal blood and keeping a straight face while the attendants goggled at me and bowed low! Like a little girl, I have known her in the joy of a compelling new gown to take me to tea in some exclusive spot in New York. I would be the press agent for her dress, for everybody was sure to look if *they* saw somebody like me strolling into the Astor or the Biltmore."[68] Hurston's account is notable for the way it emphasizes her own passivity; it is Hurst who "parades" Hurston into the restaurant, "all dressed up as an Asiatic person of royal blood." In this reminiscence, Hurston portrays herself as an exotic accoutrement strategically placed so as to dramatically accentuate Hurst's appearance. As a black woman positioned by Hurst's side at a time when such interracial couplings were rare, Hurston draws attention to Hurst's attire, which in turn was designed to highlight her best attributes, among them her "very white skin." As Hurston herself noted almost seventy years before Morrison published her statement on the "Africanist presence," the contrast results in the white person becoming "so pale with . . . whiteness" and the African American "*so* colored." Although she counted Hurst among her friends, Hurston cagily viewed their interracial friendship as a hierarchical one; it had the potential to deprive Hurst of her sense of individual identity by exoticizing and "coloring" her, while contrastingly emphasizing Hurst's privileged membership in the white majority.

While Hurston saw herself as an exotic accent placed to draw attention to and enhance Hurst's stylishness, Hurst often used their relationship to portray herself as a champion of civil rights. As the two women made several trips together (including to Hurston's hometown of Eatonville, Florida; Canada; and upstate New York), race was bound to come up, since they were crossing state lines in a segregated nation, where even in the North hotels and restaurants were restricted to white and often gentile clientele. Describing the erratic nature of these excursions,

Hurston relegates race to a subtext and attributes their frequent move-ment to Hurst's impulsive tendencies. "She was a run-away, with no re-sponsibilities," Hurston wrote.[69] She does not explain that the frequent relocations were likely orchestrated to avoid or cut down on the effects of segregation. In situating race at the forefront of her own recollections, Hurst notes that Hurston "seemed to have very little indignation for the imposed status of her race" and attempts to make up for this oversight by describing the indignations Hurston faced in her own account of their travels. Hotels regularly refused accommodations to Hurston or relegated her to the servants' quarters. When Hurst tried to present a united front by declining accommodations as well, Hurston's "attitude was swift and adamant: 'If you are going to take that stand, it will be im-possible for us to travel together. This is the way it is and I can take care of myself as I have all my life. I will find my own lodging and be around with the car in the morning.'"[70] Hurst may use the episode as an occasion to promote her own unselfish attempts to ally herself with Hurston, but the anecdote also captures Hurston's sage refusal of paternalism and her awareness that cross-racial solidarity has its boundaries.

In Hurst's take on the events described by Hurston in the "Princess Zora" story, she again places race at the forefront of her remembrances. In a tribute to Hurston written on the occasion of her death in 1961, she related how the two women "repeatedly encountered the ogre of dis-crimination" when they traveled together in the 1920s and early 1930s. Hurst recalled that as they "drove past a well-known Westchester County hotel" one summer day:

> An idea struck me. Zora, in a red head-scarf and one of her bizarre frocks of many colors, looked hot and tired from a full day's driv-ing. At my sudden request we stopped before the Inn. "Do me a favor, Zora. No questions please. Follow me." At the dining-room entrance I pushed ahead. A head-waiter appeared, his expression, when he saw Zora, as if a window shade had been drawn over his face. Before he could come through with the usual, "Sorry, every-thing reserved," I announced, "The Princess Zora and I wish a ta-ble." We were shown to the best in the room.
>
> Following a good meal and with some levity, Zora made a re-mark that revealed for an instant her mental innards: "Who would think," she soliloquized as we resumed driving, "that a good meal could be so bitter."[71]

Hurst's version presents a very different set of motives from Hurston's.

Rather than depicting herself as a self-interested party frivolously eager to show off a new dress, Hurst fashions herself as a defender of her downtrodden companion, performing the act of resistance Hurston will not, or cannot, take on herself. Although Hurst, who was not a stranger to anti-Semitism, does not indicate here that her actions were motivated by a personal understanding of discrimination, her behavior resonates with Jewish championship of African American causes that were typical of the time. Her actions may be well intentioned, but Hurst displays a paternalistic attitude in her orchestration of the episode, effectively silencing her black companion as she admonishes her not to utter a word. It is no wonder that Hurston remained attuned to the ways that Hurst might benefit from such interactions.

The "Princess Zora" tale is also notable for its incorporation of the trope of passing. According to Hurst, Hurston's style of dress—her "bizarre frocks of many colors"—facilitates her passing for African royalty. Although the story differs from the more common literary narrative of racial passing, which typically involves light-skinned African American characters passing for white, the title "Princess"—conferred upon Hurston by Hurst—allows Hurston to pass up and enter an upper-class, segregated space normally off-limits to her because of her race.[72] There is another story of subterfuge embedded in Hurst's and Hurston's narratives as well, a passing story that interestingly passes, as it goes unacknowledged in Hurst's version and perhaps only slyly acknowledged in Hurston's. Given the fact that hotels in upstate New York notoriously excluded Jewish clientele, Hurst would likely have had to pass for gentile in order to dine in the restaurant, although this did not involve the same degree of brazenness required in passing Hurston off as a princess. In one reading, Hurston's presence in the role of Princess Zora *guarantees* Hurst's own ability to pass, making her racial identity invisible, as whiteness so often is; alongside Hurston, Hurst's ethnic difference might be eclipsed, her whiteness assumed. Yet in a counter-reading, their relationship—from the outward defiance of segregation to the more surreptitious act of passing—can be understood as a willful transgression of racial taboos.

This ambivalence about whether interracial encounters end up producing whiteness or complicating racial binaries similarly pervades *Imitation of Life*. Although the circumstances differ dramatically from the story of her relationship with Hurston, *Imitation of Life*, which contains both a portrait of interracial friendship and a narrative of passing, was conceived and written at a time when the two women writers were actively engaged in personal and professional dialogue. Hurst's biographer, Brooke Kroeger, believes that the idea for the novel "started to form in [Hurst's] mind before and during" a road trip the two women took together to Canada during the summer of 1931.[73] In a letter to Hurst, Hurston addressed the possibility of her influence on the white writer as well as Sterling Brown's criticisms of the 1933 novel and its film adaptation, reassuring Hurst that she has

> a grand set of admirers in this part of the world [Durham, North Carolina] because of "Imitation of Life." So it seems that Sterling Brown is not in the majority. He picks on me all the time now. He tells people that he wants to riddle me, and otherwise deflate me because he says that I stand convicted of having furnished you with the material of "IMITATION." I let it stand without contradiction because I feel he does me honor. In so saying, he pays you an unconscious tribute because he is admitting the truth of the work. What he and his kind resent is just that.

It is notable that Hurston does not contradict Brown, and there are some suggestions that the charges may be valid, that Hurston provided Hurst with material in both general and specific ways. For example, a version of the folk song "John Henry," which appears in Hurston's folklore collection *Mules and Men*, published in 1935, appeared two years earlier in Hurst's novel, sung by Delilah. While Brown's "conviction" of Hurston for supplying Hurst with material for *Imitation* may be accurate, it does not account for the give-and-take that took place between the two women writers. In their letters to each other, Hurst and Hurston discussed possible research excursions they planned to take together to seek out sources for their writing; they shared information and territory, encouraging each other to pay visits to the areas in which they were already conducting research. In this antiterritorial spirit, Hurston ends the above letter by promising to tell Hurst stories of her experiences teaching at North Carolina College, advising, "You can get another good book out of it."[74] In the case of *Imitation of Life*, Brown's disappointment in Hurston for serving as racial informant to Hurst may be partly generated by his reaction to the interaction between *Imitation of Life*'s fictional characters, given that the novel itself is about a black woman who supplies a white woman with raw material that the latter then molds to her profit.

Hurst's multidimensional relationship with Hurston certainly gave the former enough insight to recognize that white views of black primitivism did not hold water, even if Hurston herself played into white conceptions of blacks in her personal interactions with her patrons. Yet despite being written at a time when Hurst was engaged in an intimate friendship with an African American woman whom she greatly admired for her intellectual and literary abilities, *Imitation of Life* is often read as yet another white appropriation of blackness that perpetuates stereotypes such as the mammy and tragic mulatto. Without necessarily undermining the validity of such criticisms, I want to suggest an alternative way to read the text. In the character of Delilah, we find not only a perpetuation of the mammy myth but also an incisive commentary on the way that myth is manufactured through text and image, drawing attention to its status as white fantasy rather than reality. While the story of Peola's passing could also be read as a simple appropriation of an African American theme, the juxtaposition of the racial passing narrative with two other passing tales—those of Bea Pullman, who passes as a man in the business world, and Virginia Eden, who similarly renames and reinvents herself in order to achieve upward mobility—suggests that Hurst's novel uses its racial themes to extend the two dominant concerns of her prior fiction: women's labor and ethnic assimilation.

Once a Waffle

Pancake—a humble type of Negro.
    —ZORA NEALE HURSTON, "GLOSSARY OF HARLEM SLANG"

Waffle (v.)—to speak or write equivocally
    — WEBSTER'S COLLEGE DICTIONARY

In her introduction to Hurst's speech at the National Urban League dinner in 1937, Hurston summed up the debate over *Imitation of Life* thus: "Some of us reacted very favorably to that, and some of us reacted very unfavorably, but you must say it made us think. I am afraid she brought out some things that some of us don't like to be talked about, but there are some unpleasant things about us as about everything else, and it might as well be talked about."[75] Hurston's words, carefully chosen perhaps for their vagueness, portray the controversy as a case of a white writer airing African Americans' dirty laundry. Given its themes of racial self-hatred and passing, Hurst's novel did deal with certain "unpleasant" truths, but the unfavorable reaction was concerned less with the brutality of honesty and more with the narrative's lack of realism. The attack was led by Sterling Brown, who, in an *Opportunity* review famously titled "Once a Pancake," questioned audiences' and critics' favorable opinions of the 1934 film. The film had been well received in black neighborhoods, where the portrayal of respectable African American characters was viewed as a departure from the offensive stereotypes that permeated early cinema. Some black spectators went even further, interpreting the film as a condemnation of race prejudice and the character of Peola as a race rebel, for whom passing was not an act of self-loathing, but a cry for "freedom and equal justice."[76]

While he remained unconvinced by such claims to "novelty" and found little to "cheer about" in the film, Brown reserved most of his ire for Hurst's book and her mythic "Old Negro" characterizations. Alain Locke may have laid the mammy to rest, but Hurst resuscitated her in Delilah, a figure "straight out of Southern fiction." Nor should Peola's defiance of the color line be ascribed to racial rebellion. Instead, according to Brown, Peola "is the tragic octoroon, familiar to novels more than to life."[77] Although Brown did later concede that Hurst's novel was "well-meaning perhaps," his initial review further found fault with the white writer's inauthentic use of dialect; in contrast to the "true folk-eloquence" of African American writers, Delilah's speech came across as "too designedly picturesque."[78]

Is Hurst's mammy no more than a perpetuation of a stock figure, an effort to keep "innocent sentimentalism" alive (in the words of Locke's essay on "The New Negro")? Or, given Hurst's involvement in the Harlem Renaissance, is it possible to understand her depiction of Delilah as an attempt to critique the stereotypes of old? It is difficult to imagine that Hurst, with her sympathetic understanding of race relations and outspokenness about civil rights, would uncritically employ the kind of racist stereotype we see in Delilah. Hurst takes the mammy myth to such unbelievable extremes that the novel often reads as parody, at least from the point of view of contemporary hindsight when it comes to matters of race. Based on initial reviews of the novel in the white press, however, there is little evidence to suggest that readers in her time would have picked up on such an undercurrent. Granting validity to Brown's concerns, white reviewers tended to see Delilah as a realistic embodiment of the black domestic servant rather than a lampoon of an offensive and outdated image. The black characters "stand out as real flesh and blood," wrote one reviewer, while others singled out the more stereotypical Delilah, describing her as "real and living" and applauding Hurst for her "actual . . . creation."[79] The reviewer for the Christian Science Monitor was more conflicted on the matter; commenting on Delilah's familiarity to (white) readers, the review stated that "most of us have at some time

FIGURE 2. Delilah (Louise Beavers) and Bea Pullman (Claudette Colbert) in the first film adaptation of Fannie Hurst's *Imitation of Life* (Universal, 1934).

known a servant who partook in some measure of the nature of Delilah," yet it also criticized Hurst for "overcolor[ing] her portrait a little. Delilah is just not quite authentic."[80] While black readers certainly recognized Delilah as a stereotype, it would be exceedingly unlikely for them to assume that a white writer was treating this material parodically, as Brown's reaction illustrates.

In effect, then, black and white readers shared the same blind spot: both made the assumption that Hurst was attempting to approximate the real. But Hurst's title—a title she fought to restore after the editors of *Pictorial Review* altered it in the process of serialization—was, pointedly, *Imitation of Life*. Reviewers easily applied the title to the novel's white protagonist, whose full-time devotion to her career prevented her from partaking in "authentic" life experiences as a mother, lover, and wife. As the *New York Times* reviewer understood it, "In 'Imitation of Life,' Miss Hurst wishes to point out that fame does not constitute real living, and that one who lives only in an objective sense finds life empty and bitter indeed."[81] While some critics noted that Bea's "imitation of life" was echoed in Peola's imitation of whiteness, few extended the title to Hurst's mammy figure—except, as Brown does, to accuse the author of creating characters "familiar to novels more than life."

Hurst, however, did not simply pull her character "straight out of Southern fiction"; she based her on a specific image of black womanhood derived from commodity culture, Aunt Jemima. The mammy figure in general and Aunt Jemima in particular have been the subjects of numerous works of cultural criticism. Scholars have traced the Aunt Jemima image from its origins in postbellum blackface minstrelsy (where the handkerchief-head cook was played by white men in drag) to its persistence as a trademark for pancake mix and, finally, to African American artists' reappropriation of the female domestic as a symbol of militancy. Those cultural histories that incorporate discussions of *Imitation of Life* unfailingly view Hurst's novel as a contribution to and reiteration of the mammy myth without considering how Hurst's mammy differs in some significant ways from the typical deployment of the trope in white American literature and consumer culture.[82]

With her large size and dark pigmentation, the mammy is commonly understood to function as an Africanist presence whose juxtaposition with a white mistress constructs an idealization of white femininity. Similarly, Aunt Jemima was an effective marketing tool because her smiling presence obscured traces of white women's labor in the kitchen; she upheld the myth of a harmonious slave past while nostalgically creating a new postbellum plantation imaginary, a perverse consumerist fulfillment of a democratic promise that could be extended to homes unable to afford servants. As I explore, there are indeed ways in which the character of Delilah operates as an Africanist presence for Hurst's white protagonist, but, at the same, she enables rather than obscures white women's labor. A worker and businesswoman, Hurst's Bea is far from an idealization of white femininity. The partnership between Delilah and Bea involves a division of labor whereby Delilah fulfills the domestic and traditionally feminine role while Bea, as entrepreneur, fulfills the masculine role.

Juxtaposed with white Northern working womanhood rather than Southern domestic femininity, Hurst's mammy becomes a more ambivalent figure; she operates as a stabilizing force, reigning in the white woman's transgressions, while simultaneously contributing to the destabilization of Bea's identity, highlighting her failure to conform to white feminine ideals. Even the name change suggests that there is more complexity to Hurst's use of this character. The name Jemima, derived from the Old Testament story of Job, is Hebrew for "dove." It stood for

Aunt Jemima's docility, her contentedness with her servitude, and distinguished her from other mammy figures, who were often depicted as irascible nags (more so toward black children and men than whites—witness Queenie in *Show Boat*, who is always chastising Jo for being a lazy good-for-nothing). The name Delilah may bear an aural proximity to Jemima, but its own biblical referent marks its distance. Taken from the Old Testament story of Samson and Delilah, the name is used to refer to a traitorous woman—the very opposite of the undying loyalty associated with Aunt Jemima.

Hurst's novel thus negotiates a fine line between being an additional inculcation of the mammy myth and a commentary on it. Although *Imitation of Life* does not strongly condemn the co-optation of blackness, it does expose the mammy image as the product of white fantasy, an effect enhanced by the novel's narrative point of view. Discussing the controversy over *Imitation of Life*, Anna Everett wrote that Sterling Brown was "unwilling . . . to condone the ventriloquizing discourse of one prominent white writer's view of black subjectivity."[83] However, what sets Hurst's novel apart from contemporaneous white writers' "ventriloquizing" of black discourse—texts such as O'Neill's *The Emperor Jones*, Van Vechten's *Nigger Heaven*, and Heywood's *Porgy*—is that *Imitation of Life* stakes no claim to black subjectivity. As Stephanie Thompson points out in her analysis of *Imitation of Life* (one of the few pieces of criticism to discuss the novel in its own right), Hurst's reputation as a popular or commercial writer has led critics to ignore the aesthetic construction of her work. In particular, as Everett's statement suggests, critics tend to overlook the fact that the novel is narrated from the third-person limited point of view of its white protagonist. Employing free indirect discourse, the novel places us squarely in Bea's consciousness; we see the African American characters from a distinctly white point of view that allows no access to black interiority. From Herman Melville's *Benito Cereno* to Nella Larsen's *Passing*, this technique of unreliable narration had been used to trouble readers' assumptions about race and racial epistemologies. In employing an unreliable narrator to reveal the ways that blackness is a figment of the white cultural imaginary, *Imitation of Life* begins to clear room for more complex representations of race, rendering unstable the whiteness that depends on such black images for its meaning. By outlining the disjunction between Delilah as simple stereotype and Delilah as commodity icon whose lack of authenticity is forthrightly acknowledged, I show that *Imitation of Life* does not misappropriate black subjectivity, but instead critiques the limitations of white subjectivity when it comes to imagining blackness.

The initial depiction of Delilah incorporates the major characteristics of the mammy stereotype. Hired by Bea, she is introduced into the text as an embodiment of the natural landscape, "an enormously buxom figure with a round black moon face that shone above an Alps of bosom."[84] Like Ferber's conflation of *Show Boat*'s Queenie with the "broad-bosomed" stove "whose breast would suckle numberless eager sprawling bubbling pots and pans," this description objectifies Delilah as nurturer and figurative wet nurse by twice mentioning the defining feature of her ample bosom.[85] No future description of her can ignore her enormous size, and her image is further rendered in the sharply contrasted, solid colors of minstrel iconography: "Into every cranny and crevice of the ... household there poured the red, black, and white personality of this immense woman. The red of her easily-hinged large mouth, packed with the white laughter of her stunning allotment of hound-clean teeth; the jug color of her skin ... the terrific unassailable quality of her high spirits, Baptist fervor and amplitude."[86] With her interjections of "honey chile" and "Lawd," Delilah speaks in a dialect criticized by Brown for its lack of authenticity. Delilah cheerily assumes the domestic chores of the Pullmans, named for the railway cars that employed African American porters in similarly subservient positions.

Although Delilah may deviate slightly from the mammy myth in the love she lavishes on her own baby daughter, Peola, this maternal love does not supersede her subservience to the household's white women, Bea and her infant daughter, Jessie. Hearing the two babies cry, Delilah might "run ... intuitively to her own, but the switch was without hesitancy to the white child, every labor of service adhering rigidly to that order." So dedicated is Delilah to the racial hierarchy and its insistence that white take precedence over black that she interferes with the course of nature in an effort to prevent Peola from reaching developmental milestones before Jessie; in order to ensure that Jessie begins teething before her own daughter, "Delilah had gone so far as to secretly attempt to ward off Peola's threat of triumph, by boiling up a concoction of frogs' legs in lieu of mole-feet, and standing over its boiling fumes, secretly adapt an incantation she remembered hearing her mother chant against wakeful pickaninnies." Confirming Delilah's childlike nature, the passage pokes fun at her superstitious beliefs. Delilah's rigid (though, notably, counterintuitive) adherence to the racial order is taken to such extremes that even Bea must protest weakly. With a shake of her head that conveys the hopelessness of the situation and her underlying approval of the mammy's devotion to the household's white women, Bea offers up the affectionate refrain, "Oh, Delilah!"[87]

In Hurst's version of the "Princess Zora" story, she depicted herself as Hurston's defender against racial injustice, especially when her African American companion refused to betray her own indignation about the treatment she received. Offering the "hot and tired" Hurston a break from chauffeuring Hurst herself around, Hurst passes her friend off as African royalty in order to outwit the segregated system that would deny her service at an upscale restaurant. Elements of Hurst's somewhat misguided benevolence are echoed in *Imitation of Life* when Bea makes a belated effort to right the wrongs suffered by Delilah only to be met with Delilah's reluctance to change her selfless ways. Once their business starts to operate at a profit, Bea tries to get Delilah to attend to her own needs, but the determinedly self-sacrificing Delilah has only one request: "I'd lak to see you, honey, rest up them achin' bones of yourn." Later Bea again appeals to the black woman to let her "make up to you for the way life has behaved to you. I owe you so much more than I can ever repay, even if you let me. Do you realize that instead of the hundred-dollar-a-month slave you insist upon being, you could be working for me under any financial terms you name?"[88] Repeatedly pressed by Bea, Delilah cannot name a single thing she wants for herself, other than an elaborate funeral. Nor does Bea attempt to compensate Delilah in spite of her insistence that there is nothing she wants or needs. Bea's plea to do right by Delilah, the lip service she pays to convincing Delilah to forgo martyrdom, rings insincere when we consider the white woman's complicity in the myth and the way she continues to profit from it. She absolves herself of her complicity by describing Delilah as the "slave *you insist* upon being," implying that the role is Delilah's choice and not one imposed on her by Bea or the American caste system.

Thus, seemingly at her own request, Delilah continues on in the position of maid long after the wealth Bea acquires through their joint venture makes this necessary. As Bea ascends from the pavement-pounding of her days as saleswoman to the comfortable existence of the business executive, Delilah's position in their household remains fixed, except that her tasks now cater to Bea's increasingly bourgeois needs. Toward the end of the novel, when the adult Peola arrives home to announce her decision to permanently cross the color line, she "walk[s] into the routine of Delilah preparing to deliver the nightly polished apple on its nightly polished plate." It becomes difficult to fault Peola for passing when her opportunity might be otherwise limited to the trivial polishing of apples and plates for a white mistress. Ostensibly dying of the heartbreak caused by her daughter's estrangement, Delilah's final act is to "lift . . . herself out of a hypodermic-induced sleep" and "pour hot broad kisses against the bare ankles of Bea." Bea follows out the specifications Delilah requested for her funeral in a final tribute to her, but at the funeral she tearfully expresses regret that Delilah had not been able to stall her death a few more days because it is "terrible" for Bea's daughter, Jessie, who is away at school, "not to have *her* Delilah to come home to."[89] Even in the matter of death, Bea's thoughts turn to how Delilah could have made one last sacrifice for the sake of the white family to whom she devoted her life.

Langston Hughes's acerbic parody of Hurst's novel achieves its satiric effect through role reversal. The one-act "Limitations of Life" packs a subversive punch when the white servant expresses her dogged obedience by reveling in the act of massaging her black mistress's feet. Yet Hughes, like Hurston, came to Hurst's defense in regard to accusations of racism, thanking her for her hand in creating Hollywood's "first serious treatment of the Negro problem in America."[90] Perhaps what Hughes saw to admire in *Imitation of Life* was not the dignity of Delilah (a facet of her character praised by some black audiences of the film version), but the potentially satirical undercurrents, suggested, for example, by the absurd lengths Delilah goes to assure the inferiority of her own race, even in matters of teething. In Hurst's overwrought phrasing, Delilah's request to "rub up dem white little dead-beat feet" and the "untold relief" experienced by Bea as "those warm pale-palmed fingers [were] kneading and soothing and cooling [her] tortured soles" come across as outrageous as Hughes's comic send-up. Delilah's behavior is so over the top that it is unclear whether her depiction should be read as condemnation or romanticization of the mammy role. For example, Delilah's nightly ritual of polishing an apple for Bea contains a judgment against subservience, since the term "apple polishing," equivalent to contemporary slang's "kissing ass" or "sucking up," mocks excessively submissive behavior toward a superior. Similarly, Delilah's kissing of Bea's feet as she dies may be offered as evidence of her eternal subservience to her mistress, but it can also be interpreted as a caustic commentary on the actual cause of her death. Read carefully, the text appears to imply just such causality; the chapter describing the deathbed scene between Delilah and Bea ends with the one-sentence paragraph: "In that act she died."[91] Is it possible that Hurst's novel, rather than reviving the mammy, is attempting to lay the "Old Negro" to rest?

What best supports the argument that Hurst's representation is more than a simple reiteration of a stereotype is the novel's embedded narrative about the commodification of blackness. Struggling to make ends meet by carrying on her dead husband's vocation as a peddler of maple syrup, Bea finds that her luck starts to change due not only to Delilah's assistance but also to her creativity in the kitchen. Bea expands her maple syrup line by boxing and selling the unsold blocks of maple sugar that Delilah transformed into candy creations, using the image of "Aunt Delilah" to sell her products. "The idea . . . was really Delilah's," the text slyly informs us, "although it was Bea who, on the impulse of one of her flashes, sprang out of her bed again one night with the sudden impact of a scheme."[92] Readings of Delilah as a recycled racist stereotype depend upon the belief that Hurst attempted and failed to offer an authentic portrait of a black character. But Hurst's depiction of Delilah repeatedly emphasizes the mammy image as an inauthentic white fantasy. Not only is this character too completely self-effacing to be true, but Delilah, her face adorning boxes of maple-sugar hearts and waffle flour, is a cardboard facsimile.

As Bea develops her business, the novel draws more and more attention to Delilah as image. Bea's "scheme" to begin mass-producing and selling Delilah's maple-sugar hearts is inseparable from her inspired idea to market Delilah herself: "Perhaps the Candy Corner on the Boardwalk would display a few boxes on a commission basis. Delilah's Hearts! Why not Delilah's photograph, in her great fluted white cap, and her great fluted white smile on each box. Delilah, who, though actually in no more than her late thirties, looked mammy to the world. . . . Delilah beaming and beckoning from the lid. . . ." (ellipses in text). The photographic image, described elsewhere as the "chocolate-and-cream effulgence that was Delilah," is consumed right along with the candied commodity and is likely the reason why Delilah's recipes end up selling like hotcakes.[93] Exemplifying the narrative's use of free indirect discourse, the passage describing the development of Bea's enterprise allows us to enter her consciousness, the ellipses tracing the evolution of her thought process. The passage subtly acknowledges the discrepancy between Delilah (who is "actually in no more than her late thirties") and her image in the white mind ("mammy to the world"). This discrepancy between Delilah and the image Bea manufactures of her is one of the few points of contention between servant and mistress, since Delilah futilely protests being photographed in chef's hat and apron rather than more formal attire.

Delilah supplies the raw material, which Bea then shapes to conform to a national perception. Writing advertising copy or orchestrating photographs, Bea represents the white hand molding and marketing the black image. Summarizing Delilah's attributes for a new advertising campaign, Bea finds that she is particularly adept at "writing her own copy, in a sort of rhythm that started a fashion"; the list of attributes includes "Delilah is the most indulgent hostess in the world," she "loves to spoil you," and "Delilah has a mother-complex." Bea's act of writing parallels that of Hurst herself in creating the character of Delilah. As the novel progresses, it becomes all but impossible to separate Delilah from the commodified product, since Bea's next inspiration is to open a coffee shop, where Delilah herself would preside "in her shining fluted cap, which no amount of indoor drudgery could seem to wilt."[94] In descriptions like this one, the text explicitly draws attention to Delilah's tendency to defy realism.

The commentary on white control of the black image is taken even further with Bea's next innovation to mass-produce Delilah herself. As the coffee-shop business expands into a nationwide chain, "it remained impossible for Delilah to solve the corporeal problem of being two places simultaneously," and Bea makes the decision to manufacture imitation Delilahs, creating a "corps of ample, immaculate Negro women."[95] This proves to be more difficult than it seems; Bea's difficulty in finding suitable "imitation Delilahs" acknowledges that the image does not comport with the reality: "It was no small task to find types of black women who combined sufficient of waffle-iron technique with the something benign and effulgent which must approximately, at least, correspond with the nationwide trade-mark of Delilah in her fluted crown." Rather than find employees who naturally resemble Delilah, Bea realizes that the women need to be trained to fit the image, leading to the creation of a "University of Delilah, where *nearly as possible* replicas of herself were trained for B. Pullman service."[96] The difficulty of finding black women who correspond with the trademark also reminds us of Bea's initial trials in finding a live-in domestic servant. Among the women Bea interviewed, there were no mammies willing to lay down their entire lives at the feet of a white employer. Instead, these women "demanded the freedom to return home evenings" in order to attend to their own husbands and children. Delilah is an aberration, seemingly conjured by advertising copy, since it was just as a disheartened Bea had given up on her quest and was in the process of returning home, "mentally framing an advertisement" for the help wanted section of the paper, that Delilah magically materialized before her. By detailing the process by which Bea builds her business, the text illuminates the transformation of the black woman into a "walkin' trademark," a commodity to be mass-produced and consumed.[97] Delilah's character is imitation rather than life.

Conflating *Imitation of Life* the novel with its film adaptation, critics often mistakenly refer to the product in Hurst's text as pancakes. While the adaptation substituted pancakes for Hurst's waffles in order to capitalize on the allusion to Aunt Jemima, the 1934 film also plays with the double meaning of the term "pancake," which, according to Hurston's "Glossary of Harlem Slang," was a "humble type of Negro." This wordplay is made clear in the line of the dialogue that Brown adopted for the title of his *Opportunity* review. When Stahl's Delilah refuses Bea's offer of a share in the corporation, insisting that all she wants is to continue serving her white mistress, Bea's business manager shakes his head in disbelief and declares, "Once a pancake, always a pancake." It is useful to keep in mind, however, that the pancake was once a waffle. Hurst's use of waffles rather than pancakes—like the name "Delilah"—marks her text's allusion to and distance from Aunt Jemima. A "pancake" may be a "humble type of Negro" in Harlem slang, but the verb form of "waffle" means "to speak or write equivocally." The double meaning of "waffle" makes it an apt symbol for Hurst's novel. Like *Show Boat*, *Imitation of Life* is an equivocating text, riddled with ambivalences. Its racial ideology difficult to pin down, the novel has provoked controversy because it waffles between affirming stereotypes and critiquing them, between upholding a racial binary and troubling both blackness and whiteness. Through its embedded narrative about the commodification of the black female image, however, *Imitation of Life* exposes the limitations of white perceptions of African Americans, the inability to penetrate beyond stereotype and the tendency (as white reviewers' responses to the novel indicate) to mistake myth for reality. In the section that follows, I investigate how the text employs multiple passing narratives, extending its reach to gender and ethnicity, in order to further destabilize the whiteness that depends on such fixed images of blacks for its meaning.

Imitations of White

As evidence of the impact of *Imitation of Life* on black culture, Hurston's "Glossary of Harlem Slang" contains an entry for "Pe-ola," defining the term as "a very white Negro girl."[98] Like her mother, the character of Peola in Hurst's novel ends up living her life according to a fabrication of racial identity. In crossing the color line, the fair-skinned Peola imitates whiteness. The unbridgeable distance between the submissive Delilah and the rebellious Peola appears to offer two competing models of black female identity: the self-sacrificing (Delilah) and the self-hating (Peola). However, a close analysis of Peola's subplot suggests that the mother-daughter pairing also opens a space for a more complex representation of race. I begin this section by examining how Hurst's depiction of Peola moves beyond stereotypical depictions of the mulatto character as an idolizer of whiteness. I then go on to explore how Peola's story intersects with and parallels the other passing narratives of the text: the main narrative of Bea Pullman, who passes for a man in the business world, and the additional subplot of Virginia Eden, Bea's fellow self-made business-woman. Subverting racial and gender norms, the text's multiple passing narratives contribute to its tendency to complicate, rather than stabilize, whiteness.

In *The Bluest Eye* (1970), Toni Morrison signifies on *Imitation of Life*'s passing narrative through the characters of the dark-skinned Pecola and light-skinned Maureen Peal, whose first and last names, respectively, are variations on "Peola."[99] Morrison's characters are defined by their internalization of white standards of beauty, a force that proves destructive for Pecola, who believes her black skin and lack of blue eyes doom her to a life of ugliness. In *Imitation of Life*, however, Peola's decision to pass is not motivated by an idealization of whiteness as much as a refusal to conform to the image of black inferiority embodied by her mother. Growing up in the Pullman household, Peola learns how easily the black image can be manipulated by whites for their own benefit. Describing the shared upbringing of Peola and Jessie "during [the] period of sublime democracy of childhood," the novel comments that "the dark child, . . . except for the contrast of the whiteness of Jessie, might have passed for white herself." Peola's blackness comes in to being in relation to Jessie's whiteness, and, appropriately, it is Jessie who first makes Peola aware that she is black when she begins calling her "nigger"—an interpellation Peola adamantly refuses. In one of many altercations between mother and daughter, Peola lashes out at Delilah when she reassures Bea that Jessie need not apologize: "'You! You!' she screamed, the flanges of her nose whitening and spreading like wings as she beat small fists against the checkered apron frontage of Delilah. 'You're so black! That's what makes me a nigger.'"[100] As the young Peola attacks the solidly entrenched image of the mammy, beating her fists against the "apron frontage of Delilah," it becomes clear that she is resisting the ways in which blackness is constructed by whites—a resistance that she achieves through the act of "whitening," in opposition to the legal construction of the one-drop rule.

The argument could be made that even though Peola does not idealize whiteness, her refusal to be black goes against notions of racial self-love prevalent in the Harlem Renaissance. Because of her fanatical resistance to Peola's passing, Delilah is sometimes read as a semipositive image, dignified and proud. Yet in the novel, Delilah's version of pride is, in her own terminology, "nigger-love." She is fervent in her essentialist belief that "de good Lawd . . . made us black and white," and that staying true to one's self means staying in one's place.[101] This is certainly not the kind of racial pride black intellectuals of the early twentieth century had in mind. In the hands of African American writers, passing novels (such as Larsen's *Passing*, Fauset's *Plum Bun*, and White's *Flight*) functioned as critiques of passing, often espousing messages of racial pride because the protagonists ultimately choose to return to their race. *Imitation of Life*, however, develops only part of the black writers' critique of race. Peola makes the novel's most definitive statement on racial inequality when she says, "There's nothing wrong in passing. The wrong is the world that makes it necessary."[102] Although a productive model of racial pride may be absent from Hurst's rendition of the passing story, this does not diminish its critique of the way social institutions maintain black inferiority ("the world that makes [passing] necessary"). This is illustrated not only by the manipulation of Delilah's image but also by a particularly painful scene in which a physician, called in to attend to a stricken Peola, dramatically alters his course of treatment once he discovers that she is black. Like other passing novels of the period, Hurst's narrative does more to criticize, rather than idealize, whiteness.

While Peola reads as a tragic character, she does not neatly conform to the stereotype of the tragic mulatto, despite Brown's classification of her as such. In "Negro Character as Seen by White Authors," an article that appeared in the *Journal of Negro Education* in the same year that Hurst published her novel, Brown summed up the typical fate of the mulatta: "the whole desire of her life is to find a white lover, and then go down, accompanied by slow music, to a tragic end."[103] Peola may marry a white man, but this is not "the whole desire of her life," nor the reason for her passing (in fact, it is a side effect of her decision to cross the color line). In speaking of "the world that makes [passing] necessary," Peola clarifies that her desire is not for whiteness, but for white opportunities (which is why many black spectators of the film viewed her character in such a favorably rebellious light). In the novel, Peola does undergo a kind of metaphorical death in that she is expunged from the narrative once she obtains Bea's and Delilah's concession to let her "pass completely."[104] The shocking lengths Peola goes to in order to live in the white world underline the tragedy of her fate. Not only does she remove herself to the jungles of Bolivia, ensuring her safety through her physical distance from her past life in the United States, but she also has herself sterilized so that her children will not atavistically reveal her race. Linked to an earlier episode in which she severely burned her scalp in an attempt to iron out an "imaginary kink" in her hair, Peola's sterilization serves as evidence of the self-destruction caused by impossible standards of whiteness (and it is here that Hurst's novel best presages Morrison's *The Bluest Eye*).[105]

Although her entrance into the white world comes at a tremendous cost, and sterilization could certainly be understood as a form of death, Peola, unlike the traditional mulatto figure, is not neatly recontained in the text. *Imitation of Life* is a rare example of a passing narrative in which a mixed-race female character permanently crosses the color line. The subversive implications of this ending to Peola's storyline are suggested by the significant alteration made in the 1934 film adaptation of *Imitation of Life*. Instead of disappearing from the story once she announces her decision to pass, in Stahl's film, Peola returns at Delilah's funeral and collapses in tears on the coffin. Stahl conforms to more traditional passing narratives by returning Peola to her race with the announcement that she will attend a colored teacher's college.[106] The revised ending may provide a sense of closure that might convey a message of racial pride, but more likely Hurst's chosen fate for Peola was deemed too dangerous for Hollywood, especially given the Production Code's prohibition on representations of miscegenation. Like her characterization of the mammy, Hurst's treatment of the mulatto stereotype is ideologically ambiguous; Peola at once challenges racial categories in refusing to be contained by them and submits to conventions of the tragic mulatto, her sterility assuaging fears of reproduction and rampant mongrelization.

In his analysis of *Imitation of Life*, Sterling Brown placed the novel within a tradition of white authorship on black themes and characters. More recently, however, Susan Gubar has called attention to a subtradition of Jewish women writers who take up questions of race and specifically African American identity. In surveying this tradition, Gubar singles out the novels of Ferber and Hurst, suggesting that their use of the passing genre needs to be understood in the context of their identities as Jewish women and in relation to their African American modernist contemporaries who were similarly developing the theme.[107] As

I explored earlier in this chapter, Hurst maintained enduring commitments to women's, Jewish, and civil rights issues throughout her life. *Imitation of Life* becomes an increasingly complex text when we consider the racial passing subplot in conjunction with the novel's treatment of gender, ethnicity, and assimilation.

Cultural critics have been drawn to the film versions of *Imitation of Life* precisely because the juxtaposition of racial passing with a female success story effectively reveals the co-construction of race and gender. While the ascent of the female protagonist in both film adaptations has been interpreted as a form of passing, Hurst's novel makes it explicitly so.[108] Bea's first commercial breakthrough occurs when she realizes that she can use her husband's business cards, which contain only his first initial, B.: "The accident of the initials made it all right. Beatrice or Benjamin Pullman could use those cards. . . . Naturally there was something strange and irreconcilable to a business man to have to contemplate a woman, her hands always loaded between hiking her skirts off the ground, her pocket-book, and her gloves, rushing about as salesman."[109] This passage makes clear the ways in which the patriarchal system necessitates Bea's passing. Despite the coy use of the adverb "naturally," it indicates that Bea is limited in her role as salesman because she is weighed down by *material* differences of dress. Early in the novel, we are told that Bea's mother was opposed to her daughter working because "it made a girl mannish, like those Woman's Rights advocates."[110] Indeed, Bea's work ends up transforming her into a man. The novel goes on to detail the many obstacles Bea faces in her attempt to break the gender barriers of big business and the necessity of hiding behind her first initial in order to receive equal treatment.

The novel uses a number of techniques to draw parallels between Bea's subterfuge and that of Peola. While Delilah stands in the way of Peola's passing, it is Bea, as surrogate white mother, who enables it. Hurst describes Peola's first experience of passing at age eight thus: "By one of those feats of circumstance that seemed to cerebrate and conspire, one Peola Cilla Johnston, entered into a neighborhood public school one morning by B. Pullman, as she paused long enough in her morning rush to enroll the child, was actually to pursue two years of daily attendance, unsuspected of what she chose not to reveal."[111] The fact that Bea is referred to only by her first initial in this instance recalls her similar decision to disguise her identity. Furthermore, the passage questions which of the two characters is actually obscuring her full self by juxtaposing the shortened form of Bea's name with an elongation of the girl's name; notably, this is the only time in the text that Peola's full name is used.

Hurst reinforces the identification between Peola and Bea through the technique of parataxis. Episodes that center on Peola tend to be segregated into their own chapters; thus chapter 26 sets the stage for Peola's passing by focusing on her refusal to be black after she is called "nigger" by Jessie. The chapter fades out with Peola fainting. The next chapter, rather than picking up Peola's story, shifts to Bea, announcing her meteoric rise with a series of newspaper headlines. The first reads, "FEW KNOW THAT B. PULLMAN, KNOWN BY NAME THE COUNTRY OVER, IS A WOMAN."[112] It is through a number of such textual maneuvers that Hurst analogizes Peola's subplot with her novel's central narrative: the success story of Bea's upward rise from struggling single mother to "waffle queen."

Such links between the narratives of racial and gender passing suggest that *Imitation of Life* is more than a simple appropriation of African American themes; instead, the racial angle can be read as an extension of the central preoccupations that pervade Hurst's fiction. This is nowhere more evident than in the secondary character of Bea's fellow businesswoman, Virginia Eden, who runs a line of beauty products. Virginia Eden unites the story of the working woman with the narrative of racial passing. As Kathy Peiss has shown, female entrepreneurs played crucial roles in the inception and development of the beauty industry at the beginning of the twentieth century. Virginia participates in an industry that, in Peiss's words, "redefin[es] mainstream ideals of beauty and femininity," proving both gender and racial identity to be "surprisingly malleable."[113] Much as the cosmetics she sells contribute to the construction of femininity, Eden, the text implies, has reinvented her ethnic identity. "Born Sadie Kress in Jersey City," Virginia Eden refashions herself as a blank slate, choosing a name that signifies the purity of origins (Virginia) as well as the act of creation (Eden).[114] Her former name and hometown, however, suggest that Virginia is most likely an assimilated Jew. Her act of passing is also suggested in the description of her face as "so frail [that it] had the look of a sheet of fine-grained writing-paper with careful erasures *almost marking out* what had been written on it."[115] Although Hurst's writing participates in this erasure by never definitively revealing Virginia's background, she drops enough hints to suggest that "what had been written" was almost, but not entirely, "mark[ed] out." Is this "the last carbon copy" of her Jewishness?

Although critics have been quick to point out the absence of Jewishness in *Imitation of Life*, the novel itself carries the imprint of Hurst's short fiction, which did explicitly engage with questions of immigration and assimilation. A puzzling scene, one of few in which expressly Jewish characters do appear, indicates how the presence of ethnic difference has the potential to destabilize whiteness. The beginning of the novel takes place in Atlantic City, New Jersey, whose carnivalesque and multiethnic setting foregrounds the novel's various inversions and impersonations of identity. Jews figure prominently in this setting. For example, when Bea is forced by her father into a loveless union with her family's boarder, Benjamin Pullman, their wedding dinner takes place at a "showy Boardwalk hostelry [which], catering as it did to a wealthy Semitic clientele, would not ordinarily have been first choice." As the wedding party enters the dining room, Bea "felt the rising tide of color rise and prick her face."[116] The allusion to Lothrop Stoddard's nativist tract, *The Rising Tide of Color Against White Supremacy*, is highly suggestive. The close contact with immigrants threatens to cast a pall over Bea's identity. Following her husband's death in a train wreck (more a source of relief than tears), Bea's maple-syrup selling ventures take her deeper into the seamier side of Atlantic City: "Boarding-houses with buzzing verandas spilled their commotions from lighted windows and crowded stoops. The knee-high swinging doors of saloons slapped inward and outward and family entrances were the scene of constant comings and goings. Greek restaurants poured greasy odors, kosher hotels buzzed with the activities of stout matrons in machine-stitched wigs. Nationalisms flared along these side streets, each country to its odor, complexion, and often as not, its hoisted flags." Although Bea "remain[s] unmolested" as she travels these streets, Atlantic City's ethnic population threatens to burst all bounds.[117] This is a world in which the ethnic population cannot be contained to its separate sphere, nor is it assimilable to American culture as suggested by the flaring nationalisms and the distinct odors, complexions, and flags. Bea's familiarity with these spaces of ethnic difference arises because she herself is not contained to the domestic sphere. As a working woman, she transgresses borders of race and ethnicity as well as gender.

Drawn to Virginia Eden as a fellow self-made working woman, Bea again struggles to define her own identity in relation to her friend and thus in relation to ethnic difference. Theirs begins as a mutual attraction, tinged slightly by homoerotic undertones, when Virginia courts Bea, sending her a corsage that causes Bea to note "with a sense of the growing inner dreariness which sometimes now seemed to dangle down the center of her, that is was the first corsage she had ever received."[118]

The companionship between the two women, however, turns out to be short-lived when Hurst's heroine questions the cosmetic queen's scruples in their joint real estate endeavor. In a plan that further alludes to her Anglicization of immigrant identity, Virginia proposes to transform a tenement on the Hudson into "a row of Colonial houses" on an "imitation Thames Embankment."[119] But when Virginia intends to hide the rock stratum beneath the tenement–turned–Thames Embankment from their investors, Bea decides to buy her out in order to conduct business honestly. Bea is continually conflicted over whether she and Virginia are of the same breed or whether her moral integrity places her on a higher plane. She attempts to legitimate her whiteness not only in relation to the blackness of Delilah but also by the distance established between her and a presumably Jewish character, who, in a tradition of economic stereotyping, is depicted as ethically unscrupulous. As Virginia herself reflects, her career is "strangely analogous" to that of B. Pullman but also "strangely alien to it."[120]

Even if the text conceals her ethnic background, Virginia Eden is a figure familiar to readers of Hurst's short fiction. Her stories are filled with Jewish characters who relinquish their pasts, changing their names and transforming their identities with the acquisition of material goods. In "In Memoriam" (1916), the morally bereft Becky Meyerburg, insisting that she be called "Betty," wheedles her mother into using the funds set aside for a memorial to her hard-working father (whose labor enabled the family's ascent from the ghetto to Fifth Avenue) as a dowry for a gold-digging—and likely phony—marquis. Hurst revisits similar conflicts in one of her best-known short stories, "The Gold in Fish" (1925), in which Morris Goldfish strong-arms his entire family into shortening their last name to Fish. Overriding his parents' objections that changing their name is "like cutting something so close . . . —like an arm or a something that's part of us," the hardnosed son justifies his decision: "I have changed our name legally because it was a liability and not an asset. . . . Morris Goldfish and Maurice Fish are two different human beings. Certain walks of life are closed to Morris Goldfish that I, as Maurice Fish, propose to enter."[121] For the older generation, such complete excisions of the past prove fatal. "In Memoriam" ends with Mrs. Meyerburg, now a poor woman, having given her last cent to ensure her children's upward mobility, returning to the ghetto to die. The Goldfishes suffer a similar loss when the father succumbs to anemia shortly after his son lops the "Gold" off their name: "Old man Fish was dying. . . . The rivers of his blood were running white. It was as if it was part of the fading out of old man Fish. The paling of the blood."[122]

In stories such as these, Hurst offered a trenchant indictment of American values that prized the materialistic promise of the future over connections to one's heritage and family. Exploring the underside of upward mobility, she romanticizes the immigrant past as an alternative to the sterility of the white, upper-class mainstream. In no uncertain terms, given the above description of old man Fish's demise, "whitening" is associated with death. The characters of Peola and Virginia Eden in *Imitation of Life* are holdovers from Hurst's earlier critiques of ethnic assimilation, but the novel expands this examination of the limitations of whiteness by redirecting the spotlight on to a white protagonist. The novel repeatedly attempts to situate the figures of Peola and Virginia as foils for Hurst's similarly self-made protagonist in order to differentiate Bea's racial positioning from the imitations of whiteness performed by passing African American and Jew. Ultimately, however, these characters prove stronger doubles than foils, and all three women come to represent significant challenges to the social order.

Although Bea's hiring of Delilah and appropriation of blackness may be an attempt to stabilize her identity, at every turn Bea is thwarted in her attempts at stabilization, and the novel ultimately offers a complex representation of white femininity that might be termed "queer"—and not only because Bea passes as a man. While Bea shows little interest in men and is repeatedly disturbed by thoughts of sex, the novel places a primacy on relationships formed between women. Bea and Delilah work, live, and raise their children together, enacting a separate-spheres arrangement, with Delilah performing the domestic chores and Bea operating as the financial brains behind their enterprise. As a high-powered entrepreneur whose only connection to the domestic is through the kitchens she owns and manages, Bea does not adhere to codes of heteronormativity. Absorbing herself in her business, Bea neglects romance as well as motherhood; the role of mother to Jessie falls, of course, to Delilah. It is Delilah who continually tries to operate as a force of stabilization, insisting that her employer find some "man-lovin'."[123] Seemingly in response to such expectations, Bea quite suddenly decides she is in love with her manager, Frank Flake, a man eight years younger than she is. But Bea's feelings for Flake never ring true, and, at the end of the novel, in a strange twist, she sacrifices her own happiness and allows Flake to marry her daughter. Readers might be apt to see this conclusion as a clear-cut condemnation of Bea, who is supposedly being punished for her transgression of ideological norms, but I want to emphasize the note of ambiguity on which the text ends. In the final line, Bea observes Jessie and Flake together: "They were so young, standing there. . . . so right. . . ." (ellipses in text). In a draft version of *Imitation of Life*, Hurst crossed out "so beautiful," replacing it with "so right."[124] Her revised ending works against a romanticized view of the heterosexual union, transforming it instead into a fulfillment of social expectations.[125] Furthermore, the novel's final word is no word at all but ellipses, preceded by a vision of the heterosexual lovers. This resistance to closure (especially from a writer well trained in the neat ending of the short story form) suggests that the text is leaving something unresolved, that its central identities are in flux, rather than stabilized or recontained.

Imitation of Life is structured according to competing systems of identification and disidentification in which the white protagonist's subjectivity is defined both by its contrast with and its semblance to representations of blackness and ethnic difference. As a self-made woman, Bea transgresses proper gender and sexual roles; her only sure foothold seemed to be in her whiteness, which depended upon the "Africanist presence" of Delilah (especially with Peola's disappearance into the white world). But the novel ultimately killed off the mammy figure, a violence aimed not at Delilah as an African American, but rather at the white-controlled myths of black identity; Delilah, after all, dies in the act of kissing Bea's feet. As Flake comments after the death of the mammy figure: "it will be a queer world without Delilah."[126] Not only is blackness shown to be no more than an imitation, an image molded by white fantasy, but the text's multiple passing narratives further serve to destabilize white identity. Here, we might do well to recall Hurst's earlier short story, "The Smudge." While Hattie Bertch's income from her commodification of blackness at first enables her daughter's movement into whiteness, blackface ultimately threatens to trouble the very white identity it had constructed. In *Imitation of Life*, Bea's appropriations of blackness have a similarly contradictory effect: they may initially assuage anxiety about her whiteness and femininity, but they ultimately contribute to a highly ambivalent portrait of modern womanhood that calls into questions norms of race, gender, and sexuality.

If I Were a Negro

Like Ferber, who continually returned to the theme of interracialism she explored in *Show Boat*, Hurst maintained an interest in African

American culture that did not subside with the end of the "Negro vogue." Hurst's friendship with Hurston continued well into the 1940s, and *Imitation of Life* was itself written at the tail end of the Harlem Renaissance. While Ferber's later work extends her vision of a pluralistic America to various corners of the nation and its borders, the racial themes Hurst treats in *Imitation of Life* do not surface extensively again in her fiction. The controversy over the film version of *Imitation of Life*, which was simultaneously a "sensation in Harlem" and a sore spot with African American critics such as Brown, certainly made Hurst aware of the difficulty and even futility of a white writer offering a portrait of black life.[127]

Two articles published by Hurst in 1946 provide evidence of her continued commitment to African American causes as well as her inability to shake entirely free of the contradictory racial attitudes that pervade *Imitation of Life*. In that year, Hurst received a request from *Negro Digest* to contribute to a series called "If I Were a Negro" in which prominent white Americans, from Pearl Buck to Eleanor Roosevelt, were asked to reflect on what it would be like to walk in the shoes of African Americans.[128] In her response, Hurst emphasizes the importance of interminority and cross-racial fellowship. "If I were a Negro," she writes, "I would face this shameful problem as if I were a member, not of the Negro race alone, but of any minority race confronted with the inevitable considerations of man's inhumanity to man. . . . I would work from within to reach out beyond my own race and enlist the cooperation of the white race." While Hurst draws attention to the "gargantuan social burdens" she would carry as an African American, her own empathetic response is somewhat undercut by her reference to "the godliness, the friendliness, the joyous perpetual adolescence of the Negro" that would allow her "to laugh off, sing off, pray off, some of" these burdens.[129] As Hurst assumes the guise of the black American to demand economic and social equality, her portrayal comes perilously close to devolving into minstrelsy. It is important to keep in mind, however, that Hurst wrote in accordance with an editor's request. In *Imitation of Life*, she had already taken her position on the inexorable limitations faced by white Americans who tried to ventriloquize black subjectivity.

The second article directly addresses the limitations of cross-racial understanding and attempts to move beyond such social barriers. In this article, a feature story for the *New York Times Magazine* titled "The Other, and Unknown, Harlem," Hurst offers a thoughtful depiction of segments of black life that remain unknown to most white readers and audiences. Invoking a number of mass-culture stereotypes of blacks that have barely diminished today, Hurst notes that whites have consumed the "popular whoop-'em-up, shoot-'em down, race-rioting, zoot-suited, bear-greased [sic], white man's version of New York's more infamous and famous Harlem." Because "the white mind seldom follows the Negro into his home," Hurst writes, there is little to refute the image of Harlem as a "badlands, where the chauffeur or the housemaid goes home to sleep, where the children have rickets, and no man is safe after dark," "an incubator for vice, a lunatic fringe of savage music," or the belief that "all Harlem is musically talented, unreliable, un- or amoral." Establishing her awareness of the public conception of black ghetto life, Hurst takes her readers on a tour of a number of African American homes, introducing them to "unhonored and unsung Harlem which represents decency, family unity and social stability." Although Hurst takes especial care not to neglect poor housing and other execrable conditions faced by many residents of Harlem, her goal is to present a more diverse picture of New York's primary black neighborhood, from Caribbean immigrants to native-born Americans who have migrated from various parts of the country, from white-collar families struggling to ensure that their children receive the education denied the parents to members of the professional and "intelligentsia" classes who send their children to private schools and whose apartments are filled with music and books. Encouraging her readers to see past stereotypical images of a vice-ridden underworld populated by pimps and prostitutes and dotted by seedy dives, Hurst's jeremiad exhorts whites to take an interest in the social conditions of Harlem by recognizing its diversity and the efforts of the majority of its citizens to "lead ordered, backbone-of-the-nation lives" while bearing the burden of discrimination.[130] The article serves as an important example of how Hurst's social consciousness continued to be directed at the world that made passing necessary, as well as at the implications for those who were entirely cut off from the benefits of white privilege. It may also be read as a form of self-criticism—a partial acknowledgment of her own complicity in perpetuating the erroneous conception of African Americans—and thus an attempt to right the wrongs of her fiction by presenting a broader and more complex cross section of black life.

* * *

As novels by white Jewish writers, Ferber's *Show Boat* and Hurst's *Imitation of Life* have a tendency to be read as misappropriations of blackness, lending weight to Rogin's argument that Jews transformed themselves into whites at the expense of African Americans. Having begun their careers with fiction chronicling the adventures of ethnic working women, both Ferber and Hurst have been accused of "white-washing" their heroines as their careers progressed and their fame increased. Critics have leaped to interpret this shift away from ethnically identified protagonists as an abandonment of the writers' Jewish identities, and this forsaking of their ethnic heritage was understood to erect a black-white binary. In contrast, I argue that we can also view this move as an extension of their earlier themes—a universalizing that challenges how we define the universal. When read in this light, Ferber's and Hurst's work and their careers overall do much to expose and destabilize the myths of white and black identity. Rather than understanding Jewish appropriations of blackness in the oppositional terms of identification or disidentification, we need to examine the ambivalence of such representations and the ways in which identification and disidentification operate coterminously. Furthermore, as texts that are in dialogue with the work of African American writers of the period, Hurst's and Ferber's novels are suggestive of the ways in which the relationship between blacks and Jews in the early-twentieth-century United States needs to be understood in terms of exchange and not simply unidirectional exploitation. To conclude this study, I turn now to Zora Neale Hurston, a writer well suited to comment on the black-Jewish imaginary given that her own career was marked by her association with a number of prominent Jews, including Hurst. Such associations led, in part, to Hurston's excoriation by other African American writers and critics, who accused her of participating in the minstrel tradition that her work sets out to critique.

4 / Moses and Minstrelsy: Zora Neale Hurston and the Black-Jewish Imaginary

Zora Neale Hurston came to Fannie Hurst's defense when *Imitation of Life* faced charges of racism, but in an unpublished 1934 article, titled "You Don't Know Us Negroes," Hurston made what sounds like a veiled jibe at the white author's inauthentic rendition of black life: "Whenever I pick up one of the popular magazines and read one of these mammy cut tales, I often wonder whether the author actually believes that his tale is probable or whether he knows it is flapdoodle and is merely concerned about the check." Hurston's use of universalizing masculine pronouns helps to shield Hurst from direct implication. Yet coming on the heels of Hurst's 1933 novel, which originally appeared as a magazine serial, this critique of popular representations of African Americans might very well have reminded readers of *Imitation of Life*'s controversial depiction of the mammy.[1] The contradiction between Hurston's defense of her white friend and her more oblique, and ultimately suppressed, skepticism about the ethics of Hurst's work provides evidence of the black writer's paradoxical public persona. Not averse to catering to white fascination with black culture for her own advancement (as Langston Hughes once observed, "she was always getting scholarships and things from wealthy white people"), Hurston employed double-voiced strategies that allowed her to cultivate and maintain a number of significant interracial relationships without necessarily compromising her artistic credo.[2]

While her criticism of Hurst's "mammy cut tale" may have never seen the light of day, Hurston was typically unafraid to voice her vexation about the ways that white consumption of blackness reduced African

Americans to primitive stereotypes. She expressed her distaste for popularized versions of folk culture, taking aim at the Kern-Hammerstein adaptation of *Show Boat*, for example, when she complained that the "Ol' Man Rivers ha[ve] been exploited all out of context."[3] The inability of white cultural producers to access black subjectivity was of particular concern to Hurston. Commenting on the persistence of the minstrel tradition that continued to permeate American theater in the 1920s and 1930s, she questioned why "the black-face comedians *are* black-face; it is a puzzle—good comedians, but darn poor niggers."[4] Hurston conceived of her own attempts to establish African American theater as a direct reaction to white musical appropriations such as *Porgy and Bess*, Gershwin's 1935 folk opera, which traded on stereotypes and romanticized black life. Of *Porgy and Bess*, she wrote, "The story is not too true to our lives and I want to do something more penetrating."[5] Her creative output was thus intended to counteract minstrelsy and its legacies, "debunking" what she labeled "the current mammy-song-Jolson conception of the Southern Negro."[6]

Despite her folklorist's commitment to displacing the commercial blackface tradition with an art that would draw on and do justice to the richness of African American cultural traditions, Hurston was not immune to allegations of minstrelsy simply because of her race. She herself stood accused of trying to "satisfy" the "chauvinistic tastes" of a "white audience" and maintaining black inferiority by cashing in on the "quaintness" of African American life.[7] Like Hurst and Ferber, she was found guilty of exploiting blackness through its commodification, and, to her accusers, her guilt was intensified because her writing amounted to treason—a betrayal of her race for her own gain.

Hurston's harshest critics were fellow African Americans, most often male writers and intellectuals such as Richard Wright, Ralph Ellison, and Alain Locke, all of whom reproached her for selling out to whites. *Their Eyes Were Watching God*, for example, may be revered today as a classic of American literature and feminist writing, but the novel was not as well received when it was first published in 1937. In Wright's now notorious review of *Their Eyes Were Watching God*, he takes the novel to task for lacking any "basic idea or theme that lends itself to significant interpretation" and claims that its author has "no desire whatever to move in the direction of serious fiction." Wright's initial assessment echoes views commonly held by the patriarchal literary establishment, from Nathaniel Hawthorne's invective against the "damned mob of scribbling women" to F. Scott Fitzgerald's denigration of popular writers such as Ferber and Hurst whose works were similarly aimed at a female readership. Wright's criticism, however, gets more specific, reflecting the era's racial, as well as gender, politics: "Miss Hurston *voluntarily* continues in her novel the tradition which was *forced* upon the Negro in the theater, that is, the minstrel technique that made the 'white folks' laugh. Her characters eat and laugh and cry and work and kill; they swing like a pendulum eternally in that safe and narrow orbit in which America likes to see the Negro live: between laughter and tears."[8] Equating her fiction with minstrelsy, Wright asserts that Hurston's writing shares more with white appropriations imposed upon blacks than with the tradition of African American literature formed in opposition to white domination.

Wright's accusations of minstrelsy need to be understood in terms of the shifts that took place in African American literature from the New Negro movement to the 1930s. Disappointed by the Harlem Renaissance's failure to make significant strides in racial equality through its commitment to aesthetics over propaganda, many black writers turned to unequivocal protest, leading to an era of politically conscious social realism that was shepherded in by Wright and reached its apotheosis with his publication of *Native Son* in 1940. Having declared herself "not tragically colored," Hurston refused to subscribe to what she called "the sobbing school of Negrohood."[9] Many of her works are set in all-black rural environments and thus do not deal blatantly with the social injustices faced by African Americans in a white world. Ironically then, Hurston's resistance to following white, Western modes of writing leads to accusations of minstrelsy. Because of her folk influences, her use of dialect, and her refusal of black victimization, she was viewed as pandering to white audiences and white perceptions of blacks, perpetuating stereotypes such as the "happy darky."

While initial studies of blackface minstrelsy focused on white performers, recent scholarship has turned to the phenomenon of black-on-black minstrels, contending that African American entertainers such as Bert Williams found ways to subvert stereotypes imposed by the black-face mask.[10] Hurston similarly acknowledged, played with, and counteracted conventions of minstrelsy in her fiction and in her carefully constructed public persona. Rather than simply exonerating Hurston of minstrelsy, this chapter explores how her deployment of minstrel conventions serves as a multilayered critique of racial appropriations and interminority identifications.

Although Hurston rarely called explicit attention to the Jewish identities of many of the performers and musicians whose work she disdains, the association between Jewishness and minstrelsy was unavoidable in the 1920s and 1930s. *The Jazz Singer* brought minstrelsy (and sound) to the cinema in 1927 by telling a story of Jewish assimilation. Jolson reprised his blackface roles throughout the 1930s in films such as *Wonder Bar* (1934), which includes a musical sequence, "Going to Heaven on a Mule," depicting heaven from the point of view of rural blacks and incorporating a sight gag in which a blackface Jolson reads a Yiddish newspaper. In this chapter, I consider how debates about Jewish minstrelsy that I have explored throughout this book shed light on Hurston's interracial relationships and her fiction. In turn, I demonstrate that Hurston's writing encourages a rethinking of the current paradigms circumscribing the black-Jewish imaginary; Hurston challenges the common narrative of unidirectional appropriation of blackness by Jewish producers through her own attraction to Jewish history, a cross-identification that is best exemplified by, and in, her 1939 novel, *Moses, Man of the Mountain*.

In addition to her relationships with white Negrophiles such as Carl Van Vechten and Charlotte Osgood Mason, Hurston's career was also marked by the connections she established with a trio of influential Jews. I begin this chapter by considering this subset of Hurston's interracial associations. Building upon my examination of the Hurst-Hurston friendship in the preceding chapter, I outline the circumstances of Hurston's relationships with anthropologist Franz Boas and Barnard College founder Annie Nathan Meyer. Surveying Hurston's statements on and relationships with Jews allows me to contextualize her own use of minstrel conventions within debates about Jewish paternalism and (mis)appropriations of blackness. As I show, Hurston's view of early black-Jewish relations was often contradictory; it took into account the complexity of an exchange between two historically oppressed groups, one of whom was securely at the bottom rung of the nation's social hierarchy while the other seemed to be advancing into mainstream America, as evidenced by the prominent positions of her three mentors.

This background leads me to a reevaluation of Hurston's underexamined and misunderstood novel, *Moses, Man of the Mountain* (1939), which, like the better-known *Their Eyes Were Watching God*, was excoriated for contributing to the minstrel tradition. In *Moses*, Hurston expropriates a Jewish narrative, rewriting the biblical story of Exodus by casting the enslaved and newly liberated Hebrew people as dialect-speaking, voodoo-practicing, and folktale-telling blacks. One of Hurston's most inscrutable texts because its racial politics cannot be easily pinned down, *Moses, Man of the Mountain* operates on an astonishing number of allegorical levels: it is a fulfillment of Hurston's lifelong determination to tell a story of the Jews predicated on the parallels she saw between biblical history and contemporary African American life; an exploration of the cultural exchanges between blacks and Jews, from the expropriation of the Old Testament by black theology to the appropriation of black performance styles in Jewish minstrelsy; and a political commentary on the relationship between black and Jewish leadership in the budding civil rights movement. Although *Moses* is the rare work in Hurston's oeuvre to focus mostly on men and take place in the public sphere, the narrative she devises of a mutually beneficial, yet problematic alliance between people of different backgrounds was informed by her own collaborative relationships with Jewish women. Like the masculine pronoun that partially disguises Hurston's ostensible criticism of Hurst's popular mammy tale, the homosocial setting of *Moses, Man of the Mountain* might be understood as a double-voiced technique through which she also critiqued the kinds of cross-racial identifications and appropriations associated with the figure of the white negress.

A Poetic Race of People: Hurston's Jewish Relations

In a 1925 letter to Annie Nathan Meyer, Hurston begins by praising one of her benefactor's novels, attributing Meyer's "colorful" prose to her Jewish background: "You are a poetic race of people. The Old Testament is my only reason for ever opening the Bible at all. Such powers of story telling! Such magenta speech figures."[11] Dedicated to preserving and promoting the vernacular poetry of her own race, Hurston expressed a strong fascination with the Old Testament. As an African American, she identified with the Hebrew Bible's narrative of bondage and liberation as well as its emphasis on freedom in this life above salvation in the next. Recalling her childhood reading of the Bible, Hurston wrote, "The New Testament still plays a poor second to the Old Testament for me. The Jews had a God who laid about Him when they needed Him. I could see no use waiting till Judgment Day to see a man who was just crying for a good killing, to be told to go and roast. My idea was to give him a good killing first, and then if he got roasted later on, so much the better."[12] Although her letter to Meyer was written in a period when heightened nativism could easily lead to parallels between anti-Semitism and racism, Hurston articulates her affinity with the Jewish people in transhistorical terms, turning to the rhetoric of the Old Testament, much as the black sermons and spirituals that inspired her did.

Hurston's assignment of Meyer to "a poetic race of people" is also notable because it implies that she saw her correspondent, who was of Sephardic Jewish descent, as different from other whites with whom she came into contact—indeed, a separate race. At the same time, this is a rare instance in which Hurston recognizes Meyer's Jewish identity; in many ways, Meyer could not be distinguished from Hurston's other white sponsors, given her wealth, her influence, and the fact that she did not come from a family of recent immigrants, but instead a well-connected one that proudly dated their American heritage back to the Revolution.[13] In the same letter, Hurston acknowledges her subservient position in the hierarchical relationship between the two women. Commenting on Meyer's attempt "to help your little pickaninny" and signing off "Your humble and obedient little 'pick,'" Hurston engages in the kind of minstrel performance that Wright and others found so irksome.[14] As troubling as this self-degradation seems, Hurston biographer Valerie Boyd understands her subject's actions as deliberate and strategic role-playing, explaining that "Zora was consciously *playing* Meyer . . . for her own benefit."[15] The unequal relations between Hurston and Meyer were based partly on differences in social and economic status, but the use of the derogatory term "pickaninny" also implies a hierarchy of race, even as both women were members of minority groups. The interplay between Hurston and benefactors such as Meyer speaks to the complex relationships between blacks and Jews in the early twentieth century—both as they impacted Hurston personally and as they sought to bring about change in the larger public sphere.

Among African American women writers of the period, Hurston stands out for the way that relations with Jews factored into her life. In her creative work, especially her theatrical endeavors, she contended with the popularity of Jolson, Gershwin, and other Tin Pan Alley aficionados of black culture whom she saw as motivated by profit rather than identification.[16] She benefited financially from Jewish philanthropists such as Julius Rosenwald, whose fellowship established to advance the welfare of African Americans and improve relations between the races allowed Hurston to enroll in the Ph.D. program in anthropology at Columbia.[17] During her abbreviated time as a graduate student, Hurston continued the studies she began as an undergraduate at Barnard, supervised by Jewish anthropologists Franz Boas and Melville Herskovits, whose academic work was dedicated to debunking pseudo-scientific notions of racial inferiority.[18] Boas's and Herskovits's views of race confirmed and influenced her own thinking; she, in turn, contributed to their research through her fieldwork among African Americans in Harlem and the South and among Caribbean blacks in Haiti and Jamaica. Finally, Hurston received financial assistance and participated in literary exchange with Meyer and Hurst. The fact that the two Jewish "Negrotarians" who played such crucial roles in Hurston's life were also women should not be overlooked. The bond between them and Hurston derived from the fact that all three led unconventional lives for women; while Hurston's contributions to feminist thought are well acknowledged today, Meyer and Hurst were also vocal advocates for women's rights, placing a premium on women's education and taking the struggle between career and marriage as the subject of their fiction. Yet despite such commonalities, racial differences shaped Hurston's relationships with Meyer and Hurst, which as a result were defined by patronage as well as friendship. Before discussing Hurston's personal and professional relationships with her Jewish sponsors, I consider some of Hurston's more general statements on Jews that suggest her awareness of the complex identifications, and disidentifications, underlying such interracial encounters.

Despite the suspicion Hurston reserved for the likes of Jolson and Gershwin, her attacks on white appropriations of black culture were usually made irrespective of the celebrities' Jewish backgrounds, and her attitude does not appear to translate into anti-Semitism. However, she was certainly conscious of the ways that anti-Jewish sentiment had seeped into black life. Although Hurston has written of her allegiance to the Jewish people based on her affinity for the Old Testament, many African Americans held different opinions, including the view that Jews had displaced blacks as the Chosen People.[19] The first folktale collected by Hurston in the ethnographic *Mules and Men* (1935) is an indication of these competing claims. This tale reads like an anti-Semitic joke. Before God can distribute souls equally among people of all races, "De Jew come past and heard de song from de soul-piece then he kept on passin' and all of a sudden he grabbed up de soul-piece and hid it under his clothes, and run off down de road."[20] In attempting to discredit the Jewish claim to be chosen by God, the folktale depends upon stereotypes of Jewish greed, going so far as to suggest the fraudulent myths of Jewish world domination. In her objective role as anthropologist, Hurston transcribes this tale in her collection, but her own writing, as I show, offers a more sympathetic and identificatory portrait of Jews as mistreated, misunderstood, and falsely maligned.

Hurston showed an awareness of modern anti-Semitism both in the United States and abroad and often analogized it to antiblack racism.

While Hurston's categorization of Jews as "a poetic race of people" acknowledges racial difference, it deflects any common modern experiences of oppression by harking back to the Bible. But in writings from the 1940s and 1950s (a time period, interestingly, in which Jews in the United States were seen as becoming increasingly white), Hurston describes Jews as fellow victims of white dominance, drawing attention to potential alliances between blacks, Jews, and other "darker people." Although this change of heart may have been motivated by the rise of European fascism, she refers directly to discrimination in the United States. In her 1950 essay "What White Publishers Won't Print," for example, Hurston rails against Anglo-Saxon "indifference . . . to the internal life of educated minorities," imagining an "AMERICAN MUSEUM OF UNNATURAL HISTORY" that displays the stereotypes of various racial, ethnic, and regional groups. She writes, "as long as the majority cannot conceive of a Negro or a Jew feeling and reacting inside just as they do, the majority will keep right on believing that people who do not look like them cannot possibly feel as they do, and conform to the established pattern."[21] In such statements, Hurston reveals that her own art is motivated by an urge to correct misconceptions of minorities held by the white majority. She extended her project to Jews as well as blacks in several attempts—some realized and some not—to incorporate the subject of Jewish history into her work.[22]

Even when couching her statements in biblical analogies, Hurston identifies parallels between black and Jewish experiences that supersede the transhistorical comparison between contemporary African Americans and the enslaved Jews of antiquity. Some of the best evidence of the inspiration she found in the Hebrew Bible comes from her unpublished and unfinished work, in which the Jewish struggle for self-determination became an obsession for the floundering writer toward the end of her life. In the period between 1945 and her death in 1960, Hurston planned a book, a play, and a film, all of which would tell stories of Jews. In a 1945 letter to Van Vechten, she described a proposed project, "Herod the Great," the work, it turns out, that was in progress at the time of her fatal stroke: "The story I am burning to write is one that will be highly controversial. I want to write the story of the 3000 years struggle of the Jewish people for democracy and the rights of man." Her interest in the story of the king of Judea was not only historical, for, as she writes, "The Jewish people have suffered and still suffer." The letter also suggests that she saw Jews as a symbol of universal oppression; "instead of the Jewish people being a peculiarly evil and hard-headed race of people," she intends to show "they were just people, fighting for all those things which other people hold sacred and conducing to the rights and dignity of man."[23] Hurston's view of Jewish history as a never-ending battle for freedom indicates that she saw parallels to the African American experience. This is confirmed by the title of a proposal to Scribner's, "Just Like Us: An Analysis of the Hebrews and the Modern Jews as They Were as Against Our Traditional Conceptions." In this proposal, Hurston outlines a plan for a book about "the history and philosophy of the Hebrews" that would "bring about a revision of our Sunday School literature, and alter the slovenly and inimical attitude towards the modern Jew."[24] While it is clear that Hurston is using Jews to stand in for black oppression, she also saw this as a way to address modern anti-Semitism concurrently. As these proposed plans are all dated post–World War II, she likely had the devastating effects of European anti-Semitism at the forefront of her mind, but this does not negate the possibility that she was speaking more broadly of modern attitudes toward Jews. Published in 1939, at the beginning of the Second World War, *Moses, Man of the Mountain* draws simultaneously on references to anti-Semitism in the United States and Europe.

The Jews whose lives and careers became intertwined with those of Hurston were also affected by the correspondence between antiblack racism and anti-Semitism. As discussed in the previous chapter, Hurst's interest in black causes arose out of her earlier concern with Jewish identity even when her ambivalence about her Jewish background prevented her from acknowledging the parallel; in turn, her involvement in the Harlem Renaissance and support for civil rights eventually led to a rediscovery of her Jewish roots. Similarly, for Boas and Meyer, their support of black causes can be attributed, in part, to their Jewish identities.

A pioneer in the field of anthropology credited with challenging the foundations of scientific and intellectual racism, Boas emigrated from his native Germany in 1887 because of limited career opportunities and pervasive anti-Semitism. Despite his rise to intellectual prominence, he also met with various barriers to his professional advancement in the United States due to his Jewish identity. While a few scholars assert that Boas's interest in race comes solely out of intellectual and scientific inquiry, his various biographers tend to see his work as motivated by social activism and personal experiences as well.[25] Boas's views on race and his employment of the tools of anthropological study had a tremendous influence on Hurston. Though she entered Barnard intending to pursue her interest in literature, the classes she took with Boas changed her course of study. She began taking on fieldwork for him and Herskovits, such as the anthropometric data she collected by measuring heads on Harlem street corners. After graduation, she continued her vocation as a folklorist under Boas's supervision, traveling to the South to gather folktales and voodoo ritual for the volume that became *Mules and Men*. Here and elsewhere, Hurston's views of race corresponded largely to those of Boas and his contemporaries. In her autobiography, *Dust Tracks on a Road*, for example, she defines "race" as "a loose classification of physical characteristics [that] tells nothing about the insides of people." She similarly shows her resistance to racial classification in "How It Feels to Be Colored Me," vehemently stating, "At certain times I have no race, I am *me*."[26] These statements illustrate how Boas's anthropological discoveries provided scientific grounding for Hurston's thinking about the category of race, and her belief that racial differences were determined by culture rather than biology impacted her fiction, as I explore further in my reading of *Moses, Man of the Mountain*.

Though Hurston's relationship with Boas was mostly professional, it was also marked by mutual affection that transcended that between student and teacher. Boas's preface to *Mules and Men* speaks of the intellectual value of Hurston's folklore collection, her ability to "penetrate through that affected demeanor by which the Negro excludes the White observer effectively from participating in his true inner life," but he also notes the "charm" of her "loveable personality."[27] In turn, Hurston admired Boas most for "his genius for pure objectivity," but she also comments on a more private side of the man, describing him as "full of youth and fun" when he is outside the office.[28] Rather than placing Boas on a pedestal, Hurston tended to treat him as a fatherly figure. Warned by his secretary not to call him "Papa Franz," the affectionate term his students used behind his back, Hurston confronted Boas directly, to which he replied, "Of course, Zora is my daughter. Certainly! . . . Just one of my missteps, that's all." While Boas might ambiguously joke about a "misstep," his claiming of Hurston as his daughter also shows his deep fondness for her and even alludes to shared affinities between blacks and Jews. In her recollection of the episode, Hurston concludes by emphasizing Boas's good humor, describing how "[t]he sabre cut on his cheek, which it is said he got in a duel at Heidelberg, lifted in a smile" as he defended her right to call him "Papa."[29] Hurston's reference to Boas's scar may not be as incidental as it seems. She was likely aware of the apocryphal stories, circulated by the anthropologist himself, that Boas's fencing scars were obtained in challenges provoked by anti-Semitic comments when he was a student at the University of Heidelberg.[30]

It is unlikely that Hurston would have come into contact with Boas if it were not for the timely intervention of Annie Nathan Meyer, a founder of Hurston's alma mater, Barnard College. The wife of a prominent New York physician, Meyer, dissatisfied with the education she received as a student in the Collegiate Course for Women at Columbia University, lobbied for the creation of a separate institution for women. Thanks largely to Meyer's fund-raising efforts, Barnard College was established as New York's first women's college in 1889, and Meyer remained active in the institution throughout her life. As an author of fiction, drama, and nonfiction, Meyer used her writing as a platform for several causes, from racism and anti-Semitism to a variety of women's issues, including education, labor, and antisuffrage (though a feminist, Meyer opposed the women's vote on the grounds that women would not purify democratic government, an argument that directly contrasts with the position of suffragists, including her sister, Maud Nathan). Meyer's relationship with Hurston illuminates the ways in which the former's literary interests and social activism were intertwined. When she met Hurston at the 1925 *Opportunity* dinner, where the black woman was awarded a literary prize, Meyer was determined to desegregate Barnard; she subsequently arranged for Hurston's admission and assisted her in securing tuition funds.

Although Meyer had great respect for Hurston's intellectual abilities and literary talents, their racial differences shaped the terms of their encounters. For example, Hurston reportedly did housekeeping for friends of Meyer in order to earn some of the money to finance her education.[31] It is difficult to imagine Meyer making such arrangements for a white college student in need of scholarship funds, and one can only deduce that Meyer saw this as appropriate for Hurston because of her black skin. For her part, Hurston may have played into Meyer's stereotypical view of black inferiority by casting herself as the white woman's "little pickaninny" (a term she used with other white patrons such as Charlotte Osgood Mason as well) and often obsequiously expressing her gratitude. Hurston spoke publicly of her debt to Meyer, dedicating *Mules and Men* to "my dear friend Mrs. Annie Nathan Meyer who hauled the mud to make me but loves me just the same." Yet Hurston's appreciation does not translate into praise for Meyer's literary talents. Some of the admiration Hurston expressed for Meyer's writing reads as lukewarm rather than sincere regard. For example, in the 1925 letter in which she reported reading one of Meyer's novels, she reserved the majority of her praise for the "magenta speech figures" of the Old Testament rather than Meyer's own prose and offers the carefully qualified compliment, "I don't care for detailed descriptions as a rule and often pass over them all together, but after the first line, I *had* to read yours."[32]

Meyer's literary interest in black life also took the form of the kind of theatrical appropriations that troubled Hurston. In 1925, when the two women met, Meyer was engaged in writing a play called *Black Souls*, whose title alludes to her source of inspiration, W.E.B. Du Bois's *The Souls of Black Folk*. Set on the campus of a Southern black college (a locale of which Meyer had no firsthand knowledge), the drama was about an interracial affair between an African American poet and a white senator's daughter that ends tragically in the lynching of the black man.[33] Although Meyer was an assimilationist whose philanthropy rarely extended to involvement in Jewish organizations, her activism on behalf of antilynching campaigns does appear to be rooted in her Jewish background. Her 1935 short story "The Shoe Pinches Mr. Samuels," published in an antilynching issue of the *Crisis*, centers on the rabbi of a Southern synagogue and sends a clear message: if Jews do not protest actively the practice of lynching as it has befallen their African American neighbors, they will find themselves the next target of intolerance.[34] Meyer's portrayal of lynching as an issue that should unite Jews and blacks was likely influenced by the case of Jewish factory owner Leo Frank in Georgia. In 1915, Frank met his death at the hands of a lynch mob after he was accused of sexual perversion and murder when one of his young female workers was found dead. Consistently cited by historians as a formative event in the black-Jewish alliance, Frank's lynching awakened Jews to the violent turn anti-Semitism could take and thus led to their commitment to civil rights causes.[35]

The closest Hurston came to a black-Jewish artistic collaboration was her attempt to write a novelization of Meyer's *Black Souls*, which similarly takes lynching as its subject. Hurst and Meyer's collaboration on the social problem play is documented in their correspondence. Around the time that their relationship transformed from one of patronage to partnership, the style of Hurston's letters to Meyer also changed. She began to address her letters to "Dear Friend" (rather than "Dear Mrs. Meyer") and refrained from referring to herself as Meyer's "pickaninny" and "servant." Although the two women were not on a level playing field, their relationship had begun to approximate that of intellectual equals.

Meyer shared the play with Hurston because she valued her opinion and because the black woman's stamp of authentication would assist her in getting the play produced. Hurston's view of *Black Souls* was not wholly positive, and she did not hesitate to present an honest opinion to Meyer: "Clever is not a good word for *Black Souls*. It is immensely moving. It is accurate, it is very, very brave without bathos. There are some mighty fine literary passages too. Once or twice I noted a trite figure."[36] It is unclear how the arrangements for the novelization came about, but in a later letter, Hurston offers Meyer suggestions for restructuring the plot, including opening the play with the dramatic scene of the lynching and using a flashback to tell the story of the events that preceded it. By October 1927, however, Hurston had serious doubts about the novelization project: "The more I see of the South," she wrote to Meyer, "the more am I convinced that it would strike a terribly false note." She attributes Meyer's inaccuracies to the failure of a white Northerner to understand the South's racial taboos from the perspective of an African American as well as an adherence to Du Bois, whom she dismisses as "a propaga[n]dist with all the distorted mind of his kind."[37]

Although Hurston pulled out of the plan for novelization, *Black Souls* was produced in 1932 at the Provincetown Players, the theater that was also home to Eugene O'Neill, whose plays *The Emperor Jones* (1920) and *All God's Chillun Got Wings* (1924) similarly dealt with racial themes, including miscegenation. Opening to negative reviews (the *New York Times* described it as "inept" and criticized the clumsiness of Meyer's writing[38]), *Black Souls* ran for less than a month and a total of thirteen performances. Meyer's play clearly depended on black writers for authentication. The advertisement for the play included endorsements from James Weldon Johnson ("one of the most powerful and penetrating plays yet written on the race question") and Hurston herself, who was quoted as saying, "Never before have I read anything by a white person dealing with 'inside' colored life that did not have a sprinkling of false notes."[39] Yet in 1927, Hurston had written to Meyer that the play struck a "terribly false note." Hurston's public endorsement of the play is carefully worded, using the negative to imply cagily that *Black Souls* may *not* be an exception to her previous assessment of white-authored depictions of black life. Given the apparent contradiction between Hurston's private sentiment and her public statement, it is not surprising that the collaboration, which would have been a rare instance of artistic team effort between black and Jewish women, never came to fruition.

Free-spirited and fiercely independent, Hurston did not have the best track record as an artistic collaborator. Her famous falling out with Langston Hughes over their jointly written play, *Mule Bone*, is a case in point. But with her white benefactors, in particular, Hurston actively resisted their exertion of influence, at the same time that she courted their support. From the beginning of her acquaintance with Hurst, for example, Hurston adamantly refused to be influenced by her employer and fellow writer, setting her own limits on the role the relationship would play in her work. In a letter to Meyer, Hurston speaks of Hurst's offer to send stories to editors for her, but she also sees through the older woman's largesse. Noting that she made the changes suggested by Hurst "with reservations," she states: "I do not wish to become Hurstized. There would be no point in my being an imitation Fannie Hurst, however faithful the copy while the world has the real article at hand."[40] Hurston successfully avoided Hurst's controlling hand. Her distinct voice and rich imagery take their influences from oral and folk traditions, and, as a result, her fiction has little in common with her contemporary women writers, both white and black. While the uniqueness of Hurston's vision is evident in *Moses, Man of the Mountain*, what makes this text even more fascinating to consider in the context of Hurston's relationships with Jewish benefactors is the fact that the novel is about vexed collaborations. Hurston remained skeptical about the sincerity of her patrons' friendship, attuned to the ways that they might profit from such interactions, but she also acknowledged the potential for productive cultural and political exchange between Jews and African Americans. Her own identification with Jews and Jewish history was most thoroughly articulated in *Moses, Man of the Mountain*, a novel that addresses the great promise of cross-racial identification, while also exploring its limitations.

Just Like Us?

The accusation of minstrelsy that Hurston faced with the publication of *Their Eyes Were Watching God* resurfaced when she published her subsequent novel, *Moses, Man of the Mountain*, in 1939. In one review, for instance, George Schuyler found fault with the novel's "annoying incongruities" and stated that it was "little better than burlesque, interspread with cotton-patch dialect."[41] While Ralph Ellison acknowledged that the novel's "burlesque" was "calculated," he considered it a "blight" on the text, concluding, "For Negro fiction, [*Moses*] did nothing."[42] Similar views of Hurston's work persist today. In *Required Reading* (1998), Andrew Delbanco echoes the language of the earlier reviews when he calls *Moses* "a zany burlesque of the Book of Exodus that recasts the prophet as a kind of jive godfather." Like many contemporary critics who do not hesitate to point out the unevenness of Hurston's prose, viewing her novels as ambitious attempts that fail to live up to their great promise, Delbanco arrives at a mixed verdict on *Moses*: "with a kind of antic reverence, she expropriated the story of the Jews' redemption under Moses as an exemplum for contemporary black life. The trouble is, she retells it with a mix of bombast and parody. . . . It becomes a blackface farce."[43]

Situating Hurston's work within the theatrical traditions of blackface minstrelsy and burlesque, these critics align *Moses, Man of the Mountain* with mass entertainment in order to draw attention to its failures from aesthetic and political points of view. But Hurston's use of such theatrical conventions takes on new meaning when we consider her novel in the context of the black-Jewish imaginary. Because early-twentieth-century mass entertainment joined blacks and Jews, it functions as a particularly apt site from which to explore the politics and process of cross-identification in American culture. Wright and others may have taken Hurston to task for neglecting the obligations of social protest that had come to define African American literature after the Harlem Renaissance, but, in many ways, *Moses, Man of the Mountain* is the most overtly political of Hurston's fictions. Taking place in the public rather than private sphere, the novel offers an unmitigated commentary on relations of power—both between oppressor and oppressed and between a leader and his people. It is a carefully constructed allegory that operates in multiple modalities, speaking at once to universal conditions of power and to the politics of Hurston's contemporary moment, specifically the interethnic foundations of the early civil rights movement.

Most of the existing literary criticism on *Moses* is concerned with two related aspects of the novel: its use of the biblical story as allegory and its sources. Recent critics agree that the novel does not reside in any one level of allegory, but invites multiple readings, even as many of these critics persist in seeing this multiplicity as inconsistency and hence declare it a frustrating flaw of the work. In the most basic allegorical reading, *Moses* substitutes Jews for blacks to offer a commentary on the history of slavery and its aftermath; this substitution occurs linguistically since the Hebrews in *Moses* speak in black dialect. In this respect, Hurston's source is black vernacular culture since the hermeneutical tradition of the black church also expropriated the Exodus story in spirituals and sermons, equating the bondage and liberation of African Americans with that of the biblical Israelites. Cheryl Wall, for instance, calls the novel a "very effective satire on the transition from slavery to freedom for black Americans," drawing on the "long-standing identification of blacks with enslaved Hebrews."[44] Deborah McDowell and Mark Thompson have located additional, transnational dimensions to the allegory by placing the work in its immediate historical context: the rise of National Socialism in Europe. *Moses* thus stands in for the African American experience while simultaneously commenting on the persecution of the Jews under Hitler.[45] McDowell concludes that the novel is a "political allegory analogizing Hebrew oppression in biblical antiquity, black oppression in the contemporary United States, and Jewish oppression in Nazi Germany."[46]

Although I agree with this conclusion, I want to excavate at least one more level of the text. While McDowell's analogies all transcend either time or space, *Moses, Man of the Mountain* also operates in the interstices between the experiences of African Americans and Jews in the early-twentieth-century United States. Just as *Moses* equates the political situation of blacks under Jim Crow to that of Jews under the Third Reich, it also can be read as analogizing the discrimination faced by African Americans to that of American Jews subjected to anti-Semitism and nativism that manifested in terms of immigration laws. But *Moses* does not rest comfortably with direct analogies. It also deals with the power shifts that occur when the coalition formed between two separate entities, united in their joint understanding of and fight against oppression, produces yet another hierarchy, with one group leading the other.

In the political reality of Hurston's time, this dynamic was best represented by the NAACP. As a civil rights association built on interracial cooperation, the organization depended on Jewish money and legal assistance and was headed by Jewish leadership.[47] In Hurston's novel, Moses's role as liberating intermediary between the Egyptian enslavers and Hebrew enslaved is much like that of Jews between white and black. Moses occupies a liminal position in which he has access to resources and power but identifies with those deprived of them. To underscore the ambiguity of Moses's identity, *Moses, Man of the Mountain* employs the trope of passing, if in a somewhat unconventional way; unlike more traditional uses of the passing narrative, characters in *Moses* do not pass for white, but Moses is defined by his ability to perform multiple identities, to be at once Egyptian and Hebrew. In this sense, Hurston's novel resonates with other works of modern American literature that depict Jews as chameleon-like figures, able to adapt effortlessly to their surroundings; according to Daniel Itzkovitz, such representations of Jews speak to the unsettled state of Jewishness and its ability to complicate white national identity.[48] Highlighting Moses's conflicted position by maintaining indeterminacy about his origins (while also suggesting that Moses's ambiguous origins are the source of this internal conflict), *Moses, Man of the Mountain* can be read as an exploration of the complex identificatory processes underlying black-Jewish relations. In her commentary on this unstable alliance, Hurston draws on her personal relationships and the larger-scale political associations formed between the two minorities in the fight for equal rights.

As someone whose life intersected with those of a number of Jews, Hurston was aware of the processes of empathetic identification undergirding altruism. For Hurst, Boas, and Meyer, their dedication to black causes was generated by their own identities as ethnic minorities. But given the financial security of her mentors and the relative lack of limitation they experienced in their own lives, Hurston was also cognizant of the differences in opportunities for blacks and Jews in the United States. As a fulfillment of Hurston's lifelong goal to tell a story of the Jews, *Moses* attests to the fact that she saw the relationship between Jews and blacks in terms of both its "parallels and divergences."[49] The identification between blacks and Jews she proposes is based on shared experiences of oppression, but this does not preclude her from suggesting how Jews benefited from this association and that these benefits at times included a reinforcement of white privilege.

The novel's formal strategies and thematic concerns testify to various kinds of cultural exchange between blacks and Jews. Hurston viewed Jewish appropriations of blackness in the commercial theater as outright theft, motivated by financial self-interest, but she also acknowledged the potential for more productive alliances in the realms of art and politics. Given the predominance of Jewish minstrel performers in the early twentieth century, the fact that Hurston's Hebrews in *Moses* are speaking in black folk dialect implicates the novel in this tradition of blackface—or, more accurately, blackvoice. Although the novel cautions that this kind of identification is not to be wholly trusted, *Moses* also succeeds in getting at the complexity of black-Jewish relations, suggesting that appropriation is a two-way street. In addition to satirizing such Jewish borrowings of African American culture, the novel's reliance on the Old Testament story of Exodus for its plot also refers to African Americans' borrowing from Jewish biblical and theological tradition. Are the Hebrew characters in *Moses, Man of the Mountain* Jews acting black or blacks performing as Jews? Part of the joke is that these possibilities exist simultaneously. Hurston does not sustain a single allegory through the 300-page novel; after all, the joke would eventually wear thin. Instead, *Moses, Man of the Mountain* is replete with multiple, and at times contradictory, allegories, cross-identifications, and reversals that bear the mark of Hurston's irreverent humor.

The basic allegory of Jews as blacks and Egyptians as whites is complicated further by skin color *and* the fact that the text is not clearly color coded. Critics have noted that Hurston playfully reverses skin color in that her Egyptian oppressors are dark-skinned, while the oppressed Hebrews are white-skinned. But Hurston offers few indications of characters' physical coloring other than the fact that Moses's mother, when in labor, is described as "white," and his Midianite wife, Zipporah, is described as black with "tawny" skin and "crinkly" hair.[50] The text never attributes a specific skin tone to the Egyptians or to Moses himself. In "My People, My People!" a chapter excised from the original publication of her autobiography, Hurston discusses the unreliability of racial epistemology. Using "this passing business" as her example—and stating that it "works both ways" since "all the passing is not passing for white"—she warns her readers "not to depend too much on skin."[51] This injunction applies to *Moses* as well. The reversals, as well as the absence of obvious visual signifiers of race, suggest that the allegory operates in terms of power relations and behavior. The novel's racial dynamics do not correspond to the expectations for skin color in the United States.

The text's refusal to fit neatly into a binary racial schema is complicated further by Moses's ambiguous identity. Hurston alters the biblical narrative, offers several myths side by side, and plays with the trope of passing in order to offer competing interpretations of Moses's origins. Depending on which explanation you subscribe to, he is either Hebrew, Egyptian, Assyrian, or mixed race (specifically, the son of an Egyptian mother and Assyrian father).[52] Moses's ambiguity, in turn, destabilizes his relationship to both the Egyptians and the Hebrews, as well as other groups such as the Ethiopians and Midianites (both assumed to be dark-skinned) and nations who are identified by black cultural practices rather than skin color (such as the people Moses initially encounters after crossing into Asia who play the dozens and sing the blues). In Hurston's American tale set in the ancient world, dark skin does not automatically equal inferiority and oppression, nor does light skin equal superiority and power. In fact, these associations are more often reversed or simply indeterminate. As Boyd neatly sums up the bewildering experience of reading *Moses*: "By shifting the racial dynamics this way, Hurston throws the reader off and mocks the whole notion of racial purity; a hundred pages into the novel, you're no longer sure if Moses is black or white, Egyptian or Hebrew. But you realize that it doesn't matter—and that perhaps race itself doesn't matter, at least not based on skin color."[53]

The influence of Boas in overturning earlier conceptions of race can be traced to Hurston's project in *Moses, Man of the Mountain*. But Hurston does not leave it at that. The novel also explores the politics of identification that motivated Boas and other Jewish intellectuals of the period to turn to the subject of racism. The novel addresses cross-identification on a narrative as well as a formal level; to make matters even more confusing, the narrative level does not necessarily correspond to the novel's formal substitutions, such as the casting of the Hebrews as blacks suggested by the use of dialect. Most obviously, the novel thematically addresses the process of identification through the character of Moses. While it is unclear whether Moses himself is a Hebrew, he comes to identify with the enslaved people, represents them to Pharaoh, and eventually speaks like them. Set against a history of white paternalistic interventions in African American politics and culture, Moses's position as Jewish leader of the black masses—who here, in an ironic reversal, are represented by the biblical Hebrews—is both venerated and problematized in the novel.

Hurston begins her investigation of the politics of cross-identification by alluding to shared experiences of oppression. She draws parallels between racism and anti-Semitism, analogizing the injustices faced by African Americans during slavery and under Jim Crow to the persecution of the Jewish people. Corresponding with the Hebrew Bible's Five Books of Moses, the first five chapters of the novel are told from the perspective of the Jews of Goshen, which is figured as both ghetto and slave quarters. The novel sets the stage for Moses's birth to Jochebed and Amram against the backdrop of a number of decrees passed to maintain the inferiority of the Hebrews, the most grievous of which is the prohibition against the birth of male children: "Hebrews were ... prevented from becoming citizens of Egypt, they found out that they were aliens, and from one new decree to the next they sank lower and lower."[54] The laws precluding "aliens" from becoming "citizens" strongly suggest the escalation of tightened immigration restrictions in the 1920s, as well as, for that matter, Jim Crow laws. In describing how the Hebrews were viewed in Egyptian eyes, the novel does call to mind Nazi Germany's Nuremberg Laws, given the emphasis on racial purity that led to policies designed to separate out the Jews. The planned extermination of the Jews is suggested in the murder of newborn boys, and the SS in the "secret police" who patrol Goshen. But such details are drawn vaguely enough that they could also be applied to the situation of immigrants and African Americans in the United States. The specific prohibition on the birth of male children conjures the destruction of black families during slavery, in which children were frequently sold away from their parents, and resonates with nativist fears of rampant Jewish reproduction, exemplified by Henry James's description of the "swarming" Jewish children of the ghetto as "multiplication with a vengeance."[55] The novel not only relies on transnational and transhistorical parallels in drawing analogies between African American and Jewish oppression. The opening chapters of *Moses* also evoke nativist discourse that fed immigration policies in the early decades of the twentieth century, casting Jews as foreigners who would contaminate American citizenship.

In the early twentieth century, nativist fears of racial contamination also manifested in paranoia about Jewish power, especially given Jewish involvement in the labor movement and other leftist political activities. During the 1930s, Jewish and African American activists increasingly came together around leftist political causes, including the Communist Party of the United States of America, which held its greatest sway in 1939, the year Hurston published *Moses*. In the first few chapters of *Moses*, the Hebrews speak of organizing a protest meeting with Pharaoh about their treatment, a good deal of which centers on unfair labor practices; this suggests channels used by union organizers. Furthermore, it is difficult to read lines about Hebrews "invit[ing] foreign allies to come in" and masquerading as spies in order to "overthrow the government" without conjuring associations to the branding of Jews as Communists and political agitators.[56] In the novel, Egypt's need to police its borders against the Hebrew threat is tied to anxieties about government insurrection.

Anxieties about Jewish infiltration of the national body derived, in part, from the potential for sameness, the possibility of Jewish dissemblance implied in the fear that the Hebrews could be spies. Jews' perceived ability to pass was met with attempts to mark Jewish difference. The novel plays with this notion of Jewish ambiguity in a variety of ways, employing the trope of passing to complicate myths of origins and to mediate between Jewish and African American representation. Like many biblical narratives, the story of Moses, as told in the Old Testament, is already a passing story since the Hebrew Moses is raised as a grandson of the Egyptian Pharaoh. Hurston picks up and runs with this idea, while also adding further elements of ambiguity to Moses's background. Although the first five chapters attempt to account for Moses's Egyptian upbringing, they do not provide a satisfactory explanation as to how he ends up in Pharaoh's palace. Instructing her daughter, Miriam, to keep watch over the baby Moses, whom she fears will be slain, Jochebed hopes to outwit the secret police by setting her son afloat on the Nile, apostrophizing the river: "Nile, youse such a great big river and he is such a little bitty thing. Show him some mercy, please."[57] Hurston not only deflates the seriousness of biblical rhetoric by rewriting it in folk idiom, but she also changes the biblical precedent by transforming the narrative of Moses's adoption by the Egyptian princess into a story made up by the infant's bratty older sister. In Hurston's version, Miriam falls asleep while watching Moses, wakes up to see the Egyptian princess bathing, and, to cover up her own negligence, concocts a story that the princess takes Moses in. The novel maintains a great deal of ambiguity about whether the boy in the palace is the same child as the one born to Jochebed and Amram. Although the Moses of the Bible was nursed by his biological mother, in Hurston's version, when Jochebed offers her services as wet nurse, she is told that there is no new baby other than the princess's biological son with an Assyrian prince.

Hurston's novel is not simply *about* Moses's passing, but rather it is suggested that his passing may operate as no more than a story. In making up the story and subsequently exaggerating and elaborating on details, Miriam sets the events of the novel in motion. The Hebrews immediately seize upon the possibility that the Egyptian prince is someone of Hebrew blood, and the purported passing becomes a myth of wish fulfillment for the disenfranchised community:

> Still and all, Goshen never gave up their belief in the Hebrew in the palace. It was something for men to dream about. Jochebed became a figure of importance—the mother of our Prince in the palace. Miriam told her story again and again to more believing ears. It grew with being handled until it was a history of the Hebrew in the palace, no less. Men claimed to have seen signs at the birth of the child, and Miriam came to believe every detail of it as she added them and retold them time and time again. Others conceived and added details at their pleasure and the legends grew like grass.[58]

In this reflection on the intricacies of mythmaking, the legend becomes a bravura performance of call-and-response storytelling in which multiple individuals participate, "conceiv[ing] and add[ing] details at their pleasure." In the process of retelling, the "story" grows into a "history"—that is, it becomes the unquestioned truth. Hurston also explores the psychological motivation behind such mythmaking; as she writes here, "it was something for men to dream about," and elsewhere she states that the story "kept them from feeling utterly vanquished. . . . They had something to cherish and chew on, if they could say they had a Hebrew in the palace."[59] The myth about Moses is taken up by the Hebrews as consolation or compensation for their disenfranchisement, evocative of the assimilationist strategies espoused by both Jewish and African American leaders in the early decades of the twentieth century.[60] The novel appears to be critical of this kind of passing for its tendency to placate resistance and contribute to the idealization of those in power. When some of the women even go as far to declare that "it is time we quit straining against the new order and took a active [sic] part in it," Amram accuses them of being "ready to go with the conqueror."[61] In Hurston's critique, certain forms of passing may satisfy a desire for a power, but are not particularly subversive of the structures of power.

Maintaining uncertainty about Moses's origins and fate, *Moses, Man of the Mountain* never confirms whether this act of passing took place or whether it is simply a function of storytelling and mythmaking. To this already ambiguous narrative, Hurston adds yet another level of ambiguity. In her author's note, she claims she is retrieving the story from Judeo-Christian legend, asserting that Moses is also a figure of African folklore, transported to the Americas through the African diaspora: "Wherever the children of Africa have been scattered by slavery, there is the acceptance of Moses as the fountain of mystic powers. . . . So all across Africa, America, the West Indies, there are tales of the powers of Moses and great worship of him and his powers."[62] Based on this prefatory material, Robert Hemenway concludes that Hurston's *Moses* is not a black appropriation of the Old Testament, but a reappropriation of African folklore. In other words, Moses is only a Hebrew in the Hebrew version of the story, but "his true birthright is African and . . . his true constituency is Afro-American."[63] In Hemenway's reading, Hurston proposes a corrective to the myth of Moses by restoring to him his Egyptian origins. I argue, however, that Hurston interestingly leaves the options open, for Moses's origins are never confirmed, nor does the text confirm whether we are reading a version of the Hebrew myth, as initially circulated by Miriam, or an account intended to set the record straight by "kidnap[ping] Moses from Judeo-Christian tradition."[64] If the text serves as a commentary on black-Jewish relations, it is not so much about appropriation or theft—who has the "right" to this material and who is stealing from whom. It is also about the intricacies of cultural exchanges in which origins are obscured by the processes of storytelling and about how such ambiguity of affiliation results in the ambivalence of cross-racial identification.

While the first five chapters address the Hebrews' stake in Moses's passing story, the majority of the narrative is more concerned with how Moses, raised as an Egyptian, comes to identify with and lead the Jewish people—in other words, how an individual who may or may not have legitimate ties to the oppressed comes to identify with them. And it is here that the novel's competing levels of formal and narrative substitution may throw readers into a tailspin. Moses's relationship to the Hebrews in *Moses, Man of the Mountain* signifies on the relationship of Jews to blacks in the political reality with Moses in the position of Jewish leadership and Hebrews in the position of the black masses. Moses is separated from those he leads by financial security (symbolized by his access to God, who in the text could just as easily represent a bank account as divine authority, and the corresponding ability to conjure food whenever the need arises), education, and elite status. Much as Hurston herself privately questioned the motives behind her patrons' extensions of friendship, the Hebrews continually question Moses's sincerity and the legitimacy of his identification, suspicious that he might lead them out of bondage simply to lord over them like Pharaoh. Though he acts like one of them, they resent him for his higher class status and his access to power. Moses himself is a reluctant leader, unsure whether he wants the role and how strong his identification truly is, questioning, "Why should I lead people whose ways are strange to me and who neither understand me nor trust me?"[65] While several critics have noted that Moses, in this context, can be read as a white liberal and the text a commentary on paternalism, Hurston takes her joke one step further: Moses is a *Jewish* white liberal who appears to have some legitimate connection to the oppressed even if the roots and depth of this connection are obscured.

Whether or not Moses is related to the Hebrews by blood, he comes to identify with them and sympathize with them in their oppression. The potential for more than one identity or identification is suggested in Hurston's articulation of Moses's double-consciousness: "Long ago . . . he had found out that he was two beings. In short, he was everybody boiled down to a drop. Everybody is two beings: one lives and flourishes in the daylight and stands guard. The other being walks and howls at night."[66] While growing up in the Egyptian palace, Moses is torn between his royal status as second in line to the throne and his preference for the company of the common people. Although Moses serves the state in his role of military leader of the Egyptian army, he also values his friendships with the palace servants, especially the illiterate stableman, Mentu, whose folkloric tales of talking animals captivate the young prince's imagination. Mentu, as his name suggests, is one of two mentors who play formative roles in Moses's education, but the novel also reverses the traditional power dynamics of mentorship. As Moses benefits from Mentu's folk wisdom, his feelings of affection and respect for the palace servant grow in defiance of the laws of nature. "It is natural for the stableman to love a prince, but why should a prince love a stableman?" asks Mentu, who describes himself as "little better than a Hebrew or a swineherd in Pharaoh's eyes."[67]

Transgressing social and class divisions, Moses's personal friendship with Mentu fosters his tendencies toward cross-identification, which contributes to his public championing of the rights of the Hebrews. Moses begins to advocate on behalf of the enslaved underclass, arguing to Pharaoh's court that they were "enemies . . . because they were treated as such." Asserting that the Hebrews "either [need to] be restored to citizenship or sent out of Egypt," he reasons, "It was a weak spot in any nation to have a large body of disaffected people within its confines." Although Moses presents his case in terms of what is best for the state, he is also motivated by genuine sympathy, appealing, too, to the morality of the court. When he visits Goshen and talks to the Hebrew leaders, "What he saw touched him so that he resolved in his heart to do whatever was in his power to better their condition."[68] Moses's own ambiguous identity and his pluralistic sense of between-ness, of being "two beings" at once, propel him into a position as mediator between the oppressors and the oppressed.

When Moses's defense of the Hebrews begins to endanger his own standing in the court, he does not turn away from his cause, but rather finds that his identification becomes even stronger. Moses's greatest opponent in court, Ta-Phar, seizes upon the rumor of Hebrew blood and uses it to eliminate any potential rivalry for the kingship. Whether truth or myth, the rumor that Moses is Hebrew affects his life, and his flight from Egypt is precipitated by two related events: an accusation of rape by his own wife, an Ethiopian war bride who turns against him when she hears whisperings of his Hebrew identity, and his impulsive murder of an Egyptian overseer whom he sees maltreating the Hebrew slaves. While these events may not appear to be related, the text suggests a direct connection: "Moses didn't have any more notion of killing that Egyptian overseer than he did of flying," begins chapter 9, which then backtracks to relate that "the whole thing started in the chambers of his wife." Believing the rumors of her husband's true identity, Moses's wife refuses to have anything to do with him, associating him with the Hebrew "gang of rapists and slaves." Declaring it "rape for [Moses] to even look at" her, his wife invokes the myth of the black male rapist. This detail, which is not in the biblical narrative, is significant in terms of the historical context of black-Jewish relations, given the accusations of sexual perversion that led to the lynching of Leo Frank, for example. Here, one myth is embedded in the next, for not only does Moses's wife believe the story that he is Hebrew, but she also believes the myth of the Hebrew as rapist. "If you . . . call that rape you have plenty of imagination," Moses replies, getting at false accusations generated by the notion that even a glance could be construed as physical violation. Yet Moses, attuned to his sympathetic identification, begins to question whether the rumor that the Egyptian princess passed a Hebrew child off as her own in order to guarantee her inheritance may have validity or whether it was "mob malice" manufactured by the court in "answer [to] his plea for justice against oppression." Although he is unable to convince himself one way or the other, the accusations allow him to discover "a new sympathy for the oppressed of all mankind." Rather than shunning his identification with the Hebrews based on such accusations, he embraces it.[69]

This sympathy leads Moses to put his own life in danger in the fight against racial injustice. He impulsively murders an Egyptian overseer who was in the act of brutally lashing a Hebrew slave. The slaves initially show their gratitude to Moses and protect his deed from exposure, but his actions are also viewed with doubt about why someone of his ilk would choose to defend them. The slaves misunderstand his motives, assuming he is harboring a desire to rule them himself. Although he declares himself a "friend" of the Hebrews, "decid[ing] . . . to devote his time to bettering [their] condition," they continue to hold him in suspicion, which he in turn sees as a "trampling on his sacrifices": "Moses stood hurt at the lack of appreciation of his behavior and of the motives that prompted him."[70] The motives behind Moses's cross-identification are rarely perceived as pure; instead, there persists the underlying skepticism that such altruism must hold for him ulterior benefits, in spite of the fact that he places his own life at risk.

As Moses begins to question his own identity, the novel once again makes use of the trope of passing—although this time, in the opposite direction. Moses decides to leave Egypt and reinvent himself, suppressing his identity as a warrior and prince by removing his military garb in order to cross the Red Sea into Asia. The passage that describes Moses's passage is worth quoting in full:

> Moses had crossed over. He was not in Egypt. He had crossed over and now he was not an Egyptian. He had crossed over. The short

sword at his thigh had a jeweled hilt but he had crossed over and so
it was no longer the sign of high birth and power. He had crossed
over, so he sat down on a rock near the seashore to rest himself.
He had crossed over so he was not of the house of Pharaoh. He did
not own a palace because he had crossed over. He did not have an
Ethiopian Princess for a wife. He had crossed over. He did not have
friends to sustain him. He had crossed over. He did not have enemies to strain against his strength and power. He had crossed over.
He was subject to no law except the laws of tooth and talon. He had
crossed over. The sun who was his friend and ancestor in Egypt was
arrogant and bitter in Asia. He had crossed over. He felt as empty as
a post hole for he was none of the things he once had been. He was
a man sitting on a rock. He had crossed over.[71]

Appropriating the rhetorical pose of the black preacher, Hurston uses the
call-and-response refrain, "He had crossed over," to evoke racial passing
(the crossing of the color line). In this passage, Moses appears once again
to be a blank slate, "empty as a post hole." Yet while the stripping of his
outer garments was meant to strip him of his past, this plan does not
wholly succeed. He retains, for example, the sword with the "jeweled hilt"
even if it is "no longer the sign of high birth and power." Furthermore,
when he reaches the other side, he puts his clothing back on. In fact,
Moses *fails to pass* when he crosses the Red Sea. Those he encounters on
the other side take him for a soldier and a "high-born Egyptian" based
on the very outfit he presumably renounced. Though the signs of Moses's
"high-born" identity are material, he is unable to shed completely the
trappings of privilege. This passage exposes the ambivalence underpin-
ning Moses's cross-identification, an ambivalence that becomes a source
of contention later in the novel when Moses leads the Hebrew people out
of bondage. Read as an allegory for Jewish involvement in the cause of
antiracism, the novel addresses the deeply fraught association between
African Americans and white civil rights leaders, many of whom were
upper-class and highly assimilated Jews who retained their wealth and
privilege. The passage also speaks to Hurston's multiple uses of the passing trope. Earlier in the novel, passing was associated with an assimilationist mentality, a tendency to "go with the conqueror." Here, the novel
moves to different terrain; in passing down rather than up, Moses enacts
a racial cross-identification that, while vexed, has the potential to foster
change.

Although Moses attempts to erase his past and become a blank slate, he also seeks an alternate identity with which to fill the "post hole" of his self. He eventually finds a new home with a tribe of Midianites, whose leader, Jethro, replaces Mentu as Moses's mentor and surrogate father. Even before Moses solidifies his ties to Jethro's clan by marrying his daughter, Zipporah, Jethro views Moses as a son. He imparts his wisdom to Moses as well as his knowledge of the magic of hoodoo, an arena in which Moses surpasses his teacher, becoming in Jethro's own estimation "the finest hoodoo man in the world."[72] As evidence of the influence of African American culture on Hurston's revision of the biblical tale, the plagues Moses brings down upon Egypt are not God's doing, but rather the work of a skilled hoodoo conjurer. Like the friendship with Mentu, the relationship between Moses and Jethro suggests the various apprenticeships that contributed to Hurston's own development as a writer and a folklorist. Jethro is a Boas-like father figure, guiding Moses's scientific study and nurturing his identification with the oppressed, eventually sending him out in the field when he encourages him to return to Egypt. Moses's schooling in hoodoo also recalls Hurston's experiences as an ethnographer, specifically her training with hoodoo practitioners in New Orleans, which she documents in the second half of *Mules and Men*. Portrayed as a collaboration between equals, the bond between Moses and his surrogate father is an idealized instance of mutual understanding and cooperation in the novel. Due largely to this friendship, Moses comes to see Midian as "his resting place, his eternal niche in infinity," a place where he could "blend . . . into the background."[73]

Moses's adoption of a new identity as a member of Jethro's clan is further evidence of the ways Hurston's novel troubles essentialist suppositions about familial, national, and racial ties. Significantly, linguistic shifts play an important role in Moses's assumption of a new identity and affiliation. Moses "master[s] the language of the Midianites as if he had been born to it," a technique he employs later when he masters the folk idiom of the Hebrews in order to serve as their leader. The necessity of such fluency is one of the many lessons he learns from Jethro. Viewing linguistic mastery as a skill that will serve Moses in good stead as liberator of the Hebrew people, Jethro plans to transform Moses into a leader, "making of Moses what he himself had wanted to be—a great priest . . . [a] man of science such as the world had never seen."[74] He encourages Moses to return to Egypt in order to lead the Hebrew slaves out of bondage, and when Moses shows reluctance, it is intimated that Jethro (rather than God) orchestrates the burning bush to compel his protégé to follow the destiny set out for him.

Thus Moses returns to Goshen, where he is remembered as "a friend of the race" for his past deed of killing the Egyptian overseer.[75] In order to organize the Hebrews and prepare them for liberation, Moses joins forces with his purported siblings, Aaron and Miriam, strategically using the legend of familial connection in order to convince the Hebrew masses that he is one of them. The section of the novel in which Moses returns to Egypt to negotiate with Pharaoh for the emancipation of the slaves suggests the cultural exchanges between African Americans and Jews exemplified by spirituals such as "Go Down, Moses." In addition, these episodes have corollaries in the political and legal arena of Hurston's time, specifically the cooperation between African Americans and Jews in early civil rights activism. Employing a combination of rhetorical argument and hoodoo, Moses's appeals for the liberation of the Hebrews analogize Pharaoh's court to the Supreme Court of the United States. During the early decades of the twentieth century, Jewish lawyers such as Arthur Spingarn, James Marshall, Louis Marshall, Felix Frankfurter, and Louis Brandeis (several of whom served on the legal committee of the NAACP) litigated numerous civil rights cases, winning victories that "chipped away at the Jim Crow legal structure" and paved the way for more dramatic challenges to segregation in the 1950s and 1960s.[76] The historical figure best embodied in Moses, however, was not a lawyer, but a rhetorician of another sort, literature professor Joel Spingarn. Spingarn left academia to follow a career as a civil rights leader, famously allying with W.E.B. Du Bois to play a crucial role in the formation of the NAACP and later serving as its president. The analogy between emancipation from slavery and the struggle for African American rights in the twentieth century is, of course, not unique to Hurston's allegory; it was used by civil rights activists themselves. During his publicity campaign for the NAACP, Spingarn, employing his charisma and rhetorical skill in the service of antiracism, conducted a self-funded speaking tour titled "The New Abolitionism."[77]

Like Spingarn, Moses is viewed by those in power as a "radical" who has "the common people talking about equality."[78] The relationship between Moses and Aaron, who becomes the leader's right-hand man, accompanying him when he appears before Pharaoh, strongly evokes the collaborative efforts of Spingarn and Du Bois. In "The 'Pet Negro' System," an essay critiquing how interracial friendships are tainted by white paternalism, Hurston cites the relationship between Du Bois and Spingarn as an exception: Du Bois, "the bitterest opponent of the white race that America has ever known, loved Joel Spingarn and was certainly loved in turn by him. The thing doesn't make sense. It just makes beauty."[79] In *Moses*, the collaboration between Moses and Aaron is reminiscent of the joint efforts of the two intellectuals, who, for example, appeared together in Memphis in 1914, issuing an invitation to "All Those Who Love Truth and Dare Hear It."[80] The alliance between Moses and Aaron is largely a strategic one; while Aaron's role is to reassure the masses of Moses's legitimacy and trustworthiness in advocating on their behalf, Moses's princely presence ensures their message is heard by those in power. Even as Moses argues on behalf of the Hebrews, he continues to be held in suspicion by them, and his alliance with Aaron does little to assuage fears about his own ambitions for power: "Moses had reason to believe that few if any accepted the story of his kinship with Miriam and Aaron. He was still an Egyptian noble to them. If he wanted to cast in his lot with them, well and good. But blood was thicker than missionary zeal and he would bear watching. Why should he serve them anyway? It looked mighty funny when you come to think of it, at that." Moses's greatest difficulty lies in his failure to convince the people that he is motivated by a love for "freedom and justice." Yet the novel also suggests that emancipation could not take place without Moses's presence as mediator between Pharaoh and the oppressed slaves. Pharaoh may agree to allow Aaron to appear before him in court, but "he paid little attention to the ex-slave" and "kept looking to Moses for confirmation and assurance. . . . He listened casually to the voice of Aaron. But he paid strict attention to Moses. When Aaron had finished he ignored him and acted just as Moses had spoken directly."[81] In this description, the political allegory in which Moses and Aaron correspond to Spingarn and Du Bois bleeds into a cultural one; the image of Moses speaking through Aaron is suggestive of the Jewish tradition of blackvoice, an image confirmed by the episodes of the novel in which Moses attempts to speak to the Hebrews as a Hebrew, appropriating their folk idiom.

In the scenes of the novel that take place after slavery, during the Hebrews' forty years of wandering in the desert, Hurston comically skewers the various kinds of inauthentic performance she overtly critiqued in public statements. On the one hand, Hurston was deeply disturbed by the ways that white appropriations distorted black cultural traditions. On the other hand, she was also concerned with African Americans who watered down their own culture by acting white and the complicity of black artists who capitulated to the commercial demands of white audiences by themselves engaging in minstrelsy. In an effort to convince his people that he is one of them, Moses draws on the lessons he learned from Jethro and speaks to them as a Hebrew, but the novel exposes the limits of his cross-identification, since his performance is not entirely convincing; he often "forgets" to stay in role and "goes back to talking his proper talk when he gets excited." In returning to the language of the court, Moses draws a barrier between himself and his people, reminding them of his higher social status. The novel playfully uses linguistic shifts to address how such crossings go in more than one direction. Noting the comic aspect of Moses's less-than-flawless linguistic imitations, one woman observes, "the more Moses gets natural with us, the stiffer Aaron gets. He tries to sound like some high-toned Egyptian talking proper— when he don't forget to do it."[82] Just as Moses's leadership provides Hurston with an opportunity to explore the limitations of Jewish paternalism, Aaron's leadership allows her to critique the "talented tenth," the black intellectual elite whom she scorned as propagandists out of touch with the masses and more interested in their own self-advancement. Overly concerned with the materialism of titles and "rich regalia," Aaron is depicted as a "short, squatty man who wanted things."[83] In one breath, Hurston critiques the limits of Jewish paternalism and the bourgeois pretensions of black intellectuals. Through an emphasis on language, she exposes the fissures in such cross-identifications, involving both blacks acting white and whites, and Jews, performing blackness.

In *Moses, Man of the Mountain*, no one escapes unscathed from Hurston's satiric bite, including the common people themselves. In the scenes of the novel that most threaten to devolve into minstrelsy (and hence the ones that have most offended critics), Hurston suggests that African American participation in the minstrel tradition places severe obstacles in the way of their quest for freedom. During the 1930s, the popularity of white performers in blackface, such as Jolson, had started to fade, even as the theater and screen remained largely segregated. By 1929, with the release of two studio productions, *Hallelujah!* and *Hearts in Dixie*, all-black casts began to supplant blackface performers. In films such as these, as well as the 1936 adaptation of the biblically themed play *The Green Pastures*, African American actors played stereotypical roles barely removed, if removed at all, from minstrelsy. *Moses, Man of the Mountain*'s postemancipation scenes lampoon such performances by exposing the silly antics of a people more concerned with fish fries and watermelon than freedom. "Lord, the man [Moses] come talking about making us a nation when we ain't even got garlic to season with!" complains one discontented follower. The Hebrews' minstrel antics create further divisions between Moses and his people. He first responds to the "folkses" in their down-home dialect, stating that he is "mighty sorry" that "rations are none too plentiful"; yet he grows increasingly frustrated as he listens to them grumble about hunger, and, as a result, his speech becomes more "cultivated": "I had the idea all along that you came out here hunting freedom. I didn't know you were hunting a barbecue."[84] Although these scenes are largely played to comic effect, making it difficult to sympathize with the ungrateful Hebrews, there is a legitimate political valence to the conflict as well. The scenes expose the disjunction between the Hebrews' valid concern with concrete physical conditions, such as food, and Moses's more abstract promise of freedom in his vision of a new nation.

Even as she transforms the biblical trials of the Hebrew people into a racial allegory, Hurston steers clear of the topic of color prejudice with one significant exception. Although both of Moses's wives are likely dark-skinned, the text does not offer enough information to verify his own skin color, and Moses refrains from showing signs of being "color struck," to use the title of one of Hurston's own plays that deals with the subject. The most dramatic instance of color bias in the text involves Miriam, who, as Aaron's sister, is included in Hurston's indictment of the talented tenth. Miriam harbors resentment of Moses's Midianite wife, Zipporah. Once again, in depicting this rivalry, Hurston muddies traditional color dynamics. Miriam resents Zipporah's class privilege, but takes it out on her black skin: "Look at that dark complected woman he [Moses] done brought and put up to be a Queen over the rest of us women," complains Miriam. She gathers the other women to protest against Zipporah's presence within their tribe, convincing them, "We don't want people like that among us mixing up our blood and all." In punishment, Moses afflicts Miriam with "a leprous whiteness," so that his alleged sister actually becomes white in her racism.[85]

While Miriam's attitude, on one level, reflects the internalized racism of the light-skinned African American elite, Jewish racism is also often understood in just these terms; color prejudice was a way to identify with the white majority by taking on racist sentiments toward the black underclass and solidifying their own position among whites. In Hurston's hands, however, whiteness becomes a disease rather than a privilege. Banished from the camp for seven days as a result of her leprosy, Miriam also endures a long-term punishment: "All the rest of her days, Miriam was very silent. Whole days passed by at times in which she never uttered a word." Instead of elevating Miriam's status, the whitening of her skin transforms her into an outcast, silences her, and ultimately leads to her death. In language that evokes Du Bois's *The Souls of Black Folk*, Miriam's banishment "put a veil between her and the world which never lifted."[86] In this episode, the novel makes no bones about its critique of whiteness and white color prejudice.

Curiously in this novel that focuses mostly on men, Miriam, the most prominent female character, is the one to display virulently racist attitudes and consequently suffers one of the harshest penalties. The fact that her punishment by Moses has the effect of silencing her is further notable because it was Miriam's storytelling that set the narrative in motion in the first place. As the one to devise the story of Moses's adoption by the Egyptian princess, she is responsible for his ability to reinvent himself. Although she may later state her aversion to the mixing of blood, her story initiated the text's theme of racial mixing and created its various destabilizations of identity; the cross-identification that makes possible the Hebrews' quest for freedom can be attributed to her actions. Following her death, which occurs, at her own behest, before the Israelites reach the Promised Land, Moses eulogizes her as a "patriot," recognizing that without her the Exodus might not "have taken place at all. . . . If she had not come to the palace gates to ask for him and to claim him as a brother, would he have left Egypt as he did? He doubted it. . . . A mighty thing had happened in the world through the stumbling of a woman who couldn't see where she was going. She needed a big tomb so the generations that come after would know her and remember."[87]

Miriam is certainly no saint; even her invention of the story of Moses's adoption was selfishly motivated by a need to cover up her own negligence and a desire to establish a kinship with the ruling class. Yet her conception of a passing story ultimately had the effect of troubling, rather than upholding, difference, opening a space for the deliverance of an enslaved nation. Moses may claim the mantle of savior of the Hebrew people, but his speech concedes that Miriam might have been the greater force behind their freedom. At once severely rebuked and highly honored by Moses, the character of Miriam encapsulates the contradictions that characterized Hurston's relationships with Jewish women such as Hurst and Meyer, whose own storytelling and advocacy for black causes simultaneously upheld and challenged the binary between black and white.

Like Miriam, Moses himself remains a venerated and problematic figure in the novel's conclusion. Echoing the form of its biblical precedent, the book of Exodus, *Moses, Man of the Mountain* is divided into forty chapters. The final chapter transports the Hebrews to the gates of

Canaan, where Moses takes leave of them. As the Hebrews prepare to cross the River Jordan into the Promised Land, Moses reflects on the limits of such crossings, including his own, and the novel ends on a somewhat pessimistic note about the future of the newly formed nation. In an alteration from the biblical plot, Hurston once again downplays the role of God. Rather than being prohibited from entering the Promised Land as punishment for his smashing of the Ten Commandments, Moses himself refuses to enter Canaan in order to forsake his position as ruler. Throughout the novel, Moses remained vigilant of the fact that even the reverence of the Hebrew people was dangerous as it could too easily translate into a reinstatement of tyranny. Recognizing that the people are unable to see his motives as pure because he is not one of them, Moses decides that the new nation is better off defining freedom on their own terms without an outsider in their midst. Surveying Israel from the top of Mount Nebo, Moses reflects, "he wasn't sure he had succeeded. He had found out that no man may make another free. Freedom was something internal. The outside signs were just signs and symbols of the man inside. All you could do was to give the opportunity for freedom and the man himself must make his own emancipation."[88]

Moses's reflections on his attempt to deliver the Hebrews into freedom further suggest the novel's allegory to the Jewish leadership of the NAACP. Despite his extensive involvement in the early civil rights movement, Joel Spingarn, for example, continually struggled with the problem of white leadership, a dilemma that several times brought him to the brink of resignation from the various high offices he held in the organization. In speeches, he proclaimed to his black constituency to be "tired . . . of the philanthropy of rich white men toward your race" and urged African Americans not to rely on white supporters, but to "fight [their] own battles with [their] own leaders and [their] own money."[89] Asserting the limits of cross-identification and even the best-intentioned of intergroup alliances, Moses does not become a part of the new nation by entering the Promised Land. Instead, in the final lines of the novel, he "turned with a firm tread and descended the other side of the mountain and headed back over the years."[90]

Although I have argued that *Moses, Man of the Mountain* can be understood in terms of the historical and cultural context of black-Jewish relations, this is not the only allegorical level on which the novel operates. The novel's accomplishment rests in its shifting allegories and its invitation to multiple interpretations. My reading is intended to add one more in order to complicate the various analogies, cross-identifications, and displacements. Nor do I want to argue that this reappropriation of the myth of the Chosen People by an African American writer is really a text about Jews after all. Instead, it is an exploration of interminority relations in which the ambiguity of Jewish identity, represented in the uncertain origins and tenuous cross-identifications of Moses, complicates racial dichotomies, mediating between black and white. Hurston's rewriting of the biblical epic attests to the messiness of racial affiliations and interracial identifications, constructing a unique passing story in which "true" identity remains forever indeterminate.

Hurston's narrative about the complexities of cross-racial identification and collaboration arose from her personal experiences with Jewish women such as Meyer and Hurst. At the same time, her use of the biblical story of Exodus is reminiscent of another contemporary, Edna Ferber, whose *Show Boat* employed multiple forms of passing to similar effect and who justified her decision to portray African American life by declaring herself "a little Jewish slave girl on the Nile." *Moses, Man of the Mountain* similarly asserts that Jews are "just like us," but the transhistorical and transnational dimensions of this analogy speak to dissimilarities between Jewish American and African American experiences as well. The genius of Hurston's *Moses* lies in its thematic and formal inconsistencies, the very aspect of the novel that other critics have singled out as its flaw. These inconsistencies enable Hurston to affirm commonalities that unite minority groups *and* acknowledge the tensions that divide them, staging the hierarchical alliance in realistic, rather than idealistic, terms. Hurston may employ minstrel conventions in her expropriation of the Old Testament, but in so doing, her novel also becomes a form of minstrelsy in reverse. An elaborate performance of blackface and Jewface, *Moses, Man of the Mountain* critiques the processes of cross-identification that led Jews to appropriate African American narratives and African Americans to see themselves in Jewish ones.

Conclusion

Danzy Senna's 1998 novel, *Caucasia*, narrates the coming-of-age story of a mixed-race protagonist named Birdie Lee. The offspring of a civil rights movement union between a black intellectual father and a white activist mother, Birdie appears white, but actively identifies with her dark-skinned sister and openly embraces her African American heritage. When the onset of the Black Power movement leads to the dissolution of her parents' marriage, Birdie and her paranoid mother leave their Boston home to go underground, eventually re-creating lives for themselves in predominantly white small-town New Hampshire. According to Birdie's mother, the fact that her daughter could pass for white would allow them to elude the Federal Bureau of Investigation (FBI), whose agents are on her trail, she presumes, for her involvement with a militant radical group. In describing Birdie's transformation into a white girl, Senna makes an important innovation in the traditional passing narrative. In *Caucasia*, whiteness is not represented as a monolithic category. Instead, Birdie must pass for a specific kind of white. Although Birdie, "a blank slate," could be anything—"Puerto Rican, Sicilian, Pakistani, Greek"—her mother insists on inventing a Jewish identity and history for her, reasoning that passing for Jewish would allow Birdie to retain her African American identity. In fact, passing for Jewish "wasn't really passing," explains Birdie's mother, "because Jews weren't really white, more like an off-white. . . . They were the closest [Birdie] was going to get to black and still stay white. 'Tragic history, kinky hair, good politics. . . . It's all there.'" And so, outfitted with a cheap Star of David necklace, an invented dead assimilated father whose defining feature was his "curly black" Jewfro, a copy of *The Diary of Anne Frank*, and a sprinkling of Yiddish phrases, Birdie Lee is transformed into a half-Jewish girl named Jesse Goldman.[1]

A significant contribution to the discourse on multiracialism that emerged in the 1990s, *Caucasia* speaks to the ambivalent place of Jewishness within race and ethnic studies and to its central locus within the field of whiteness studies. Although Birdie is mixed race, it is only by taking on a Jewish identity that she can be simultaneously black and white. *Caucasia*'s reinvention of the passing trope underscores the debate about whether Jewish identity should be aligned with a dominant whiteness or with the minoritarian position of racial otherness. On the one hand, the theme of passing for Jewish places Jewishness within the framework of ethnic and racial difference. While the trope of passing alone often works to question ontology and reveals how racial identity has come to be defined socially and legally, the concept of passing for Jewish takes the challenge to essentialism one step further since the theme evolved due to another construction that took place over the course of the twentieth century: the historical transformation of Jewishness into whiteness through the process of assimilation. On the other hand, the theme of "passing for Jewish" depicts Jewishness *as* whiteness and thus as a part of the dominant culture. Once "almost white but not quite," to play on Homi Bhabha's formulation, Jews are now almost ethnic but not quite.[2] Occupying multiple positions at once, Jewishness simultaneously signifies whiteness and racial difference; furthermore, the confusion over whether the term "Jewish" refers to race, ethnicity, religion, nation, or culture is emblematic of its complex meanings across categories of identity.

While Senna's novel effectively conveys the ambivalence of Jewish identity by classifying Jews as "off-white" and "close" to black, another contemporary multiracial narrative, Rebecca Walker's 2001 memoir, *Black, White, and Jewish*, speaks more unequivocally to the movement of Jews into the white, middle-class mainstream. The daughter of African American writer Alice Walker and Jewish civil rights attorney Mel Leventhal, Rebecca Walker, like the fictional Birdie Lee, experienced the break-up of her parents' marriage with the demise of the integrationist politics of the civil rights era. Subtitling her book an "autobiography of a shifting self," Walker details how she transforms herself from a rebellious black adolescent living with her mother in the bohemia of San Francisco to an upper-middle-class Jewish girl living with her father and stepmother in the suburbs of New York City. Trying out a variety of identities in the course of her memoir, Walker ultimately comes to disidentify with her Jewish roots. As an adult, she changes her last name from Leventhal to Walker, moving her father's surname to the "more obscure middle position." As she explains, she changes her name "because I do not feel an affinity with whiteness, with what Jewishness has become."[3]

Taken together, *Caucasia* and *Black, White, and Jewish* represent the paradoxical impulses that continue to define the black-Jewish imaginary. In *Caucasia*, the admittedly uneasy affinities between blackness and Jewishness work to upset binary racial schemas. Birdie displays a "postethnic" sensibility, acquiring her identity through processes of social affiliation; although she at first operates as a tabula rasa on which others inscribe identities, by the end of the novel she moves toward defining herself outside a black-white binary, and her adopted Jewish identity provides the impetus for this redefinition.[4] In contrast, *Black, White, and Jewish* highlights the white privilege of Jews in order to restore a black-white binary. In effect, Walker's complete erasure of "Leventhal" from her name when she publishes her book serves as a rejoinder to her own title, subsuming its final word to rewrite the terms of identity as simply "black and white."

In this book, I have argued for a more dynamic rendering of the black-Jewish imaginary, one that encompasses both Walker's and Senna's viewpoints. We need to allow for the possibility that whiteness can be both produced and destabilized through cross-racial performances and encounters. While I have demonstrated that considerations of women and gender complicate the masculinist paradigms that have dominated scholarship on appropriations of blackness, the four case studies in this book are not intended to be conclusive. Instead, it is my hope that these examples—chosen in part because they are high-profile cases that have had a significant (if at times unacknowledged) impact on literary and popular culture—will spur further scholarship in race and whiteness studies. There is more work to be done not only in regard to gender and sexuality but also in terms of the ways other categories of identity, including class and region, impact processes of comparative racialization. Imperatively, there is also a need to incorporate a more diverse range of voices, most notably those of Jews of color whose perspectives on race and whiteness would radically redefine the terms of Jewish identity.

* * *

I began this book with fictional and historical narratives about female blackface performance, and it is with a recent example of this phenomenon that I would like to end. In 2007, controversial Jewish co-median Sarah Silverman took on the topic of Jewish minstrelsy for an episode of her television show, *The Sarah Silverman Program*, on Comedy Central. The episode, titled "Face Wars," opens with Sarah (as I will refer to Silverman's television persona) claiming to be "the victim of a hate crime" after she is denied use of a tennis court at a local country club, presumably because of her Jewish surname. As she sits in a coffee shop, complaining, in her usual self-absorbed manner, of her second-class citizenship and hyperbolically declaring that there is "nothing harder than being Jewish in the entire world," she is confronted by an African American waiter who challenges her to try walking in his shoes. Taking him up on the challenge, Sarah enlists a makeup artist who paints a shining black oval and oversized white lips on her face and supplies her with a red bandanna. As soon as she steps out into the street, Sarah faces a battery of insults, aimed at her as a racist for adopting blackface. Naively understanding herself to be a victim rather than a perpetrator of racism, Sarah, who had donned blackface intending to prove that it is worse to be Jewish than black, realizes how very wrong she was and undergoes a sympathetic identification with African Americans. "I had no idea how cruel white people could be to us," she muses and, conveniently spotting a Baptist church, decides that she needs to be "with my own kind." But just as the white people on the street took offense at Sarah's *blackface*, not her black skin, she is forcibly ejected by the African American con-gregants ("Forsaken by my own people") after she attempts to join in the gospel singing by breaking into a shuffle. Subsequently arrested in what she believes is a case of racial profiling (but actually turns out to be the rather mundane misdemeanor of unpaid parking tickets), Sarah finds herself embraced by a group of white supporters who also don blackface and stage a protest outside the police station, demanding "the freedom to explore issues of race in American culture through the use of post-modern irony."

Played to hilarious comic effect, sustained by the exaggerated inno-cence and bratty overentitlement of Silverman's Jewish American Prin-cess persona, "Face Wars" invokes and deconstructs the major critical frameworks of black-Jewish relations. Sarah's initial donning of black-face is motivated not by empathetic identification, nor a conscious or subconscious desire to achieve whiteness by participating in the racist practices of the dominant culture. Instead, it is initiated in the competi-tive spirit of one-upmanship (what Stanley Crouch in another context has described as a "big-time martyr ratings contest"[5]) as Sarah and the

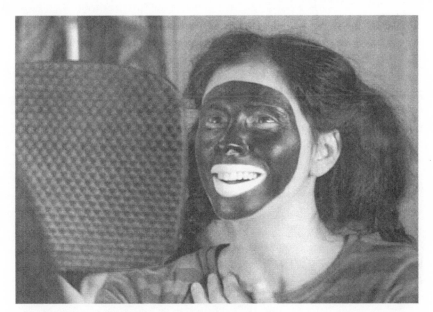

FIGURE 3. Sarah Silverman in blackface in the "Face Wars" episode of *The Sarah Silverman Program* (Comedy Central, 2007).

African American waiter square off over whose suffering was worse: that of the Jews, who in Sarah's words, were subjected to the "murder showers" of the Holocaust, or that of African Americans, whose centuries of servitude got them "great singing voices and really catchy songs." The episode thus mocks the comparative atrocities debate that has stymied many attempts to reforge alliances between blacks and Jews. Even when Sarah arrives at an empathetic identification with African Americans, however, blackface comes to mark the distance between black and Jew, since she becomes an accusatory target for the racism visually displayed in her over-the-top face paint. In this respect, the episode traces the paradigm shift from Irving Howe to Michael Rogin; once interpreted as a means of identification with a fellow oppressed minority, Jewish minstrelsy came to be viewed as a racist and self-aggrandizing act that ushered Jews into the white majority by elevating them above the black underclass. The episode addresses the inevitable obstacles to cross-racial identification, but it also suggests that these limitations extend in both directions. Just as Sarah's attempt to experience blackness comes across as racist, the African American waiter makes a misguided effort to transform himself into a Jew, resulting in an equally offensive and stereotypical exhibition of hooked nose, side-locks, and "I Love Money" T-shirt.

The end of "Face Wars" finds Sarah in the hospital after she is accidentally shot in the arm while delivering a rallying speech to her supporters outside the police station. With the remaining traces of her black makeup leaving the imprint of a Hitler mustache upon her upper lip, Sarah is visited by the country club attendant who had earlier denied her a court. Apologizing for what she openly admits was her anti-Semitism, the attendant confesses that when she saw Sarah on a news broadcast as a black woman, she realized it could have been "a lot worse" and invites her back to the club to play tennis—as long as it is not during peak hours. The episode acknowledges that Jews may rise "on the backs of blacks," but it also suggests that this ascent does not translate into full membership in the club and comes at a high price for all involved. In "Face Wars," the wiping away of blackface does more than transform Jews into white folks: it also leaves a stain in the form of a Hitler mustache. This partial access to white privilege entails a dangerous forgetting in which the history of Jewish persecution is blacked out to recast Jews in the role of white oppressor.

"Face Wars" is one example of Silverman's predilection for politically incorrect comedy that often has the effect of laying bare white privilege, an exposé that is as much inflected by gender and sexuality as it is by Jewishness. In her one-woman stand-up show, *Jesus Is Magic*, for example, the comedian wonders what the world is coming to when a self-described "totally cute white girl" cannot go on network television and say the word "chink" (a reference to her skirmish with an Asian media watchdog group following the delivery of a joke on *Late Night with Conan O'Brien*). At another point, she puts forth the incisive one-liner, "I don't want to be labeled as straight or labeled as gay; I just want people to look at me and see me, you know, as white." During the 2008 presidential election, Silverman's much-ballyhooed Internet campaign video for Barack Obama provided certain proof of the political undercurrent to her outrageous humor on the subjects of race and black-Jewish relations. Promoting a voting drive known as "The Great Schlep," Silverman exhorts Jewish grandkids to "schlep" down to Florida in order to convince (and, if necessary, bribe) their grandparents to vote for Obama. Seated on a couch between an elderly Jewish woman and a young African American man, Silverman attempts to bridge the gulf between Jew and black by drawing a number of meaningless comic comparisons, such as the fact that they both say "yo"—except "Jews go right to left." Predictably,

Silverman oversteps the line when she suggests that the two might find common ground because "all their friends are dying," causing the black man to get up and leave in disgust. Silverman remains undeterred by having given offense.

Earning the comedian a postelection "mazel tov" from *New York Times* columnist Frank Rich, the video is believed to have had some effect in securing Florida for Obama.[6] Silverman may have succeeded in using irony to open a dialogue about race and, in the process, preserved some remnant of a now highly fraught black-Jewish alliance. In its brashness and willingness to push the envelope of acceptability, Silverman's shtick is most often likened to the Jewish comedy of Lenny Bruce, but I also like to think of her as heiress to another taboo-defying, onetime-blackface Jewish comedienne, Sophie Tucker. Like Tucker's, Silverman's performances hold out the promise of social and political change that can come through willfully affronting norms of race, gender, and sexuality—with the addition of postmodern irony and a forthright acknowledgment of the limitations of cross-racial solidarity.

In "Eating the Other," her well-known critique of the commodifications of racial otherness that take place in contemporary mass culture, black feminist theorist bell hooks argues that racial and ethnic differences function as the "seasoning" that spices up the "dull dish that is mainstream white culture." Hooks pessimistically views acts of cultural appropriation as objectifications of the other, who will be "eaten, consumed, and forgotten." In the conclusion of her essay, hooks turns to another Jewish performer, Sandra Bernhard, who also sent up minstrel conventions in her 1990 concert film *Without You I'm Nothing.* Hooks reserves guarded optimism for Bernhard's one-woman performance piece, which consists of her impersonations of black divas performed, in its film version, before a diegetic all-black nightclub audience, who registers undisguised contempt for the star's imitations of blackness. Describing Bernhard's "sense of blackness as both problematic and complex," hooks attributes the complexity to Bernhard's Jewish identity and her sexual ambiguity, both of which are important components of the film as well.[7]

For the women who have been the subject of this book, the cross-racial identifications enacted in their lives and in their art can similarly be categorized as "both problematic and complex." Critics, however, have been more likely to downplay or overlook entirely the complexity; applying masculinist theoretical paradigms, they have written off the cultural productions of Jewish women, in particular, as simply problematic. *The White Negress* works against this impulse. By moving questions of sexuality and gender (including, especially, working womanhood) to the forefront, this book has argued that appropriations of blackness in literature and minstrelsy have the potential to offer up multifaceted representations of ethno-racial relations and of white and racialized femininity. These texts perform balancing acts that compel us to move beyond the critical tendency to reify the black-white binary, clearing a path for more nuanced accounts of the black-Jewish imaginary in which cross-racial affinities and tensions function concomitantly to make and unmake whiteness and thus to define and redefine the terms of race.

NOTES

Introduction

1. Fannie Hurst, "The Smudge," in *The Vertical City* (New York: Harper & Brothers, 1922), 145–177.

2. Carol Batker, *Reforming Fictions: Native, African, and Jewish American Women's Literature and Journalism in the Progressive Era* (New York: Columbia University Press, 2000), 10.

3. Biographical information on Jolson can be found in Herbert G. Goldman, *Jolson: The Legend Comes to Life* (New York: Oxford University Press, 1988).

4. A listing of the various versions of *The Jazz Singer* can be found in J. Hoberman, "*The Jazz Singer*: A Chronology," in *Entertaining America: Jews, Movies, and Broadcasting*, ed. J. Hoberman and Jeffrey Shandler (Princeton, N.J.: Princeton University Press, 2003), 84–92. They include the 1952 version starring Danny Thomas and Peggy Lee; the 1959 *Ford Showtime* version starring Jerry Lee Lewis; and the 1980 Neil Diamond vehicle. The animated versions include Warner Brothers' "Merrie Melody" *I Love to Singa* (1936), featuring Owl Jolson, and *The Simpsons* episode "Like Father, Like Clown" (1991). The influence of *The Jazz Singer* can be seen most recently on the Warner Brothers' animated film *Happy Feet* (2006). For further discussion of *The Jazz Singer*'s impact on cinema, see Andrew Sarris, "The Cultural Guilt of Musical Movies: *The Jazz Singer*, Fifty Years After," *Film Comment* (September–October 1977): 39–41.

5. For an interpretation of *The Jazz Singer* as emblematic of the experiences of the Jewish film moguls, see Neal Gabler, *An Empire of Their Own: How the Jews Invented Hollywood* (New York: Random House, 1988), 139–145.

6. Irving Howe, *World of Our Fathers* (New York: Harcourt Brace Jovanovich, 1976), 563. Howe's insights are based in part on Ronald Sanders, "Jewish Composers and the American Popular Song," in *Next Year in Jerusalem*, ed. Douglas Villiers (New York: Penguin, 1976), 197–218.

7. Michael Rogin, *Blackface, White Noise: Jewish Immigrants in the Hollywood Melting Pot* (Berkeley: University of California Press, 1996), 95, 112.

8. See Toni Morrison, "On the Backs of Blacks," *Time*, December 2, 1993; Toni Morrison, *Playing in the Dark: Whiteness and the Literary Imagination* (New York: Vintage, 1993); Eric Lott, *Love and Theft: Blackface Minstrelsy and the American Working Class* (New York: Oxford University Press, 1993); and David Roediger, *The Wages of Whiteness: Race and the Making of the American Working Class* (New York: Verso, 1991).

9. The persistence of Rogin's paradigm is exemplified in Eric Lott's recent essay memorializing Rogin and celebrating the publication of *Blackface, White Noise*. See Eric Lott, "Semi-mojo, or Shaft in Scarsdale: Michael Rogin and Comparative American Studies," *Comparative American Studies* 6.1 (2008): 85–91. For useful critiques of Rogin's reading, see Hasia Diner, "Trading Faces," *Common Quest* (Summer 1997): 40–44; Ann Pellegrini, *Performance Anxieties: Staging Psychoanalysis, Staging Race* (New York: Routledge, 1997), 49–64; Joel Rosenberg, "What You Ain't Heard Yet: The Languages of *The Jazz Singer*," *Prooftexts* 22 (Winter/Spring 2002): 11–54; Joel Rosenberg, "Rogin's Noise: The Alleged Historical Crimes of *The Jazz Singer*," *Prooftexts* 22 (Winter/Spring 2002): 221–239; Daniel Itzkovitz, "Passing Like Me: Jewish Chameleonism and the Politics of Race," in *Passing: Identity and Interpretation in Sexuality, Race, and Religion*, ed. Maria Carla Sanchez and Linda Schlossberg (New York: New York University Press, 2001), 38–63; Michael Alexander, *Jazz Age Jews* (Princeton, N.J.: Princeton University Press, 2003); and Stephen J. Whitfield, *In Search of American Jewish Culture* (Hanover, N.H.: Brandeis University Press, 1999), 139–167. For a response to Rogin arguing that it is performance in general, rather than blackface specifically, that transforms Jews into Americans, see Andrea Most, *Making Americans: Jews and the Broadway Musical* (Cambridge, Mass.: Harvard University Press, 2004), especially chapters 1 and 2.

10. Jonathan Freedman, *Klezmer America: Jewishness, Ethnicity, Modernity* (New York: Columbia University Press, 2007), 197. For more on the ways that the "Jew-as-white-person-model" has marginalized the experiences of Jews of color, see Melanie Kaye/Kantrowitz, *The Colors of the Jews: Racial Politics and Radical Diasporism* (Bloomington: Indiana University Press, 2007).

11. Feminist critics Susan Gubar and Linda Williams also offer readings of *The Jazz Singer* that take into account gender and sexuality; Gubar, in particular, sheds light on the protagonist's non-normative masculinity. See Susan Gubar, *Racechanges: White Skin, Black Face in American Culture* (New York: Oxford University Press, 1997), 66–75; and Linda Williams, *Playing the Race Card: Melodramas of Black and White from Uncle Tom to O. J. Simpson* (Princeton, N.J.: Princeton University Press, 2001), 136–158. Other critics have similarly called for more attention to gender in discussions of black-Jewish relations and Jews and race, but overwhelmingly considerations of gender have been confined to the lens of masculinity. See, for example, Jeffrey Melnick, "Rattling the Cage of Black-Jewish Relations," in *"Jewishness" and the World of "Difference" in the United States*, ed. Marc Lee Raphael (Williamsburg, Va.: College of William and Mary, 2001), 50–64; Daniel Itzkovitz, "Race and Jews in America: An Introduction," *Shofar* 23.4 (2005): 1–8; and Jeffrey Melnick, "Some Notes on the Erotics of Black-Jewish Relations," *Shofar* 23.4 (2005): 9–25.

12. Hurst, "Smudge," 157, 151.

13. Ibid., 146.

14. Ibid., 170.

15. Ibid., 163. In this respect, the text evokes Kate Chopin's remarkable short story "Desiree's Baby" (1893), which offers a feminist critique of the ways that women, rather than men, carry the burden of racial stains and miscegenation. For a discussion of Brazil as a signifier of race mixing in the cultural imaginary of the time, see Zita Nunes, "Phantasmatic Brazil: Nella Larsen's *Passing*, American Literary Imagination, and Racial Utopianism," in *Mixing Race, Mixing Culture*, ed. Monika Kaup and Debra Rosenthal (Austin: University of Texas Press, 2002), 50–61.

16. Hurst, "Smudge," 172.

17. Ibid., 151. While Hattie's coloring and freckles are suggestive of Irish origins, the color red was also used to demarcate Jewish difference, especially in the anti-Semitic iconography of the stage Jew. The story never firmly establishes Hattie's background, but it clearly paints a portrait of her as a white ethnic character.

18. Ibid., 153.

19. Fannie Hurst, *Anatomy of Me: A Wonderer in Search of Herself* (Garden City, N.Y.: Doubleday, 1958), 43.

20. Ann Douglas, *Terrible Honesty: Mongrel Manhattan in the 1920s* (New York: Farrar, Straus, and Giroux, 1995); George Hutchinson, *The Harlem Renaissance in Black and White* (Cambridge, Mass.: Harvard University Press, 1995); Michael North, *The Dialect of Modernism: Race, Language, and Twentieth-Century Literature* (New York: Oxford University Press, 1994).

21. Horace Kallen, "Democracy versus the Melting-Pot," in *Jewish American Literature: A Norton Anthology*, ed. Jules Chametzky, John Felstiner, Hilene Flanzbaum, and Kathryn Hellerstein (New York: W. W. Norton, 2001), 216.

22. See, for example, Lois Rudnick, "The New Woman," in *1915, The Cultural Moment*, ed. Adele Heller and Lois Rudnick (New Brunswick, N.J.: Rutgers University Press, 1991), 69–81; Elizabeth Ammons, "The New Woman as Cultural Symbol and Social Reality: Six Women Writers' Perspectives," in Heller and Rudnick, *1915*, 82–97; Martha H. Patterson, *Beyond the Gibson Girl: Reimagining the American New Woman, 1895–1915* (Urbana: University of Illinois Press, 2005); Catherine Rottenberg, *Performing Americanness: Race, Class, and Gender in Modern African-American and Jewish-American Literature* (Hanover, N.H.: Dartmouth University Press, 2008), 92–107; and Charlotte Rich, *Transcending the New Woman: Multiethnic Narratives in the Progressive Era* (Columbia: University of Missouri Press, 2009). A number of these studies and others also consider New Negro Womanhood in relation to New Womanhood. See, for example, Rottenberg, *Performing Americanness*, 92–107; Patterson, *Beyond the Gibson Girl*, 50–79; and Cherene Sherrard-Johnson, *Portraits of New Negro Women* (New Brunswick, N.J.: Rutgers University Press, 2007). Also relevant here is Susan A. Glenn's *Daughters of the Shtetl: Life and Labor in the Immigrant Generation* (Ithaca, N.Y.: Cornell University Press, 1990), which focuses on Jewish immigrants as models of New Womanhood.

23. Norman Mailer, "The White Negro," in *Advertisements for Myself* (Cambridge, Mass.: Harvard University Press, 1985), 337–358; James Baldwin, "The Black Boy Looks at the White Boy," in *The Price of the Ticket* (New York: St. Martin's, 1985), 290. For an interpretation of the role that Jewishness plays in Mailer's conception of the white Negro, see Andrea Levine, "The (Jewish) White Negro: Norman Mailer's Racial Bodies," *MELUS* 28.2 (2002): 59–81.

24. Emily Miller Budick, *Blacks and Jews in Literary Conversation* (Cambridge: Cambridge University Press, 1996); Ethan Goffman, *Imagining Each Other: Blacks and Jews in Contemporary American Literature* (Albany: State University of New York Press, 2000); Adam Zachary Newton, *Facing Black and Jew: Literature as Public Space in Twentieth-Century America* (Cambridge: Cambridge University Press, 1999); Eric J. Sundquist, *Strangers in the Land: Blacks, Jews, Post-Holocaust America* (Cambridge, Mass.: Harvard University Press, 2005). Although they do not necessarily take up questions of black-Jewish relations, comparative studies of modern Jewish and African American literature do exist. They include Martin Japtok, *Growing Up Ethnic: Nationalism and the Bildungsroman in African American and Jewish American Fiction* (Iowa City: University of Iowa Press, 2005); and Rottenberg, *Performing Americanness*. Several studies also compare modern Jewish and African American literature within broader frameworks of multiethnic literature that include other ethnic traditions as well. See, for example, Batker, *Reforming Fictions*; Delia Caparoso Konzett, *Ethnic Modernisms: Anzia Yezierska, Zora Neale Hurston, Jean Rhys, and the Aesthetics of Dislocation* (New York: Palgrave Macmillan, 2002); Steven Belluscio, *To Be Suddenly White: Literary Realism and Racial Passing* (Columbia: University of Missouri Press, 2006); Alicia Kent, *African, Native, and Jewish American Literature and the Reshaping of Modernism* (New York: Palgrave Macmillan, 2007); and Werner Sollors, *Ethnic Modernism* (Cambridge, Mass.: Harvard University Press, 2008).

25. Hasia Diner, *In the Almost Promised Land: American Jews and Blacks, 1915–1935* (Baltimore: Johns Hopkins University Press, 1977); David Levering Lewis, "Parallels and Divergences: Assimilationist Strategies of Afro-American and Jewish Elites from 1910 to the Early 1930s," in *Bridges and Boundaries: African Americans and American Jews*, ed. Jack Salzman (New York: Jewish Museum, 1991), 17–35; Cheryl Lynn Greenberg, *Troubling the Waters: Black-Jewish Relations in the American Century* (Princeton, N.J.: Princeton University Press, 2006).

26. Matthew Frye Jacobson, *Whiteness of a Different Color: European Immigrants and the Alchemy of Race* (Cambridge, Mass.: Harvard University Press, 1998); Karen Brodkin, *How the Jews Became White Folks and What That Says About Race in America* (New Brunswick, N.J.: Rutgers University Press, 1999); Eric L. Goldstein, *The Price of Whiteness: Jews, Race, and American Identity* (Princeton, N.J.: Princeton University Press, 2006).

1 / From White Negress to Yiddishe Mama

1. Brooke Kroeger, *Fannie: The Talent for Success of Writer Fannie Hurst* (New York: Random House, 1999), 80.

2. On "coon songs," see Lynn Abbott and Doug Seroff, *Ragged But Right: Black Traveling Shows, "Coon Songs," and the Dark Pathway to Blues and Jazz* (Jackson: University Press of Mississippi, 2007); and James H. Dormon, "Shaping the Popular Image of Post-Reconstruction American Blacks: The 'Coon Song' Phenomenon of the Gilded Age," *American Quarterly* 40.4 (1988): 450–471.

3. A useful discussion of Tucker's tendency to reinvent her autobiographical narrative can be found in Susan Ecker and Lloyd Ecker, album notes to *Origins of the Red Hot Mama, 1910–1922* (Archeophone, 2009). In the book accompanying this CD, the Eckers present various versions of stories that Tucker tells about her life side by side. Their forthcoming film biography of Tucker should also be enlightening in this

regard. For information on the film and the Eckers' research, see www.sophietucker. com.

4. Alexander Saxton, *The Rise and Fall of the White Republic: Class Politics and Mass Culture in Nineteenth-Century America* (New York: Verso, 1990), 165; David Roediger, *The Wages of Whiteness: Race and the Making of the American Working Class* (New York: Verso, 1991). A history of blackface can be found in Robert C. Toll, *Blacking Up: The Minstrel Show in Nineteenth-Century America* (New York: Oxford University Press, 1974).

5. Eric Lott, *Love and Theft: Blackface Minstrelsy and the American Working Class* (New York: Oxford University Press, 1993); W. T. Lhamon, *Raising Cain: Blackface Performance from Jim Crow to Hip Hop* (Cambridge, Mass.: Harvard University Press, 1998). Of particular relevance here is Lhamon's reading of *The Jazz Singer* in which he argues that the 1927 film uses blackface to acknowledge, rather than disguise, the ethnic self as a means to success.

6. Lott, *Love and Theft*, 53.

7. Marjorie Garber, *Vested Interests: Cross-dressing and Cultural Anxiety* (New York: Routledge, 1997), 277.

8. Cited in Lott, *Love and Theft*, 160.

9. See Annemarie Bean, "Transgressing the Gender Divide: The Female Impersonator in Nineteenth-Century Blackface Minstrelsy," in *Inside the Minstrel Mask: Readings in Nineteenth-Century Blackface Minstrelsy*, ed. Annemarie Bean, James V. Hatch, and Brooks McNamara (Hanover, N.H.: Wesleyan University Press, 1996), 245–256; Annemarie Bean, "Black Minstrelsy and Double Inversion, circa 1890," in *African American Performance and Theater History: A Critical Reader*, ed. Harry J. Elam Jr. and David Krasner (New York: Oxford University Press, 2001), 171–191; and William J. Mahar, *Behind the Burnt Cork Mask: Early Blackface Minstrelsy and Antebellum American Popular Culture* (Urbana: University of Illinois Press, 1999).

10. Recent scholarship in the field of African American performance studies investigates how entertainers worked within minstrel conventions to create their own brand of subversive spectacle. See, in particular, Louis Chude-Sokei, *The Last "Darky": Bert Williams, Black-on-Black Minstrelsy, and the African Diaspora* (Durham, N.C.: Duke University Press, 2006). The deployment of performance as a mode of subversion also figures prominently in the work of Daphne Brooks, *Bodies in Dissent: Spectacular Performances of Race and Freedom, 1850–1910* (Durham, N.C.: Duke University Press, 2006); Jayna Brown, *Babylon Girls: Black Women Performers and the Shaping of the Modern* (Durham, N.C.: Duke University Press, 2008); and Karen Sotiropolous, *Staging Race: Black Performers in Turn of the Century America* (Cambridge, Mass.: Harvard University Press, 2006).

11. See, for example, Ted Merwin, *In Their Own Image: New York Jews in Jazz Age Popular Culture* (New Brunswick, N.J.: Rutgers University Press, 2006); Pamela Brown Lavitt, "Vaudeville," in *Jews and American Popular Culture*, ed. Paul Buhle (Westport, Conn.: Praeger, 2007), 15–35; and D. Travis Stewart, *No Applause—Just Throw Money* (New York: Farrar, Straus, and Giroux, 2005).

12. Andrew Erdman, *Blue Vaudeville: Sex, Morals, and the Marketing of Amusement, 1895–1915* (Jefferson, N.C.: McFarland, 2004), 5.

13. John E. DiMeglio, *Vaudeville, U.S.A.* (Bowling Green, Ohio: Bowling Green Popular Press, 1973). In addition to the major vaudeville circuits, which

are my main focus here, there were separate venues for Yiddish and black vaudeville.

14. Michael Rogin, *Blackface, White Noise: Jewish Immigrants in the Hollywood Melting Pot* (Berkeley: University of California Press, 1996); Harley Erdman, *Staging the Jew: The Performance of an American Ethnicity, 1860–1920* (New Brunswick, N.J.: Rutgers University Press, 1997); Jeffrey Melnick, *A Right to Sing the Blues: African Americans, Jews, and American Popular Song* (Cambridge, Mass.: Harvard University Press, 1999).

15. The quip can be heard in Ada Jones and Len Spencer, "The Original Cohens," recorded October 19, 1905, *Jewface* (Reboot Stereophonic, 2006).

16. Merwin, *In Their Own Image*, 17–60.

17. Pamela Brown Lavitt, "First of the Red Hot Mamas: 'Coon Shouting' and the Jewish Ziegfeld Girl," *American Jewish History* 87.4 (1999): 290.

18. Susan Glenn, *Female Spectacle: The Theatrical Roots of Modern Feminism* (Cambridge, Mass.: Harvard University Press, 2000), 3. See also M. Alison Kibler, *Rank Ladies: Gender and Cultural Hierarchy in American Vaudeville* (Chapel Hill: University of North Carolina Press, 1999).

19. See Glenn, *Female Spectacle*; and Sarah Bernhardt, *My Double Life* (London: William Heinemann, 1907), 81. Another figure worthy of consideration in this context is the burlesque performer Adah Isaacs Menken, who, as several scholars have recently shown, maintained an ambiguous identity but had links to Jewishness and blackness. See Renée Sentilles, *Performing Menken: Adah Isaacs Menken and the Birth of American Celebrity* (New York: Cambridge University Press, 2003); and Brooks, *Bodies in Dissent*, chapter 3.

20. Unidentified clipping in Locke Collection Envelope #2391, Sophie Tucker Scrapbooks, Billy Rose Theatre Collection, New York Public Library of the Performing Arts (hereafter cited as Sophie Tucker Scrapbooks); Antoinette Donnelly, "Sophie Tucker Gives Advice on Streamlines," *Chicago Daily Tribune*, March 7, 1937.

21. Midler, in particular, acknowledges Tucker's influence when she assumes her "Soph" persona for telling raunchy jokes.

22. June Sochen, "Fanny Brice and Sophie Tucker: Blending the Particular with the Universal," in *Hester Street to Hollywood: The Jewish American Stage and Screen*, ed. Sarah Blacher Cohen (Bloomington: Indiana University Press, 1983), 55. See also June Sochen, "From Sophie Tucker to Barbra Streisand: Jewish Women Entertainers as Reformers," in *Talking Back: Images of Jewish Women in American Popular Culture*, ed. Joyce Antler (Hanover, N.H.: Brandeis University Press, 1998), 68–84; and Joyce Antler, *The Journey Home: Jewish Women and the American Century* (New York: Free Press, 1997), 136–147.

23. Sarah Blacher Cohen, "The Unkosher Comediennes: From Sophie Tucker to Joan Rivers," in *Jewish Wry: Essays on Jewish Humor*, ed. Sarah Blacher Cohen (Bloomington: Indiana University Press, 1987), 106–107.

24. Eddie Cantor, *Take My Life* (Garden City, N.J.: Doubleday, 1957), 34, cited in Lewis A. Erenberg, *Steppin' Out: New York Nightlife and the Transformation of American Culture, 1890–1930* (Westport, Conn.: Greenwood Press, 1981); Sophie Tucker, *Some of These Days* (New York: Doubleday, Doran, 1945), 54.

25. See David Biale, *Eros and the Jews: From Biblical Israel to Contemporary America* (New York: Basic Books, 1992), 204–227; Erenberg, *Steppin' Out*, 191; and Irving

Howe, *World of Our Fathers* (New York: Harcourt Brace Jovanovich, 1976), 12–13, 558. See also some of the essays collected in Nathan Abrams, ed., *Jews and Sex* (Nottingham, U.K.: Five Leaves, 2008).

26. Tucker, *Some of These Days*, 139.

27. For a book-length biography of Tucker, see Armond Fields, *Sophie Tucker: First Lady of Show Business* (Jefferson, N.C.: McFarland, 2003). Some of Fields's research has been challenged by Susan Ecker and Lloyd Ecker. See Ecker and Ecker, album notes to *Origins of the Red Hot Mama*.

28. Wilson Midgley, BBC review of *Some of These Days*, July 17, 1948, Sophie Tucker private recordings collection, 1925–1953, Rodgers and Hammerstein Archives of Recorded Sound, New York Public Library of the Performing Arts.

29. Tucker, *Some of These Days*, 1.

30. Ibid., 2.

31. Ibid., 22, 137.

32. Ibid., 33.

33. Ibid., 33–34.

34. Ibid., 44.

35. Antler, *Journey Home*, 139.

36. Tucker, *Some of These Days*, 35, 40.

37. Ibid., 40–41.

38. Antler, *Journey Home*, 139.

39. Tucker, *Some of These Days*, 63. The story of Tucker's liberation from blackface is yet another autobiographical narrative that the performer alters with different tellings. See, for example, Ecker and Ecker, album notes to *Origins of the Red Hot Mama*, 15.

40. Sophie Tucker autobiographical writings, New York Public Library.

41. Alan Trachtenberg, *Shades of Hiawatha: Staging Indians, Making Americans, 1880–1930* (New York: Hill and Wang, 2005), 140–169.

42. A related use of the word "squaw" to racialize the difference of a Jewish immigrant woman occurs in Abraham Cahan's *Yekl* (1896). To the disgust of her Americanized husband, Jake (formerly Yekl), Gitl, his wife, "naturally dark of complexion," appears fresh off the boat with "her face [covered] with a deep bronze, which combined with her prominent cheek bones, inky little eyes, and, above all, the smooth black wig, to lend her resemblance to a squaw" (Abraham Cahan, *Yekl and the Imported Bridegroom and Other Stories of the New York Ghetto* [New York: Dover, 1970], 34). For an important reading of this scene that situates Cahan's novella in relation to African American writing, see Werner Sollors, *Beyond Ethnicity: Consent and Descent in American Culture* (New York: Oxford University Press, 1986), 149–173.

43. Tucker, *Some of These Days*, 63.

44. Untitled clipping from *Cleveland Dealer* (1909), Locke Collection Envelope #2391, Sophie Tucker Scrapbooks.

45. Tucker, *Some of These Days*, 63.

46. Buzzy Jackson, *A Bad Woman Feeling Good: Blues and the Women Who Sang Them* (New York: W. W. Norton, 2005), 24–27.

47. Melnick, *Right to Sing the Blues*, 114.

48. Brown, *Babylon Girls*, 214–215.

49. On Williams and Cantor, see Chude-Sokei, *Last "Darky,"* 20–21; and Douglas, *Terrible Honesty*, 77. On Brice and Cantor, see Barbara Grossman, *Funny Woman: The*

Life and Times of Fanny Brice (Indianapolis: Indiana University Press, 1992), 94. As Linda Mizejewski points out and I discuss further later, the very fact that Williams appeared alongside Brice suggested that Brice, as a Jew, was not considered a white American woman, especially since Williams had a clause in his contract saying he could not appear on stage with the Ziegfeld chorus girls, for fear that he would sully their whiteness. See Linda Mizejewski, *Ziegfeld Girl: Image and Icon in Culture and Cinema* (Durham, N.C.: Duke University Press, 1999), 6.

50. Brown, *Babylon Girls*, 213–214; Henry T. Sampson, *Blacks in Blackface: A Source Book on Early Black Musical Shows* (Metuchen, N.J.: Scarecrow Press, 1980), 364–366.

51. Cited in Daphne Harrison, *Black Pearls: Blues Queens of the 1920s* (New Brunswick, N.J.: Rutgers University Press, 1988), 209.

52. Ethel Waters, *His Eye Is on the Sparrow* (New York: Da Capo Press, 1989), 135. According to Susan Ecker and Lloyd Ecker, rumors also appeared in black newspapers that Tucker had been tutored by Bessie Smith. See Ecker and Ecker, album notes to *Origins of the Red Hot Mama*, 46.

53. Whitney Balliett, *American Singers* (New York: Oxford University Press, 1979), 29, cited in Robert Dawidoff, *Making History Matter* (Philadelphia: Temple University Press, 2000), 145.

54. Harrison, *Black Pearls*, 210.

55. The relationship between Tucker and Mom Chung is discussed in detail in Judy Tzu-Chun Wu, *Doctor Mom Chung of the Fair-Haired Bastards* (Berkeley: University of California Press, 2005), 170–183. Wu analyzes the homoerotic undertones of this friendship and speculates that Tucker does not mention Chung in her memoir out of respect for the other woman's privacy.

56. Tucker, *Some of These Days*, 70.

57. Ibid., 83.

58. Sophie Tucker autobiographical writings, New York Public Library.

59. Ibid.

60. Tucker, *Some of These Days*, 83.

61. Ibid., 85. Differences between the draft and published memoir as they relate to Elkins are significant here. For example, the draft version of this scene leaves out the adjective "inborn," which suggests that it might have been an editorial addition rather than Tucker's own choice of words. Editorial changes to Tucker's memoir were also made by Dorothy Giles, who collaborated with Tucker on the writing.

62. "Married 3 Times, Sophie Finds Out Her Act's a Single," *Daily News,* November 24, 1961, in Sophie Tucker Clippings, 1932–1959, Billy Rose Theatre Collection, New York Public Library of the Performing Arts.

63. Sophie Tucker autobiographical writings, New York Public Library.

64. Sophie Tucker Story, October 16, 1953, Sophie Tucker private recordings collection, 1925–1953, Rodgers and Hammerstein Archives of Recorded Sound.

65. Tucker, *Some of These Days*, 248.

66. Ibid., 114. Susan Ecker and Lloyd Ecker have found evidence that suggests Tucker's version of her initial meeting with Brooks was slightly romanticized. See Ecker and Ecker, album notes to *Origins of the Red Hot Mama*, 29–30.

67. "Songstress Heads Bill," *Los Angeles Times*, November 13, 1935; "Sophie Tucker Pays Tribute to Shelton Brooks," *Los Angeles Sentinel*, December 10, 1953.

68. Sophie Tucker autobiographical writings, New York Public Library.

69. Sophie Tucker, "Some of These Days," recorded 1911, *Origins of the Red Hot Mama, 1910–1922* (Archeophone, 2009).

70. Sophie Tucker, "I Know That My Baby Is Cheating On Me," recorded 1928, *The Great Sophie Tucker* (Jasmine, 2005).

71. "One Arrest Not Enough," *Variety*, November 10, 1910, n.p., in Locke Collection Envelope #2391, Sophie Tucker Scrapbooks; Frank Cullen, Florence Hackman, and Donald McNeilly, *Vaudeville, Old and New* (New York: Routledge, 2007), 1129; Fields, *Sophie Tucker*, 44.

72. Melnick, *Right to Sing the Blues*, 111.

73. Mizejewski, *Ziegfeld Girl*, 6.

74. Peter Antelyes, "Red Hot Mamas: Bessie Smith, Sophie Tucker, and the Ethnic Maternal Voice in American Popular Song," in *Embodied Voices: Representing Female Vocality in Western Culture*, ed. Leslie C. Dunn and Nancy A. Jones (New York: Cambridge University Press, 1994), 212–229.

75. Hazel Carby, "It Jus Be's Dat Way Sometime: The Sexual Politics of Women's Blues," in *The Jazz Cadence in American Culture*, ed. Robert G. O'Meally (New York: Columbia University Press, 1998), 469–482; Angela Davis, *Blues Legacies and Black Feminism* (New York: Vintage, 1998); Harrison, *Black Pearls*.

76. Amiri Baraka as Leroi Jones, *Blues People: Negro Music in White America* (New York: William Morrow, 1963), 99; Dan Burley, "The 'Crazy Blues,'" *New York Amsterdam News*, March 2, 1940; Ken Smikle, "Black Music History," *New York Amsterdam News*, February 27, 1982.

77. Ecker and Ecker, album notes to *Origins of the Red Hot Mama*, 46; Harrison, *Black Pearls*, 187, 234.

78. "Bill Bristles with Novelties," *New York Telegraph*, July 4, 1916, in Locke Collection Envelope #2391, Sophie Tucker Scrapbooks.

79. Tucker, *Some of These Days*, 139.

80. See assorted unidentified clippings covering Tucker's London tour in Sophie Tucker Scrapbooks; and "Sophie Tucker Fined for Smuggling Silk Dresses," *Chicago Daily Tribune*, March 27, 1931.

81. "Sophie Here, Foils Age Query," *San Francisco Call*, March 12, 1929, in Sophie Tucker Scrapbooks.

82. Zora Neale Hurston, "Characteristics of Negro Expression," in *Folklore, Memoirs, and Other Writings*, ed. Cheryl A. Wall (New York: Library of America, 1995), 844–845.

83. Baraka as Jones, *Blues People*, 148; Davis, *Blues Legacies and Black Feminism*, 4.

84. J. Saunders Redding, *A Scholar's Conscience: Selected Writings of J. Saunders Redding, 1942–1977* (Lexington: University Press of Kentucky, 1992), 217.

85. Baraka as Jones, *Blues People*, 150.

86. Davis, *Blues Legacies and Black Feminism*, 13.

87. Ethel Waters, "No Man's Mamma Now," *Ethel Waters, 1925–1926* (Classics, 1997); Sophie Tucker, "I'm Living Alone and I Like It," *The Golden Jubilee Album* (Sepia, 2005). While black women's blues also warn against financial dependency on men, there is a marked difference in their attitude toward labor and greater skepticism about the liberating effects of consumerism. Showing the influence of slave songs, blues women often expressed the drudgery of work in their music, a theme not present in Tucker's.

88. Sophie Tucker, "If Your Kisses Can't Hold the Man You Love," recorded October 1930, *The Great Sophie Tucker*.

89. Cited in Tucker, *Some of These Days*, 217–218.

90. It is worth noting another key difference: unlike Tucker, many black blues women did renounce *heterosexual* sex, either through subtle implications that "a good man is hard to find" or more blatantly as in Ma Rainey's "Prove It On Me Blues," which states, "Went out last night with a crowd of my friends / They must've been women, 'cause I don't like no men."

91. Bessie Smith, "I Need a Little Sugar in My Bowl," *Greatest Hits* (Acrobat Music, 2005).

92. Ethel Waters, "My Handy Man," *Ethel Waters, 1926–1929* (Classics, 1993).

93. Such covert naughtiness could, of course, cross the line into more explicit obscenity, depending on context. A case in point is the Jewish comedy of Belle Barth, who also got her start in vaudeville and whose impersonations of Tucker and overtly vulgar renditions of jazz numbers like "Darktown Strutters' Ball" became staples of her nightclub act. See Cohen, "Unkosher Comediennes," as well as Barth's own recording, *If I Embarrass You Tell Your Friends*, available at Dartmouth Jewish Sound Archive, www.darthmouth.edu/djsa.

94. On management requests that she remove "Who Paid the Rent for Mrs. Rip Van Winkle?" see *New York Telegraph*, July 30, 1914, in Locke Collection Envelope #2391, Sophie Tucker Scrapbooks.

95. Cohen, "Unkosher Comediennes."

96. Sophie Tucker, "If Your Kisses Can't Hold the Man You Love," recorded 1930, *The Great Sophie Tucker*.

97. Sophie Tucker, "No One Man Is Every Going to Worry Me," recorded 1937, *The Great Sophie Tucker*.

98. Sophie Tucker, "Too Much Lovin'" and "Hollywood Will Never Be the Same," recorded November 1930, *The Great Sophie Tucker*.

99. Sophie Tucker, "Is He the Boy Friend?" recorded August 28, 1928, *The Great Sophie Tucker*. Latter quotation cited in Cohen, "Unkosher Comediennes," 107.

100. Sophie Tucker, "I Don't Want to Get Thin," recorded April 2, 1929, *The Great Sophie Tucker*.

101. Ida Cox, "Four Day Creep," cited in Baraka as Jones, *Blues People*, 92.

102. Tucker, "I Don't Want to Get Thin."

103. Sophie Tucker, "There's Something Spanish in My Eyes," recorded June 13, 1928, *The Great Sophie Tucker*.

104. Sochen, "Fanny Brice and Sophie Tucker."

105. Herbert G. Goldman, *Fanny Brice: The Original Funny Girl* (New York: Oxford University Press, 1992), 46.

106. Grossman, *Funny Woman*, 11.

107. Brice, cited in ibid., 102.

108. Ibid., xiv.

109. Parker, cited in ibid., 149.

110. Untitled review in *Variety*, March 19, 1920, Locke Collection Envelope #2391, Sophie Tucker Scrapbooks.

111. Riv-Ellen Prell, *Fighting to Become American: Assimilation and the Trouble between Jewish Women and Jewish Men* (Boston: Beacon Press, 1999), 43.

112. On Jewish female garment workers as New Women, see Susan A. Glenn, *Daughters of the Shtetl: Life and Labor in the Immigrant Generation* (Ithaca, N.Y.: Cornell University Press, 1990).

113. Tucker, *Some of These Days*, 28.

114. Cited in ibid., 218.

115. An unidentified review in Locke Collection Envelope #2391, Sophie Tucker Scrapbooks, states, "Laughing, rollicking, captivating Sophie Tucker, with her 'colored' voice, her naughty wink and her nerve, is back again."

116. Tucker, *Some of These Days*, 275.

117. Jean-Paul Sartre, *Nausea*, trans. Lloyd Alexander (New York: New Directions, 1964), 175–178; Jonathan Judaken, *Jean-Paul Sartre and the Jewish Question* (Lincoln: University of Nebraska Press, 2006), 42–48.

118. Sophie Tucker Story, October 16, 1953, Sophie Tucker private recordings collection, 1925–1953, Rodgers and Hammerstein Archives of Recorded Sound.

119. Tucker, *Some of These Days*, 203.

120. Armond Fields also reports an incident in which Tucker bucked management by refusing to perform on Yom Kippur. See Fields, *Sophie Tucker*, 166.

121. Howe, *World of Our Fathers*, 563.

122. Sophie Tucker, *Some of These Days*, script by Dr. Sidney Marks, musical score and accompaniment by Shmuel Fershko, issued by the Membership Department of the Zionist Organization of America, n.d., Sophie Tucker private recordings collection, 1925–1953, Rodgers and Hammerstein Archives of Recorded Sound.

123. Tucker, *Some of These Days*, 280.

124. Sophie Tucker, "Some of These Days," recorded September 2, 1927, *The Great Sophie Tucker*.

125. Sophie Tucker, "My Yiddishe Momme," recorded June 20, 1928, *The Great Sophie Tucker*.

126. Joyce Antler, *You Never Call! You Never Write! A History of the Jewish Mother* (New York: Oxford University Press, 2007), 21.

127. Tucker, "My Yiddishe Momme."

128. Mark Slobin, *Tenement Songs: The Popular Music of Jewish Immigrants* (Chicago: University of Illinois Press, 1982), 203–205.

129. Tucker, *Some of These Days*, 260, 188.

130. Ibid., 260.

131. Ashton Stevens, unlabeled clipping, circa 1910–1911, in Sophie Tucker Scrapbooks.

132. Sophie Tucker studio performances in Sophie Tucker private recordings collection, 1925–1953, Rodgers and Hammerstein Archives of Recorded Sound.

133. These records can be found in the Dartmouth Jewish Sound Archive, www.darthmouth.edu/djsa. There are notable differences in meaning and context between the Yiddish and English versions of these songs that are worth further analysis. On "Yiddishe Mama," see Slobin, *Tenement Songs*, 202–205. And special thanks to Josh Lambert for his translation of "Mama Goes Where Papa Goes."

134. For further discussion of African American vocalizations of Hebrew and Yiddish songs, see Hasia Diner, *In the Almost Promised Land* (Baltimore: Johns Hopkins University Press, 1977), 67–68; Leslie Fiedler, "Negro and Jew: Encounter in America," in *No! In Thunder* (Boston: Beacon Press, 1960), 244; Melnick, *A Right to Sing the*

Blues, 180; and Stephen Whitfield, *In Search of American Jewish Culture* (Hanover, N.H.: Brandeis University Press, 1999), 139–167.

135. Billie Holiday, *Rare Live Recordings, 1934–1959* (Esp Disk, 2007). On "Strange Fruit," see Jackson, *Bad Woman Feeling Good*, 112–117; and Whitfield, *In Search of American Jewish Culture*, 147.

136. Gabler's view has been challenged by several scholars, including Ted Merwin in *In Their Own Image*.

2 / The Same Show Boat?

1. Edna Ferber, *A Peculiar Treasure* (New York: Doubleday, 1939), 53, 102, 287.

2. Ibid., 53.

3. *Show Boat* is dedicated to *Minick*'s producer, "Winthrop Ames Who First Said Show Boat to Me." After a dismal opening night for *Minick*, made worse by an infestation of bats in the theater, Ames suggested that next time they would charter a showboat and play the rivers, prompting Ferber's interest in, as she put it, "one of the most melodramatic and gorgeous bits of Americana that had ever come my way." For further details on Ferber's writing of *Show Boat*, see Ferber, *Peculiar Treasure*, 283–306.

4. Ann Douglas, *Terrible Honesty: Mongrel Manhattan in the 1920s* (New York: Farrar, Straus, and Giroux, 1995).

5. Lauren Berlant, *The Female Complaint: The Unfinished Business of Sentimentality in American Culture* (Durham, N.C.: Duke University Press, 2008), 69–106; Linda Williams, *Playing the Race Card: Melodramas of Black and White from Uncle Tom to O. J. Simpson* (Princeton, N.J.: Princeton University Press, 2001), 136–186.

6. Michael Rogin, *Blackface, White Noise: Jewish Immigrants in the Hollywood Melting Pot* (Berkeley: University of California Press, 1996), 112.

7. Ferber and Tucker were later to have professional dealings through the American Federation of Actors. See Joyce Antler, *The Journey Home: Jewish Women and the American Century* (New York: Free Press, 1997), 144–145.

8. June Sochen, *Consecrate Every Day: The Public Lives of Jewish American Women, 1880–1980* (Albany: State University of New York Press, 1981), 103–105; Carol Batker, *Reforming Fictions: Native, African, and Jewish American Women's Literature and Journalism in the Progressive Era* (New York: Columbia University Press, 2000), 10, 108–130. For a similar view, see also Diane Lichtenstein, *Writing Their Nations: The Tradition of Nineteenth-Century American Jewish Women Writers* (Bloomington: Indiana University Press, 1992), 129–141.

9. Technically, the term "integrated book musical" was not used until 1943 to describe Rodgers and Hammerstein's *Oklahoma!* but looking back, theater historians have noted that *Show Boat* originated the form. Scholars have also debated whether to classify Kern and Hammerstein's *Show Boat* as a musical, opera, or operetta. Following from Leonard Bernstein's designation, Andrea Most calls it an operetta, while Peter Rabinowitz identifies it as opera. The debate over classification arises, in part, because *Show Boat* is the first of its kind. Since it is commonly viewed as inaugurating modern musical theater, I refer to it here as a musical. See Andrea Most, *Making Americans: Jews and the Broadway Musical* (Cambridge, Mass.: Harvard University Press, 2004), 28–29; and Peter Rabinowitz, "Music, Genre, and Narrative Theory," in *Narrative Across Media: The Languages of Storytelling*, ed. Marie-Laure Ryan (Lincoln: University of Nebraska Press, 2004), 305–328. On Bernstein's classification, see

Stephen Whitfield, *In Search of American Jewish Culture* (Hanover, N.H.: Brandeis University Press, 1999), 74. For more on *Show Boat*'s status in musical theater history, see Ethan Mordden, *Make Believe: The Broadway Musical in the 1920s* (New York: Oxford University Press, 1997), 205–232; Geoffrey Block, *Enchanted Evenings: The Broadway Musical from "Show Boat" to Sondheim* (New York: Oxford University Press, 1997), 19–40; John Bush Jones, *Our Musicals, Ourselves: A Social History of the American Musical Theatre* (Hanover, N.H.: Brandeis University Press, 2003), 73–78; and Raymond Knapp, *The American Musical and the Formation of National Identity* (Princeton, N.J.: Princeton University Press, 2005), 185–194. Knapp offers a particularly useful discussion of the musical's racial politics.

10. Information about *Show Boat*'s production history from its 1927 Broadway premiere through the 1970s can be found in Miles Kreuger, *Show Boat: The Story of a Classic American Musical* (New York: Oxford University Press, 1977). See also Alberta Hunter interview, *Alberta Hunter: Jazz at the Smithsonian*, produced and directed by Clark Santee and Delia Gravel Santee (Adler Enterprises, 1982).

11. "Speakin' o' Performers," *New York Amsterdam News*, December 14, 1927; J. A. Rogers, "European Correspondent of 'News' Threatens to Become a Philosopher," *New York Amsterdam News*, October 3, 1928. Discussion of the African American response can also be found in Martin Duberman, *Paul Robeson* (New York: New Press, 1989), 114–115.

12. Interestingly, *Jewish American Literature: A Norton Anthology*, which includes the lyrics of "Ol' Man River" in a section on "The Golden Age of the Broadway Song," uses "colored folks" and incorrectly attributes the words to Hammerstein. Some of the revisions of the lyrics have been attributed to Paul Robeson, who would make the changes in performance, much to the consternation of Hammerstein, who stated, "As the author of these words, I have no intention of changing them or permitting anyone else to change them. I further suggest that Paul write his own songs and leave mine alone." See Jules Chametzky, John Felstiner, Hilene Flanzbaum, and Kathryn Hellerstein, eds., *Jewish American Literature: A Norton Anthology* (New York: W. W. Norton, 2001), 969. Hammerstein's statement on the lyrics is cited in Robin Breon, "*Show Boat*: The Revival, the Racism," *Drama Review* 39.2 (Summer 1995): 95.

13. Frank Rich, "The Seminal American Musical Is Rebuilt from the Ground Up," *New York Times*, October 20, 1993; Jack Kroll, "Stormy Trip for 'Show Boat,'" *Newsweek*, November 1, 1993, 76.

14. For scholarly treatments of the controversy over the revival, see Breon, "*Show Boat*," 86–105; the chapter on *Show Boat* in Carol Tator, Frances Henry, and Winston Mattis, *Challenging Racism in the Arts* (Toronto: University of Toronto Press, 1998), 159–213; and Leslie Sanders, "American Scripts, Canadian Realities: Toronto's *Show Boat*," in *Pop Can: Popular Culture in Canada*, ed. Lynne Van Luven and Priscilla L. Walton (Scarborough, Ont.: Prentice Hall Allyn, 1999), 13–26. Most reviews of the Toronto revival concur with Rich and Kroll that the protests were overstated; almost all the reviews single out the performances of black actors, especially Lonette McKee as Julie and Michel Bell as Joe, over white ones. For a generally positive review of the Broadway production that also focuses on the musical's progressive politics, see Vincent Canby, "Confronting a Classic, Head On," *New York Times*, October 9, 1994. William Henry III, in contrast, lends validity to the protestors' complaints, arguing for the show's persistent racism. See William Henry III, "Rough Sailing for a New

Show Boat," Time, November 1, 1993, 84. For more on the conflicts between blacks and Jews in Toronto, see Clyde H. Farnsworth, "Blacks Accuse Jews in 'Show Boat' Revival," *New York Times*, May 1, 1993; and Howard Adelman, "Blacks and Jews: Racism, Anti-Semitism, and *Show Boat*," in *Multiculturalism, Jews and Identities in Canada*, ed. Howard Adelman and John Simpson (Jerusalem: Magnes Press, 1996), 128–178. For more on the continuation of the controversy despite the positive reviews, see the op-ed by Michael Valpy, "Surely There's Something Better Than *Show Boat*," *Globe and Mail*, October 19, 1993.

15. John Lahr, "Mississippi Mud," *New Yorker*, October 25, 1993, 124.

16. Marlene Nourbese Philip, *Showing Grit: Showboating North of the 44th Parallel* (Toronto: Pouli, 1993), 17.

17. References to minstrelsy appear in several of Ferber's other works as well. Noting such references in the Emma McChesney stories, for example, William Gleason argues that the allusions are sympathetic, showing that black Americans "in the 1910s were contained within cripplingly restrictive social (and literary) roles," much like women. See William Gleason, "'Find Their Place and Fall in Line': The Revisioning of Women's Work in *Herland* and *Emma McChesney & Co.*," *Prospects* 21 (1996): 39–87.

18. Edna Ferber, *Show Boat* (1926; repr., New York: Signet, 1994), 22, 48, 90, 53.

19. As scholars have shown, Stowe, though she in all likelihood never attended a minstrel show, was influenced by blackface minstrelsy in her characterizations. See, for example, Jason Richards, "Imitation Nation: Blackface Minstrelsy and the Making of African American Selfhood in *Uncle Tom's Cabin*," *Novel: A Forum on Fiction* 39.2 (Spring 2006): 204–220; and W. T. Lhamon, Jr., *Raising Cain: Blackface Performance from Jim Crow to Hip Hop* (Cambridge, Mass.: Harvard University Press, 1998), 96–99. For a further comparison of *Show Boat* and *Uncle Tom's Cabin*, see Berlant, *Female Complaint*, 69–106.

20. Ferber, *Peculiar Treasure*, 6.

21. For biographical information on Ferber, see Julie Goldsmith Gilbert, *Ferber: A Biography* (New York: Doubleday, 1978); Carolyn Heilbrun, "Edna Ferber," in *Notable American Women: The Modern Period*, ed. Barbara Sicherman and Carol Hurd Green (Cambridge, Mass.: Harvard University Press, 1980); Antler, *Journey Home*, 150–172; Marion Meade, *Bobbed Hair and Bathtub Gin: Writers Running Wild in the Twenties* (New York: Harcourt, 2004); and Ferber's two autobiographies, *A Peculiar Treasure* and *A Kind of Magic* (New York: Lancer, 1966).

22. Edna Ferber, foreword to *Buttered Side Down* (1912; repr., East Bridgewater, Mass.: Signature Press, 2007), xi.

23. Joyce Kilmer, "Business Woman Most Domestic," *New York Times*, April 4, 1915. The character's astounding appeal was due in part to the fact that modern American women identified with Ferber's protagonist as they, too, sought vocations outside the home. Cast as Emma in the stage adaptation of the series *Our Mrs. McChesney*, actress Ethel Barrymore spoke to the impact this character had on popular images of American womanhood. "I shan't be playing a part in this," stated Barrymore of her role. "For the first time in my life I'll be able to act, and talk, and walk, and dress just as I do every day of my life. I'll be taking the part of an American woman possessed of brains, and initiative, and a taste in clothes." Cited in Edna Ferber, "Hats Off to the Business Woman!" *New York Times*, October 24, 1915. Emma even captured the attention of President Franklin D. Roosevelt, who wrote to Ferber, advising her to

marry off her heroine—a piece of advice she ended up following, contributing to a somewhat more conventional narrative for her iconoclastic protagonist. Roosevelt's letter to Edna Ferber is cited in Gilbert, *Ferber*, 409.

24. Edna Ferber, *Fanny Herself* (1917; repr., Urbana: University of Illinois Press, 2001), 121, 107, 136, 261.

25. Werner Sollors, *Beyond Ethnicity: Consent and Descent in American Culture* (New York: Oxford University Press, 1986); Ferber, *Fanny Herself*, 121.

26. Horace Kallen, "Democracy versus the Melting-Pot," in Chametzky et al., *Jewish American Literature*, 216.

27. Randolph Bourne, "Trans-National America," in *War and the Intellectuals* (New York: Harper & Row, 1964), 107–123.

28. Kallen, "Democracy versus the Melting-Pot," 217. The philosophy was not labeled "cultural pluralism" until Kallen named it such in 1924. David Hollinger differentiates between Kallen and Bourne, noting that Bourne "envisioned a dynamic interaction while Kallen stressed the autonomy of each group." See David Hollinger, *Postethnic America: Beyond Multiculturism* (1995; repr., New York: Basic Books, 2000), 11.

29. Kallen, "Democracy versus the Melting-Pot," 213. See also Bourne, "Trans-National America," 113–114; and Randolph Bourne, "The Jew and Trans-National America," in *War and the Intellectuals* (New York: Harper & Row, 1964), 124–133, originally published in the *Menorah Journal* 2 (1916): 277–284. Bourne also mentions in the latter essay that a Jewish classmate coined the term "transnationalism."

30. Ferber, *Fanny Herself*, 130.

31. In his study of the Jewish diaspora, for example, German ethnographer Richard Andree wrote: "Even when he adopts the language, dress, habits, and customs of the people among whom he lives, he still remains everywhere the same. All he adopts is but a cloak, under which the eternal Hebrew survives; he is the same in his facial features, in the structure of his body, his temperament, his character." Cited in Sander Gilman, *The Jew's Body* (New York: Routledge, 1991), 76. For similar examples, see Madison Grant, *The Passing of the Great Race* (New York: Charles Scribner's Sons, 1916), 81; and E. A. Ross, *The Old World in the New* (New York: Century, 1914), 285–286.

32. Similar images of fashion as a symbol of cultural hybridity pervade American Jewish fiction set in the garment industry, from Abraham Cahan's *The Rise of David Levinsky* (1917) to the writings of Anzia Yezierska. In Yezierska's 1923 novel, *Salome of the Tenements*, for example, the fashion designer protagonist, Sonya Vrunsky, makes her name by bringing seemingly contradictory elements together. Her legendary creation, "The Sonya Model," is described as "a costume, plain enough for everybody but distinctive enough to make it effective for any occasion," allowing "the wearer to have the joy of a dress that could be slipped on in a moment, and yet give the luxurious sense of a fitted gown. A supple, clinging thing in everyday serge, veiling yet revealing the lovely curves of a woman's body" (Anzia Yezierska, *Salome of the Tenements* [Chicago: University of Illinois Press, 1995], 169).

33. Ferber, *Fanny Herself*, 257.

34. The original dedication to the novel read, "To Adolf Hitler who has made of me a better Jew and a more understanding and tolerant human being, as he has of millions of other Jews, this book is dedicated in loathing and contempt." See Gilbert, *Ferber*, 291.

35. Ferber, *Peculiar Treasure*, 9, 10. On the Jew as national allegory, see Daniel Itzkovitz, "Secret Temples," in *Jews and Other Differences*, ed. Jonathan Boyarin and Daniel Boyarin (Minneapolis: University of Minnesota Press, 1997), 177.

36. For further discussion of Ferber's statements on her Jewish identity in *A Peculiar Treasure*, see Antler, *Journey Home*, 159–172; Steven Horowitz and Miriam Landsman, "The Americanization of Edna: A Study of Ms. Ferber's Jewish American Identity," *Studies in American Jewish Literature* 2 (1982): 69–80; Ann Shapiro, "Edna Ferber, Jewish American Feminist," *Shofar* 20.2 (2002): 52–60; and Eileen Watts, "Edna Ferber, Jewish American Writer: Who Knew?" in *Modern Jewish Women Writers in America*, ed. Evelyn Avery (New York: Palgrave Macmillan, 2007), 41–61.

37. Cited in "Edna Ferber, Novelist, 82, Dies," *New York Times*, April 17, 1968.

38. Joel Porte, review of *Writing Their Nations: The Tradition of Nineteenth-Century American Jewish Women Writers*, by Diane Lichtenstein, *AJS Review* 20.1 (1995): 264.

39. On Ferber's intent to satirize the western, see Ferber, *Peculiar Treasure*, 339.

40. Harold Bloom, *Jewish Women Fiction Writers* (Philadelphia: Chelsea House, 1998), 16.

41. Ferber, *Peculiar Treasure*, 340, 344.

42. Lewis Nichols, "Talk with Edna Ferber," *New York Times*, October 5, 1952.

43. For more on Ferber's film adaptations, see J. E. Smyth, *Edna Ferber's Hollywood: American Fictions of Gender, Race, and History* (Austin: University of Texas Press, 2009).

44. "Edna Ferber, Novelist, 82, Dies."

45. In 1930, for example, the merits of her prose were debated in the pages of the *English Journal*. See William Allen White, "A Friend's Story of Edna Ferber," *English Journal* 19.2 (February 1930): 101–106; and William R. Parker, "A Stranger's Story of Edna Ferber," *English Journal* 19.6 (June 1930): 447–449. For an additional positive evaluation of Ferber's career up until the release of *Show Boat*, the novel that earns her the reputation as "the keenest social critic among our fiction writers," see Grant Overton, "The Social Critic in Edna Ferber," *Bookman* 64 (October 1926): 138.

46. F. Scott Fitzgerald to Maxwell Perkins, January 10, 1920, in *Dear Scott/Dear Max: The Fitzgerald-Perkins Correspondence*, ed. John Kuehl and Jackson Bryer (New York: Scribner's, 1971), 25. Known for his ironic, trick endings, O. Henry denoted tightly crafted formulaic fiction that suffered even more from doses of sentimentality. For modernists like Fitzgerald, who shunned the prioritizing of plot (and clever plot twists) above formal innovation, O. Henry was synonymous with hack writer. Fitzgerald was far from the only critic to align Ferber with O. Henry, the pseudonym of turn-of-the-century short story writer William Sydney Porter. As Christopher Wilson has shown, it is likely that Ferber consciously adopted O. Henry as a role model, especially in her early fables, which focused on ordinary people and were aimed at mass magazine readership. See Christopher Wilson, *White Collar Fictions* (Athens: University of Georgia Press, 1992), 56–94.

47. F. Scott Fitzgerald, *This Side of Paradise*, in *F. Scott Fitzgerald: Novels and Stories, 1920–1922* (New York: Library of America, 2000), 188.

48. Nichols, "Talk with Edna Ferber." Ferber also discusses some of her limitations as a writer, especially her tendency toward purple prose, in the first chapter of *A Kind of Magic*.

49. Dwight MacDonald, "Masscult and Midcult," *Partisan Review* 27.2 (1960): 203–233.

50. Joan Shelley Rubin, *The Making of Middlebrow Culture* (Chapel Hill: University of North Carolina Press, 1992); Janice Radway, *A Feeling for Books: The Book-of-the-Month Club, Literary Taste, and Middle-Class Desire* (Chapel Hill: University of North Carolina Press, 1997). Spearheaded by feminist critics, this project of recuperating middlebrow literature has its roots in the recoveries of works by nineteenth-century sentimental women writers that began in the 1970s. Although Fitzgerald places Ferber within a patriarchal tradition as a descendant of O. Henry, his comments are reminiscent of the commonly cited opinions that nineteenth-century male writers held of their female counterparts, authors like Harriet Beecher Stowe and Louisa May Alcott, who might be considered Ferber's foremothers. Most famously, in an 1855 letter to his publisher, Nathaniel Hawthorne complained of Stowe and her ilk: "America is now wholly given over to a damned mob of scribbling women, and I should have no chance of success while the public taste is occupied with their trash—and should be ashamed of myself if I did succeed. . . . Worse they could not be, and better they need not be, when they sell by the hundred thousand" (cited in Fred Lewis Pattee, *The Feminine Fifties* [New York: D. Appleton-Century, 1940], 110). Hawthorne's and Fitzgerald's condemnations of women's writing as "trash" are in part motivated by envy; successfully tapping into the mind-sets and fantasies of their female readers, writers like Stowe and Ferber enjoyed commercial success and accompanying financial rewards.

51. Lisa Botshon and Meredith Goldsmith, eds., introduction to *Middlebrow Moderns: Popular American Women Writers of the 1920s* (Boston: Northeastern University Press, 2003), 3–21.

52. For more on the links between progressive politics and middlebrow women's fiction in the interwar period, see Jaime Harker, *America the Middlebrow: Women's Novels, Progressivism, and Middlebrow Authorship between the Wars* (Boston: University of Massachusetts Press, 2007).

53. Jonathan Freedman, *The Temple of Culture: Assimilation and Anti-Semitism in Literary Anglo-America* (New York: Oxford University Press, 2000), 174.

54. In *The Modern Jewish Canon*, for example, Ruth Wisse includes Ferber on a list of writers whose art is so devoid of "*Jewish* energy . . . that one could invent parlor games over the ethnic or religious identity of its authors." See Ruth Wisse, *The Modern Jewish Canon* (New York: Free Press, 2000), 25. This view was also espoused in Ferber's own time. A 1930 essay surveying representations of Jews in American fiction, for example, notes that Jewish writers who "might have revealed the Jew have preferred, with some profit to themselves, to exploit the American folkways, as Miss Edna Ferber has done in *Show Boat* and *Cimarron*." See Florence Kiper Frank, "The Presentment of the Jew in American Fiction," *Bookman* 71 (June 1930): 270. For further discussion of Ferber's marginalization in Jewish American literature, see Horowitz and Landsman, "Americanization of Edna," 69–80. Though this article was published in 1982, most of the points remain applicable. The title of an essay published as recently as 2007 by Eileen Watts may say it all: "Edna Ferber, Jewish American Writer: Who Knew?"

55. Shapiro, "Edna Ferber, Jewish American Feminist," 52–60; Watts, "Edna Ferber, Jewish American Writer," 41–61; Antler, *Journey Home*, 150–172. Other discussions of Ferber's work in the context of Jewish women's writing can be found in Janet

Burstein, *Writing Mothers, Writing Daughters* (Urbana: University of Illinois Press, 1996); and Diane Lichtenstein, *Writing Their Nations: The Tradition of Nineteenth-Century American Jewish Women Writers* (Bloomington: Indiana University Press, 1992), 129–141. A somewhat dated consideration of Ferber's portrayal of women that does not take into account issues of Jewish identity can be found in Mary Rose Shaughnessy, *Women and Success in American Society in the Works of Edna Ferber* (New York: Gordon Press, 1977).

56. Ferber, *Peculiar Treasure*, 289.

57. Irving Howe, *World of Our Fathers* (New York: Harcourt Brace Jovanovich, 1976), 563.

58. Louis Kronenberger, "'Show Boat' Is High Romance," *New York Times*, August 22, 1926.

59. Fanny Butcher, "Edna Ferber and 'Show Boat' Due for Praise Friday," *Chicago Daily Tribune*, August 14, 1926.

60. Langston Hughes, "The Negro Artist and the Racial Mountain," in *The Portable Harlem Renaissance Reader*, ed. David Levering Lewis (New York: Penguin, 1994), 93.

61. Douglas, *Terrible Honesty*, 76–77; Michael North, *The Dialect of Modernism: Race, Language, and Twentieth-Century Literature* (New York: Oxford University Press, 1994); George Hutchinson, *The Harlem Renaissance in Black and White* (Cambridge, Mass.: Harvard University Press, 1995). Of these critics, the only one to specifically mention *Show Boat*, albeit briefly, is Douglas. For a historical treatment of the era, see David Levering Lewis, *When Harlem Was in Vogue* (New York: Penguin, 1997).

62. Langston Hughes, *The Big Sea* (New York: Hill and Wang, 1940), 223.

63. An accurate transcription of *Show Boat*'s lyrics can be found in Amy Asch, ed., *The Complete Lyrics of Oscar Hammerstein II* (New York: Alfred A. Knopf, 2008). The song itself has been a point of contention in black-Jewish cultural relations. Though it appears to be a song of resignation, Paul Robeson's performances also transformed it into a song of protest, in part by changing the most problematic lyrics, as discussed above. In a comic sketch, comedian Phil Silvers depicts Jerome Kern teaching Paul Robeson how to sing "Ol' Man River"—the irony being, of course, that the song is supposed to be "authentically" black; in the sketch, "Robeson" interrupts the lesson to ask what "taters" are, which gets at the fact that the vernacular of "Ol' Man River" and other such white appropriations was not authentic at all. A description of Silvers's sketch can be found in Gerald Bordman, *Jerome Kern: His Life and Music* (New York: Oxford University Press, 1980), 400. Further analysis of the sketch can be found in a chapter on Robeson in Richard Dyer, *Heavenly Bodies: Film Stars and Society* (New York: Routledge, 2004), 64–136.

64. Ferber, *Show Boat*, 2, 3.

65. Ibid., 7–8.

66. Ibid., 2.

67. Ibid., 20, 21.

68. Ibid., 46.

69. Ibid., 22, 19.

70. Ibid., 287, 88.

71. Ibid., 157.

72. Ibid., 166.

73. Ibid., 158.

74. For a discussion of historical incidents that inspired this scene in Ferber's novel, see Stephen Talty, *Mulatto America* (New York: HarperCollins, 2003), 51–73.

75. Ferber, *Show Boat*, 109.

76. Susan Gubar, "Jewish American Women Writers and the Race Question," in *The Cambridge Companion to Jewish American Literature*, ed. Hana Wirth-Nesher and Michael P. Kramer (New York: Cambridge University Press, 2003), 234.

77. Two anthologies, in particular, offer insight into the diverse approaches scholars have taken to the topic of passing. Elaine Ginsberg's *Passing and the Fictions of Identity* (Durham, N.C.: Duke University Press, 1996) focuses largely on narratives of racial passing, while Maria Carla Sanchez and Linda Schlossberg's *Passing: Identity and Interpretation in Sexuality, Race, and Religion* (New York: New York University Press, 2001) covers a variety of approaches. Influential scholarship on the literature of passing includes Werner Sollors, *Neither Black Nor White Yet Both* (Cambridge, Mass.: Harvard University Press, 1999), 246–284; Pamela Caughie, *Passing and Pedagogy: The Dynamics of Responsibility* (Urbana: University of Illinois Press, 1999); Gayle Wald, *Crossing the Line: Racial Passing in Twentieth-Century U.S. Literature and Culture* (Durham, N.C.: Duke University Press, 2000); Kathleen Pfeiffer, *Race Passing and American Individualism* (Boston: University of Massachusetts Press, 2003); Julie Cary Nerad, "Slippery Language and False Dilemmas: The Passing Novels of Child, Howells, and Harper," *American Literature* 75.4 (December 2003): 813–841; Wendy Doniger, *The Woman Who Pretended to Be Who She Was: Myths of Self-Imitation* (New York: Oxford University Press, 2005); and Martha Cutter, "An Intricate Act of Passing: Strategies of Racial and Textual Subversion in Charles Chesnutt's 'The Passing of Grandison,'" *CEA Critic* 70.2 (2008): 46–56. Baz Dreisinger's recent contribution, *Near Black: White-to-Black Passing in American Culture* (Amherst: University of Massachusetts Press, 2008), focuses on whites who pass for black, a topic also taken up in Wald.

78. See, for example, Lori Harrison-Kahan, "Passing for White, Passing for Jewish: Mixed Race Identity in Danzy Senna and Rebecca Walker," *MELUS* 30.1 (2005): 19–48; Jennifer Glaser, "The Jew in the Canon: Reading Race and Literary History in Philip Roth's *The Human Stain*," *PMLA* 123.5 (October 2008): 1465–1478; and Jonathan Freedman, *Klezmer America: Jewishness, Ethnicity, Modernity* (New York: Columbia University Press, 2007), chapter 4.

79. Daniel Itzkovitz, "Passing Like Me: Jewish Chameleonism and the Politics of Race," in Sanchez and Schlossberg, *Passing*, 45, 39.

80. Daniel Itzkovitz, "Secret Temples," in *Jews and Other Differences*, ed. Jonathan Boyarin and Daniel Boyarin (Minneapolis: University of Minnesota Press, 1997), 177.

81. See, for example, Warren Hoffman, *The Passing Game: Queering Jewish American Culture* (New York: Syracuse University Press, 2009); Melanie Levinson, "'To Make Myself for a Person': 'Passing' Narratives and the Divided Self in the Work of Anzia Yezierska," *Studies in American Jewish Literature* 13 (1994): 2–9; and Meredith Goldsmith, "Dressing, Passing, and Americanizing: Anzia Yezierska's Sartorial Fictions," *Studies in American Jewish Literature* 16 (1997): 34–45. Studies that consider Jewish and African American literature alongside each other through the lens of passing include Adam Zachary Newton, "Incognito Ergo Sum: 'Ex' Marks the Spot in Cahan, Johnson, Larsen, and Yezierska," in *Race and the Modern Artist*, ed. Heather

Hathaway, Josef Jarab, and Jeffrey Melnick (New York: Oxford University Press, 2003), 140–183; Martin Japtok, *Growing Up Ethnic: Nationalism and the Bildungsroman in African American and Jewish American Fiction* (Iowa City: University of Iowa Press, 2005); Steven Belluscio, *To Be Suddenly White: Literary Realism and Racial Passing* (Columbia: University of Missouri Press, 2006); and Catherine Rottenberg, *Performing Americanness: Race, Class, and Gender in Modern African-American and Jewish-American Literature* (Hanover, N.H.: Dartmouth University Press, 2008).

82. Rottenberg, *Performing Americanness*, 6. For an important discussion of the theatricality of assimilation, see also Most, *Making Americans*, 101–118.

83. Ferber, *Show Boat*, 69.

84. See, for example, Werner Sollors's discussion of fingernails as a racial sign in *Neither Black Nor White Yet Both*, 142–161.

85. Mark Twain, *Pudd'nhead Wilson* (1894; repr., New York: Bantam Dell, 2005), 8.

86. Ferber, *Show Boat*, 109, 110–111.

87. Ferber includes a brief discussion of racist language in Edna Ferber, "Remedies for Hate," *English Journal* 35.6 (June 1946): 320–322.

88. Williams, *Playing the Race Card*, 182.

89. Ferber, *Show Boat*, 116.

90. Philip, *Showing Grit*, 24.

91. Ferber, *Show Boat*, 269.

92. Ibid., 275, 276.

93. Ibid., 275.

94. Ibid.

95. On the motif of homecoming in passing narratives, see Wald, *Crossing the Line*, 25–52.

96. Ferber, *Show Boat*, 301–302, 303. Not surprisingly, this finale was significantly altered in the musical and film versions because it does not fit the Hollywood prototype for a happy ending. Instead of killing off Gaylord, Hammerstein reunites husband and wife at the end of the musical. In the 1936 film version, Magnolia never returns to the showboat; the film ends with the reunion of Magnolia and Gaylord at one of their daughter's performances. In quite a different move (which is telling of the dominant ideologies of their times), the 1951 film does not even allow Magnolia to reach stardom; she returns with her daughter to what is suggested will be a *domestic* life on the showboat, where she is soon reunited with her wayward husband.

97. Edna Ferber, *Saratoga Trunk* (1941; repr., New York: HarperCollins, 1968), 14, 37.

98. Ibid., 37.

99. Ibid., 87.

100. Ibid., 190.

101. Ibid., 250.

102. Ibid., 96.

103. Ibid., 275–277. The 1945 film adaptation of *Saratoga Trunk*, starring Ingrid Bergman as Clio and Gary Cooper as Clint, leaves out the blackface scene.

104. Ibid., 100.

105. Langston Hughes, "Some Practical Observations: A Colloquy," *Phylon* 11 (Winter 1950): 307–311, repr. in *The Collected Works of Langston Hughes*, vol. 9, ed. Christopher De Santis (Columbia: University of Missouri Press, 2002), 310. Hughes also recommends Ferber as a possible model for black writing in his 1946 essay "It's

About Time," in which he urges black writers to write about Negroes "who do *not* come to a bad end." See Langston Hughes, "It's About Time" (May 22, 1946), repr. in *Collected Works of Langston Hughes*, vol. 9. For Hughes's discussion of Ferber as an early literary influence, see Hughes, *Big Sea*, 33–34.

3 / Limitations of White

1. Correspondence between Hurst and *Pictorial Review* editor T. Von Ziekursch indicates that Hurst was not happy with the magazine's decision to change her title, *Imitation of Life*, to "Sugar House" and tried to get the magazine to change the title back before the issue with the first installment went to press. Von Ziekursch reassures Hurst that "Sugar House" is a "swell and grand title." T. Von Ziekursch to Fannie Hurst (FH), August 23, 1932, Box 154, Folder 4, Fannie Hurst Papers, Harry Ransom Center (HRC), University of Texas at Austin.

2. Florence L. Strauss to FH, October 6, 1932, Box 154, Folder 4, Fannie Hurst Papers, HRC. This folder contains extensive correspondence between Hurst and the various movie studios about the rights to *Imitation of Life*. For a full discussion of *Imitation of Life* and the Production Code, see Susan Courtney, *Hollywood Fantasies of Miscegenation* (Princeton, N.J.: Princeton University Press, 2005), 142–190.

3. As evidence of the popularity of *Imitation of Life* among film critics, a volume of the Rutgers Films in Print series is dedicated to the film with a focus on Sirk's 1959 version. See Lucy Fischer, ed., *Imitation of Life* (New Brunswick, N.J.: Rutgers University Press, 1991). In addition to the essays collected in this volume, see Jane Caputi, "Questions of Race and Place: Comparative Racism in *Imitation of Life* and *Places in the Heart*," *Cineaste* 15 (1987): 16–21; Michael Selig, "Contradiction and Reading: Social Class and Sex Class in *Imitation of Life*," *Wide Angle* 10.4 (1988): 13–23; Judith Butler, "Lana's 'Imitation': Melodramatic Repetition and the Gender Performative," *Genders* 9 (Fall 1990): 1–18; Mary Ann Doane, *Femmes Fatales: Feminism, Film Theory, Psychoanalysis* (New York: Routledge, 1991), 209–248; bell hooks, "The Oppositional Gaze: Black Female Spectators," in *Black Looks: Race and Representation* (Boston: South End Press, 1992), 115–131; Richard Henke, "Imitation World of Vaudeville," *Jump Cut* 39 (1994): 31–39; Marianne Conroy, "'No Sin in Lookin' Prosperous': Gender, Race, and the Class Formations of Middlebrow Taste in Douglas Sirk's *Imitation of Life*," in *The Hidden Foundation*, ed. David E. James and Rick Berg (Minneapolis: University of Minnesota Press, 1996), 114–137; Miriam Thaggert, "Divided Images: Black Female Spectatorship and John Stahl's *Imitation of Life*," *African American Review* 32.3 (1998): 481–491; Adrienne Johnson Gosselin, "Racial Etiquette and the (White) Plot of Passing: (Re)Inscribing 'Place' in John Stahl's *Imitation of Life*," *Canadian Review of American Studies* 28.3 (1998): 47–67; Peter Verstraeten, "The (Dis)Illusion of White Masquerade: An Overidentification with Stock Images in Sirk's Melodrama *Imitation of Life* (1959)," *Thamyris* 7 (Summer 2000): 201–213; Tina M. Harris and Deidra Donmoyer, "Is Art Imitating Life? Communicating Gender and Racial Identity in *Imitation of Life*," *Women's Studies in Communication* 23.1 (Winter 2000): 91–110; Matthew H. Bernstein and Dana F. White, "*Imitation of Life* in a Segregated Atlanta: Its Promotion, Distribution, and Reception," *Film History* 19 (2007): 152–178; and Hiram Perez, "Two or Three Spectacular Mulatas and the Queer Pleasure of Overidentification," *Camera Obscura* 23.1 (2008): 113–143. Scholarship that compares the two film versions through the lens of motherhood includes E. Ann Kaplan, *Motherhood and*

Representation: The Mother in Popular Culture and Melodrama (New York: Routledge, 1992); and Ruth Feldstein, *Motherhood in Black and White: Race, Sex, and American Liberalism 1930–1965* (Ithaca, N.Y.: Cornell University Press, 2000). An important comparison of Hurst's novel to both of its film adaptations can be found in Lauren Berlant, *The Female Complaint: The Unfinished Business of Sentimentality in American Culture* (Durham, N.C.: Duke University Press, 2008), 107–144, originally published as "National Brand/National Body: *Imitation of Life*," in *Comparative American Identities*, ed. Hortense Spillers (New York: Routledge, 1991), 110–140.

4. Claude McKay, *A Long Way from Home* (New York: Furman, 1937), 112.

5. Sterling A. Brown, "*Imitation of Life*: Once a Pancake," *Opportunity: Journal of Negro Life* 12.3 (March 1935): 87–88.

6. "Miss Fannie Hurst," letter to the editor, *Opportunity* 13.4 (April 1935): 121. For correspondence between Hurst and *Opportunity* about her response to Brown, see Box 189, Folder 5, Fannie Hurst Papers, HRC.

7. Donald Bogle, *Toms, Coons, Mulattoes, Mammies and Bucks* (New York: Viking Press, 1973), 57–60; Anna Everett, *Returning the Gaze: A Genealogy of Black Film Criticism, 1909–1949* (Durham, N.C.: Duke University Press, 2001), 218–232.

8. A modest and growing Hurst revival is in evidence. This effort has been spearheaded by Susan Koppelman, who started the Fannie Hurst Society in the early 1990s and published the *Fannie Hurst Newsletter* from 1991 to 1995. Koppelman also edited the recently published *The Stories of Fannie Hurst* (New York: Feminist Press, 2004). Brooke Kroeger's thoroughly researched biography, *Fannie: The Talent for Success of Writer Fannie Hurst* (New York: Random House, 1999), has spurred further interest in the author. The only full-length work of literary criticism on Hurst is Abe C. Ravitz, *Imitations of Life: Fannie Hurst's Gaslight Sonatas* (Carbondale: University of Southern Illinois Press, 1997). General studies of Hurst include Ellen Serlen Uffen, "The Novels of Fannie Hurst: Notes Toward a Definition of Popular Fiction," *Journal of American Culture* 1 (1978): 574–583; Cynthia Ann Brandimarte, "Fannie Hurst: A Missouri Girl Makes Good," *Missouri Historical Review* 81 (April 1987): 275–295; Diane Lichtenstein, "Fannie Hurst and Her Nineteenth-Century Predecessors," *Studies in American Jewish Literature* 7 (1988): 26–39; and Susan Koppelman, "Fannie Hurst," *Belles Lettres* (Fall 1994): 72–76. One of the few works of literary criticism to focus solely on Hurst's *Imitation of Life* is Priscilla Leder, "Sugar Hearts: Female Power in Fannie Hurst's *Imitation of Life*," *Journal of the American Studies Association of Texas* 31 (October 2000): 47–63.

9. Here, I play on Homi Bhabha's famous formulation, "almost the same but not quite," in "Of Mimicry and Man." See Homi Bhabha, *The Location of Culture* (New York: Routledge, 1994), 85–92.

10. On Hurst's ambivalence toward her Jewish identity, see Joyce Antler, *The Journey Home: Jewish Women and the American Century* (New York: Free Press, 1997), 161–166.

11. "Fannie Hurst, Popular Author of Romantic Stories, Dies at 78," *New York Times*, February 24, 1968. The term "sob sister" comes from the title of one of Hurst's own stories. For a reading of this and other Hurst stories that challenges the view of her as a sentimental writer for the masses, see Susan Koppelman, "Fannie Hurst's Short Stories of Working Women—'Oats for the Woman,' 'Sob Sister,' and Contemporary Reader Responses: A Meditation," in *American Women Short Story Writers*, ed. Julie Brown (New York: Garland, 1995), 137–150.

12. "Fannie Hurst, Popular Author of Romantic Stories, Dies at 78"; T. Von Ziekursch to FH, May 31, 1932, Box 154, Folder 4, Fannie Hurst Papers, HRC.

13. Susan Koppelman, introduction to *Stories of Fannie Hurst*; Stephanie Lewis Thompson, *Influencing America's Tastes: Realism in the Works of Wharton, Cather, and Hurst* (Gainesville: University Press of Florida, 2002); Ann Douglas, *Terrible Honesty: Mongrel Manhattan in the 1920s* (New York: Farrar, Straus, Giroux, 1995), 500.

14. "She Chose to Suffer!" advertisement for King Features Syndicate, Inc., Box 252, Folder 2, Fannie Hurst Papers, HRC.

15. Antler, *Journey Home*, 169; Beatrice Kean Seymour, "World's Highest Paid Short Story Writer Joins Everybody's," *Everybody's Weekly*, June 2, 1928, 15, Box 252, Folder 2, Fannie Hurst Papers, HRC.

16. "Business Woman," *New York Times Book Review*, February 5, 1933, 7:4, 14:1. Several critics have noted comparisons between Stein and Hurst. Ann Douglas makes the comparison, albeit qualifiedly, when she labels Hurst a "Steinian of sorts" in the bibliographic essay of *Terrible Honesty*, 500. See also Lisa Botshon and Meredith Goldsmith, introduction to *Middlebrow Moderns: Popular American Women Writers of the 1920s* (Boston: Northeastern University Press, 2003). For a reading of *Lummox* that is attentive to Hurst's "Steinian" literary techniques, see Thompson, *Influencing America's Tastes*, 155–193.

17. *San Francisco Chronicle*, December 21, 1926, in Fannie Hurst Scrapbook II, HRC.

18. Gladys Baker, "Fannie Hurst on Marriage," *Birmingham News*, February 3, 1929, in Box 252, Folder 2, Fannie Hurst Papers, HRC.

19. "Fannie Hurst Wed, Hid Secret 5 Years," *New York Times*, May 4, 1920.

20. Douglas, *Terrible Honesty*, 500.

21. Exceptions include June Sochen, *Consecrate Every Day: The Public Lives of Jewish American Women, 1880–1980* (Albany: State University of New York Press, 1981), 84–113; Diane Lichtenstein, "Fannie Hurst and Her Nineteenth-Century Predecessors," *Studies in American Jewish Literature* 7 (1988): 26–39; and Janet Burstein, *Writing Mothers, Writing Daughters: Tracing the Maternal in Stories by American Jewish Women* (Urbana: University of Illinois Press, 1996).

22. Secondary Jewish characters, however, do make frequent appearances throughout Hurst's work; examples include the Jewish family that employs Bertha as a domestic servant in *Lummox* and Ray's lover in *Back Street*.

23. As Susan Koppelman discusses, Hurst, an American-born Jew of German descent, did not speak or write Yiddish; thus, the accents of Hurst's Jewish immigrant characters are rendered through English dialect spellings rather than Yiddish or Yinglish. See Koppelman, introduction to *Stories of Fannie Hurst*, xxii.

24. In fact, while Hurst is rarely more than a footnote in Jewish literary history today, early in her career she was decreed the newest member of an emerging group of Jewish writers. Fitzgerald may have denigrated her as a "Yiddish descendant of O. Henry," but influential writer and editor William Dean Howells, who had nurtured the fiction-writing career of journalist Abraham Cahan, took a more positive view when he identified her in 1915 as the latest "writer of the Hebraic school." Comparing the stories of her 1914 collection, *Just Around the Corner*, to the work of Cahan, Israel Zangwill, and Montague Glass, Howells wrote that Hurst "shows the same artistic qualities, the same instinct for reality, the same confident recognition of the

superficial cheapness and commonness of the stuff she handles." Hurst's 1919 short story collection, *Humoresque*, brought similar encomia. "No American author today can interpret the life of the Jewish people with the humor, the pathos and the delicacy of this young author," wrote Frieda Friedman of *Humoresque* in the *Jewish Tribune*. "I like to think of her as the interpreter of the Jews to Christian America, as Israel's contribution to American literature." In 1922, the *Jewish Tribune* reprinted an excerpt from "Roulette," a short story about a Vodna pogrom that appeared in Hurst's collection *The Vertical City*, promoting the author as a "true daughter of Israel" with a "deep race consciousness" and the story itself as "a passionate Jewish outburst against the age-long sufferings and sorrows of her race." See W. D. Howells, "Editor's Easy Chair," *Harper's Monthly Magazine*, May 1915, 959, in Fannie Hurst Scrapbook XXXVII, HRC; Frieda Friedman, "Fannie Hurst's Success," *Jewish Tribune*, July 10, 1925, n.p., in Fannie Hurst Scrapbook II, HRC; and Fannie Hurst, "When the Pogrom Came to Vodna," *Jewish Tribune*, April 7, 1922, 1. One of the few studies to consider Hurst alongside Yezierska is Carol Batker, *Reforming Fictions: Native, African, and Jewish American Women's Literature and Journalism in the Progressive Era* (New York: Columbia University Press, 2000), 108-130.

25. Ray Long to FH, September 21, 1912, cited in Ravitz, *Imitations of Life*, 18.

26. For example, Michael Rogin's claim that Hurst passed for gentile appears in *Blackface, White Noise: Jewish Immigrants in the Hollywood Melting Pot* (Berkeley: University of California Press, 1996), 123, and is often cited by other critics. See also Tiffany Patterson, *Zora Neale Hurston and a History of Southern Life* (Philadelphia: Temple University Press, 2005), 165-170. Hurst's relationship to passing is complex. She never went to great lengths to obscure her Jewish identity, and based on my research, her Jewish background remained public knowledge throughout her life; at the same time, given her success and high degree of assimilation, she was at times taken for gentile, and she may have passed on occasion—for example, as I will discuss, by dining in restricted restaurants that excluded Jewish clientele.

27. H. Allen Smith, "Behaviorist Defends Christmas against Fannie Hurst's Attacks," *Rocky Mountain News*, December 20, 1929, in Fannie Hurst Scrapbook III, HRC; Program for Statue of Liberty Anniversary Dinner, "A Tribute to the Contributions of the Foreign Born to America," October 27, 1946, in Fannie Hurst Scrapbook XXII, HRC; Rabbi Abraham Burstein to FH, November 30, 1961, Box 156, Folder 1, Fannie Hurst Papers, HRC. Correspondence between Hurst and Louis Harap, managing editor of the *Jewish Survey*, and between Hurst and the Jewish Publication Society can be found in Box 156, Folder 3, Fannie Hurst Papers, HRC.

28. Nathaniel Zalowitz to FH, June 7, 1949, Box 156, Folder 1, Fannie Hurst Papers, HRC.

29. Frieda Friedman, "Fannie Hurst's Success," *Jewish Tribune*, July 10, 1925, n.p., in Fannie Hurst Scrapbook II, HRC.

30. Joseph Brainin, "Fannie Hurst—The Jewess," *Jewish Standard: Canadian Jewish Weekly*, January 30, 1931, in Fannie Hurst Scrapbook IV, HRC. Eric Goldstein offers a useful and applicable discussion of the ways that Jewish women adopted racial language to express their Jewish identities. See Eric Goldstein, *The Price of Whiteness: Jews, Race, and American Identity* (Princeton, N.J.: Princeton University Press, 2006), 11-31.

31. For discussions of the relationship between Hurst and Hurston, see Virginia

Burke, "Zora Neale Hurston and Fannie Hurst as They Saw Each Other," *CLA Journal* 20 (1977): 435–447; Gay Wilentz, "White Patron and Black Artist: The Correspondence of Fannie Hurst and Zora Neale Hurston," *Library Chronicle of the University of Texas* 35 (1986): 21–43; Jane Caputi, "'Specifying' Fannie Hurst: Langston Hughes's 'Limitations of Life,' Zora Neale Hurston's *Their Eyes Were Watching God*, and Toni Morrison's *The Bluest Eye* as 'Answers' to Hurst's *Imitation of Life*," *Black American Literature Forum* 24.4 (1990): 697–716; and Patterson, *Zora Neale Hurston*, 1–3, 165–170. Kroeger discusses this relationship in some detail in her biography of Hurst, as do Hurston's biographers. See, for example, Robert Hemenway, *Zora Neale Hurston: A Literary Biography* (Urbana: University of Illinois Press, 1977); and Valerie Boyd, *Wrapped in Rainbows: The Life of Zora Neale Hurston* (New York: Scribner, 2003).

32. Langston Hughes, *The Big Sea* (New York: Hill and Wang, 1940), 225.

33. Zora Neale Hurston, "How It Feels to Be Colored Me," in *Folklore, Memoirs, and Other Writings*, ed. Cheryl A. Wall (New York: Library of America, 1995), 828, 829.

34. A list of the contents of Hurst's library can be found in Box 273, Folder 4, Fannie Hurst Papers, HRC.

35. Alain Locke, "The New Negro" (1925), repr. in *The Norton Anthology of African American Literature* (New York: W. W. Norton, 2003), 984–993.

36. Although Van Vechten's novel was praised by some black writers, including Langston Hughes, James Weldon Johnson, and Zora Neale Hurston, for its positive portrayal of middle-class black intellectuals (Hughes maintained that it was an accurate depiction of "a whole rainbow of life above 110th Street," while Hurston found its portrait of "Negroes of wealth and culture" to be "written in the deepest sincerity"), it was attacked by others for upholding caricatures of primitive blacks. In the opinion of W.E.B. Du Bois, for example, Van Vechten's portrayal of Harlem was "neither truthful nor artistic." Hughes's views on *Nigger Heaven* are cited in Jervis Anderson, *This Was Harlem* (New York: Farrar, Straus, Giroux, 1981), 219–220; Du Bois's opinion can be found in "Critiques of Carl Van Vechten's *Nigger Heaven*," in *The Portable Harlem Renaissance Reader*, ed. David Levering Lewis (New York: Penguin, 1994), 106–109; Hurston's comments appear in Zora Neale Hurston, "What White Publishers Won't Print," in Wall, *Folklore, Memoirs, and Other Writings*, 954.

37. FH to Carl Van Vechten, November 15, 1943, Box 237, Folder 4, Fannie Hurst Papers, HRC.

38. Van Vechten to H. L. Mencken, May 29, 1925, H. L. Mencken Collection, Manuscript Division, New York Public Library, cited in David Levering Lewis, *When Harlem Was in Vogue* (New York: Penguin, 1997), 98.

39. Lewis, *When Harlem Was in Vogue*, 100. See also David Levering Lewis, "Parallels and Divergences: Assimilationist Strategies of Afro-American and Jewish Elites from 1910 to the Early 1930s," in *Bridges and Boundaries: African Americans and American Jews*, ed. Jack Salzman (New York: Jewish Museum, 1991), 17–35.

40. Cheryl Lynn Greenberg, *Troubling the Waters: Black-Jewish Relations in the American Century* (Princeton, N.J.: Princeton University Press, 2006).

41. Hasia Diner, *In the Almost Promised Land: American Jews and Blacks, 1915–1935* (Baltimore: Johns Hopkins University Press, 1977), 237, 136. On this point, see also Michael Alexander, *Jazz Age Jews* (Princeton, N.J.: Princeton University Press, 2001).

42. Goldstein, *Price of Whiteness*, 70, 3.

43. Hurst, *Anatomy of Me*, 350.

44. "Air Bias Question," *New York Amsterdam News*, August 16, 1947.

45. Hurst, *Anatomy of Me*, 350.

46. Fannie Hurst, "Our Wayside Trees Are Gibbets," *Crisis* (January 1935): 7.

47. Proceedings of the Annual Dinner Meeting, New York Urban League, January 13, 1937, HRC.

48. FH to Belle Davis, July 23, 1938, Box 189, Folder 3, Fannie Hurst Papers, HRC.

49. See Wilentz, "White Patron and Black Artist"; and Burke, "Zora Neale Hurston and Fannie Hurst." Hurst's problematic views of Hurston are also in evidence in the lukewarm Guggenheim recommendation she wrote for her in 1933; the letter contains ample praise but also comments on Hurston's "natural" and "humble" characteristics as well as her "erratic" and "undisciplined" work ethic. (Needless to say, Hurston did not receive a fellowship that year.) For transcriptions of Hurst's recommendation and introduction to *Jonah's Gourd Vine*, see Carla Kaplan, ed., *Zora Neale Hurston: A Life in Letters* (New York: Doubleday, 2002), 284–285.

50. Proceedings of the Annual Dinner Meeting, New York Urban League, January 13, 1937.

51. Cited in Kroeger, *Fannie*, 188–189.

52. Proceedings of the Annual Dinner Meeting, New York Urban League, January 13, 1937.

53. See especially Wilentz, "White Patron and Black Artist."

54. Zora Neale Hurston, *Dust Tracks on a Road* (New York: Harper Perennial, 1942), 193.

55. Ibid., 269; Zora Neale Hurston (ZNH) to Constance Sheen, February 2, 1926, in Kaplan, *Zora Neale Hurston*, 80.

56. Hurst's support of Dorothy West is discussed in Kroeger, *Fannie*, 158. As a judge in the 1933 *Opportunity* contest, Hurst selected Marita Bonner's "A Possible Triad in Black Notes," writing that she "was struck by the power and quality of the three stories." Set in Bonner's multiethnic enclave of Frye Street, Chicago, "A Possible Triad in Black Notes" is a series of interrelated sketches, with the first two featuring mixed-race black families and the last featuring a Jewish family. Bonner did not win the contest, and Hurst expressed regret that she was unable to attend the *Opportunity* dinner since she was particularly interested in meeting Bonner. This near-relationship was indeed a missed opportunity, given that Bonner, a talented and versatile writer, remains one of the little-known women writers of the Harlem Renaissance. See FH to Elmer A. Carter, editor of *Opportunity*, April 29, 1933; and FH to Elmer A Carter, May 1, 1933, both in Box 189, Folder 5, Fannie Hurst Papers, HRC.

57. Fannie Hurst, "Zora Hurston: A Personality Sketch," in *Imitation of Life*, ed. Lucy Fischer (New Brunswick, N.J.: Rutgers University Press, 1991), 174. This essay was originally published in the *Yale University Library Gazette* 35 (1961): 17–22.

58. Langston Hughes, "Limitations of Life," in *Black Theatre USA: Plays by African Americans*, ed. James V. Hatch and Ted Shine (New York: Free Press, 1974), 632.

59. Hurst, "Zora Hurston," 174.

60. Ibid., 173.

61. Hurston, *Dust Tracks on a Road*, 195, 269.

62. ZNH to FH, January 30, 1940, in Kaplan, *Zora Neale Hurston*, 451–452.

63. FH to ZNH, February 19, 1943, Fannie Hurst Collection, Folder 1a.66, Robert D. Farber University Archives and Special Collections Department, Brandeis University.

64. Hurston, *Dust Tracks on a Road*, 194.

65. Hemenway, *Zora Neale Hurston*, 21.

66. Hurst, "Zora Hurston," 176.

67. Hurston, *Dust Tracks on a Road*, 197.

68. Ibid., 269.

69. Ibid., 197.

70. Hurst, "Zora Hurston," 174–175.

71. Ibid., 175–176.

72. In this sense, the episode shares a certain resonance with a famous scene in Nella Larsen's *Passing* (1929), in which two light-skinned African American women fatefully encounter each other as they take tea on the rooftop of a posh Chicago hotel whose doors would be barred to them if they were not masquerading as white.

73. Kroeger, *Fannie*, 194.

74. ZNH to FH, February 6, 1940, in Kaplan, *Zora Neale Hurston*, 453.

75. Proceedings of the Annual Dinner Meeting, New York Urban League, January 13, 1937.

76. Faye Jackson, "Fredi Washington Strikes New Note in Hollywood Film," *Pittsburgh Courier*, December 15, 1934, cited in Everett, *Returning the Gaze*, 221. See also Thomas Cripps, *Slow Fade to Black: The Negro in American Film, 1900–1942* (New York: Oxford University Press, 1993), 301–303.

77. Brown, "Once a Pancake."

78. Sterling Brown, *The Negro in American Fiction* (Port Washington, N.Y.: Kennikat Press, 1937), 144; Brown, "Once a Pancake."

79. Viola White Walker, Weekly Book Review, *Lawrence (Mass.) Tribune*, March 10, 1933; review of *Imitation of Life*, *New Haven (Conn.) Register*, February 12, 1933; Mary Ross, "From a Waffle Shop to a Worldwide Business: In Delilah Fannie Hurst Creates Her Finest Character since *Lummox*," *New York Herald Tribune Books*, February 5, 1933, 4.

80. "Successor to Lummox," *Christian Science Monitor*, February 25, 1933.

81. "Business Woman."

82. For analyses of Aunt Jemima that include discussions of Hurst's novel, see M. M. Manring, *Slave in a Box: The Strange Career of Aunt Jemima* (Charlottesville: University of Virginia Press, 1998); and Doris Witt, *Black Hunger: Soul Food and America* (Minneapolis: University of Minnesota Press, 2004). Although Witt challenges the reliability of previous scholarship on Aunt Jemima, she gets many of the details about Hurst's novel wrong (for example, she calls the protagonist Jewish and attributes lines from the film to the novel). Other relevant studies of Aunt Jemima include Arthur F. Marquette, ed., *Brands, Trademarks, and Good Will: The Story of the Quaker Oats Company* (New York: McGraw-Hill, 1967), 137–158; and Marilyn Kern-Forworth, *Aunt Jemima, Uncle Ben, and Rastus: Blacks in Advertising, Yesterday, Today and Tomorrow* (Westport, Conn.: Greenwood Press, 1994). On the mammy image more generally, see Barbara Christian, *Black Women Novelists* (Westport, Conn.: Greenwood Press, 1980), 7–12; Trudier Harris, *From Mammies to Militants: Domestics in Black American Literature* (Philadelphia: Temple University Press, 1982); and Kim-

berly Wallace Sanders, *Mammy: A Century of Race, Gender and Southern Memory* (Ann Arbor: University of Michigan Press, 2008).

83. Everett, *Returning the Gaze*, 192.

84. Fannie Hurst, *Imitation of Life* (1933; repr., Durham, N.C.: Duke University Press, 2004), 75.

85. Edna Ferber, *Show Boat* (1926; repr., New York: Signet, 1994), 53.

86. Hurst, *Imitation of Life*, 79.

87. Ibid., 83, 84.

88. Ibid., 143, 216.

89. Ibid., 241, 267, 273. Emphasis mine.

90. Langston Hughes to FH, July 13, 1937, Box 151, Folder 1, Fannie Hurst Papers, HRC.

91. Hurst, *Imitation of Life*, 82–83, 267.

92. Ibid., 85.

93. Ibid., 86–87.

94. Ibid., 145, 105.

95. Ibid., 117, 145.

96. Ibid., 191, 152. Emphasis mine.

97. Ibid., 74, 75, 105.

98. Zora Neale Hurston, "Glossary of Harlem Slang," in *Spunk: The Selected Stories of Zora Neale Hurston* (New York: Marlowe, 1985), 94.

99. Morrison's signification on Hurst (or at least the 1934 film adaptation of Hurst's novel) is supported by Maureen's reply when she first hears Pecola's name: "Pecola? Wasn't that the name of the girl in *Imitation of Life*? . . . The picture show . . . [w]here this mulatto girl hates her mother cause she is black and ugly but then cries at the funeral." See Toni Morrison, *The Bluest Eye* (New York: Plume 1993), 67. For more on the relationship between Hurst and Morrison, see Caputi, "'Specifying' Fannie Hurst."

100. Hurst, *Imitation of Life*, 92, 148.

101. Ibid., 118.

102. Ibid., 244.

103. Sterling Brown, "Negro Character as Seen by White Authors," *Journal of Negro Education* 2 (April 1933), repr. in *Callaloo* 14/15 (February–May 1982), 77–78.

104. Hurst, *Imitation of Life*, 246.

105. Ibid., 144.

106. Douglas Sirk's 1959 remake maintains Stahl's revised end, but is much more ambiguous, leaving the fate of Sarah Jane (Sirk's version of the Peola character) open.

107. Susan Gubar, "Jewish American Women Writers and the Race Question," in *The Cambridge Companion to Jewish American Literature*, ed. Hana Wirth-Nesher and Michael P. Kramer (New York: Cambridge University Press, 2003), 231–249. This phenomenon of Jewish women writers using the passing narrative has also been noted by Joyce Antler. See Antler, *Journey Home*, 171.

108. Sirk's transformation of the Bea Pullman character into Lora Meredith, a film and stage actress, also serves to highlight her social performances.

109. Hurst, *Imitation of Life*, 61–62.

110. Ibid., 16.

111. Ibid., 184.

112. Ibid., 151.

113. Kathy Peiss, *Hope in a Jar: The Making of America's Beauty Culture* (New York: Henry Holt, 1998), 5, 262.

114. Hurst, *Imitation of Life*, 198.

115. Ibid., 158. Emphasis mine. Lauren Berlant and Daniel Itzkovitz similarly argue that Virginia Eden's origins can be read as Jewish, although I also believe it is significant that the novel resists definitively stating the character's ethnic origins. See Berlant, *Female Complaint*, 120; and Daniel Itzkovitz, "Passing Like Me: Jewish Chameleonism and the Politics of Race," in *Passing: Identity and Interpretation in Sexuality, Race, and Religion*, ed. Maria Carla Sanchez and Linda Schlossberg (New York: New York University Press, 2001), 48.

116. Hurst, *Imitation of Life*, 36–37.

117. Ibid., 72.

118. Ibid., 157.

119. Ibid., 162, 198.

120. Ibid., 201.

121. Fannie Hurst, "The Gold in Fish," in Koppelman, *Stories of Fannie Hurst*, 258, 256–257.

122. Ibid., 275.

123. Hurst, *Imitation of Life*, 181.

124. Ibid., 292; "Imitation of Life," Box 28, Folder 3, Fannie Hurst Papers, HRC.

125. For a similar reading of the ending, which relies in more detail on differences between the draft and published versions of the novel, see Thompson, *Influencing America's Tastes*, 155–193.

126. Hurst, *Imitation of Life*, 273.

127. "A Sensation in Harlem," *New York Amsterdam News*, January 26, 1935.

128. John H. Johnson to FH, February 14, 1946, Box 189, Folder 5, Fannie Hurst Papers, HRC.

129. Fannie Hurst, "The Sure Way to Equality," *Negro Digest* (February 26, 1946): 27–28.

130. Fannie Hurst, "The Other, and Unknown, Harlem," *New York Times Magazine*, August 4, 1946, 18–19, 38–39.

4 / Moses and Minstrelsy

1. Zora Neale Hurston, "You Don't Know Us Negroes," 1934, unpublished essay written for the *American Mercury*, Manuscript Division, Library of Congress, cited in Valerie Boyd, *Wrapped in Rainbows: The Life of Zora Neale Hurston* (New York: Scribner, 2003), 267. Boyd further reads the word "flapdoodle" as a reference to "flapjacks," the featured product in *Imitation of Life* (though, as discussed in the previous chapter, it was the film adaptation that substituted pancakes for Hurst's waffles).

2. Langston Hughes, *The Big Sea* (New York: Hill and Wang, 1940), 239. I remain aware of such contradictory tendencies in my own use of Hurston's autobiographical statements and letters, especially since my intent is to explore how her cross-racial interactions *were* shaped by contradictions. Critics have attempted to make sense of the many contradictions that seem to mar Hurston's reliability as an autobiographical narrator, including her strategy of presenting herself differently to black and white audiences. Her autobiography, *Dust Tracks on a Road*, which is at times overly conciliatory toward her white supporters, has been of particular interest in this regard.

See, for example, Alice Walker, "Forward: Zora Neale Hurston—A Cautionary Tale and a Partisan View," in Robert Hemenway, *Zora Neale Hurston: A Literary Biography* (Urbana: University of Illinois Press, 1977), xi–xviii; Nellie Y. McKay, "Race, Gender, and Cultural Context in Zora Neale Hurston's *Dust Tracks on a Road*," in *Life/Lines: Theorizing Women's Autobiography*, ed. Bella Brozki and Celeste Schenck (Ithaca, N.Y.: Cornell University Press, 1988), 175–188; Pierre A. Walker, "Zora Neale Hurston and the Post-Modern Self in *Dust Tracks on a Road*," *African American Review* 32.3 (1998): 387–399; and Robert Seguin, "Cosmic Upset: Cultural Revolution and the Contradictions of Zora Neale Hurston," *Modernism/Modernity* 16.2 (2009): 229–253.

3. Zora Neale Hurston, "What White Publishers Won't Print," in *Folklore, Memoirs, and Other Writings*, ed. Cheryl A. Wall (New York: Library of America, 1995), 954.

4. Zora Neale Hurston, "Characteristics of Negro Expression," in Wall, *Folklore, Memoirs, and Other Writings*, 844–845.

5. Zora Neale Hurston (ZNH) to Claude Barnett, June 3, 1944, in *Zora Neale Hurston: A Life in Letters*, coll. and ed. Carla Kaplan (New York: Doubleday, 2002), 499. Given her feelings on the matter, it is not surprising that Hurston refused to conceal her annoyance when her white collaborator on the musical "Polk County" advised her to maintain a "sort of Gershwinesque feeling"; she replied, "You don't know what the hell you're talking about." Cited in Hemenway, *Zora Neale Hurston*, 298.

6. Cited in Hemenway, *Zora Neale Hurston*, 205.

7. Richard Wright, "Between Laughter and Tears," *New Masses* (October 5, 1937): 22–23.

8. Ibid.

9. Zora Neale Hurston, "How It Feels to Be Colored Me," in Wall, *Folklore, Memoirs, and Other Writings*, 827.

10. See, for example, Louis Chude-Sokei, *The Last "Darky": Bert Williams, Black-on-Black Minstrelsy, and the African Diaspora* (Durham, N.C.: Duke University Press, 2006); and Karen Sotiropolous, *Staging Race: Black Performers in Turn of the Century America* (Cambridge, Mass.: Harvard University Press, 2006). For a discussion of black female minstrelsy, see Jayna Brown, *Babylon Girls: Black Female Performers and the Shaping of the Modern* (Durham, N.C.: Duke University Press, 2008).

11. ZNH to Annie Nathan Meyer, July 18, 1925, in Kaplan, *Zora Neale Hurston*, 62.

12. Zora Neale Hurston, *Dust Tracks on a Road* (1942; repr., New York: HarperPerennial, 1995), 40.

13. For biographical information on Meyer, see Joyce Antler, *The Journey Home: Jewish Women and the American Century* (New York: Free Press, 1997), 63–72. Carla Kaplan's forthcoming group biography, *Miss Anne in Harlem: The White Women of the Black Renaissance*, should also shed light on this underexamined figure.

14. ZNH to Annie Nathan Meyer, July 18, 1925, in Kaplan, *Zora Neale Hurston*, 63.

15. Boyd, *Wrapped in Rainbows*, 102.

16. Hurston occasionally voiced specific concerns about Jewish theft of black folk material, though in private rather than public. In a 1931 letter to Charlotte Osgood Mason, for instance, she commented on the "ethics" of Tin Pan Alley Jews who made their living by stealing ideas from African Americans. However, this comment is made in the context of a complaint about black cultural producers who sell out: "They stand around tin-pan alley and imitate the Jews. If a Negro comes along with an idea

they attempt first to steal it & then crush the idea-bearing individual. Crush him so that he wont [sic] be around accusing them. . . . They all attempt to clean themselves with their tongues like a cat by saying 'other people do it.' And the worst of it is they choose to take their ethics from the tin-pan alley Jew, who in turn despises them for being not only petty crooks, but lacking in originality in even that" (ZNH to Charlotte Osgood Mason, October 15, 1931, in Kaplan, *Zora Neale Hurston*, 233–235). When Hurston embarked on a research expedition in 1940 to collect spirituals in South Carolina, her partner, anthropologist Jane Belo, sent her recording equipment, which, to Hurston's dismay, was accompanied by "two very enthusiastic Jews who want to take the Spirituals for commercial purposes." Refusing to "let all that swell music get away from us like that," Hurston acquiesced to showing the Jews around, but refused to take them to "the fattest and juiciest places" (cited in Hemenway, *Zora Neale Hurston*, 274–275). According to Valerie Boyd, Hurston's fears turned out to be unfounded and the collaboration with the Jewish filmmakers more fruitful than expected. See Boyd, *Wrapped in Rainbows*, 344.

17. The Rosenwald fellowship was a source of controversy as part of it was subsequently rescinded.

18. Hasia Diner explains that although their research rarely focused directly on Jews (in part, in order to maintain objectivity), these social scientists "were conscious of a direct link between Jewish identity and an interest in destroying the foundations of racism." See Hasia Diner, *In the Almost Promised Land: American Jews and Blacks, 1915–1935* (Baltimore: Johns Hopkins University Press, 1977), 149.

19. For more on the conflicting claims of Jews and blacks to be the Chosen People of God, see the primary documents and essays collected in Part 2 of Maurianne Adams and John Bracey, eds., *Strangers and Neighbors: Relations Between Blacks and Jews in the United States* (Amherst: University of Massachusetts Press, 1999).

20. Zora Neale Hurston, *Mules and Men* (1935; repr., New York: HarperPerennial, 1990), 4.

21. Hurston, "What White Publishers Won't Print," 950–955.

22. Throughout her career, Hurston read widely in Jewish history and religion, and she repeatedly turned to the Bible in her work, incorporating biblical references in her figurative language (several appear in her short story "The Gilded Six-Bits"), drawing on biblical allegories (as in "Sweat"), and rewriting biblical myths. In addition to *Moses*, she wrote a play called *The First One*, which addressed the myth of Ham, and at least one short story about Moses called "The Fire and the Cloud," which became the basis for the longer novel; several of the folktales she published were also retellings of biblical myths.

23. ZNH to Carl Van Vechten, September 12, 1945, in Kaplan, *Zora Neale Hurston*, 529–532.

24. Cited in Hemenway, *Zora Neale Hurston*, 343.

25. On Boas's experiences with anti-Semitism, see Vernon J. Williams Jr., *Rethinking Race: Franz Boas and His Contemporaries* (Lexington: University Press of Kentucky, 1996), 8–9, 104–106; and Diner, *In the Almost Promised Land*, 142–149.

26. Hurston, *Dust Tracks on a Road*, 249; Hurston, "How It Feels to Be Colored Me," 829.

27. Franz Boas, introduction to Zora Neale Hurston, *Mules and Men*, xiii.

28. Hurston, *Dust Tracks on a Road*, 143, 140.

29. Ibid., 140.

30. Diner, *In the Almost Promised Land*, 143.

31. Boyd, *Wrapped in Rainbows*, 109.

32. ZNH to Annie Nathan Meyer, July 18, 1925, in Kaplan, *Zora Neale Hurston*, 62.

33. Meyer's "Black Souls" can be found in *Strange Fruit: Plays on Lynching by American Women*, ed. Kathy A. Perkins and Judith L. Stephens (Bloomington: Indiana University Press, 1998), 138-173.

34. Annie Nathan Meyer, "The Shoe Pinches Mr. Samuels," *Crisis* (January 1935): 8-9, 24-25.

35. For more on the Frank case, see, for example, Jeffrey Melnick, *Black-Jewish Relations on Trial: Leo Frank and Jim Conley in the New South* (Jackson: University Press of Mississippi, 2000); and Diner, *In the Almost Promised Land*, 14-15.

36. ZNH to Annie Nathan Meyer, January 15, [1926], in Kaplan, *Zora Neale Hurston*, 78.

37. ZNH to Annie Nathan Meyer, October 7, 1927, in Kaplan, *Zora Neale Hurston*, 108.

38. J.H., "Inscrutable Query," *New York Times*, March 31, 1932.

39. Cited in Antler, *Journey Home*, 69.

40. ZNH to Annie Nathan Meyer, December 13, 1925, in Kaplan, *Zora Neale Hurston*, 72.

41. Cited in M. Genevieve West, *Zora Neale Hurston and American Literary Culture* (Gainesville: University Press of Florida, 2005), 165.

42. Ralph Ellison, "Recent Negro Fiction," *New Masses*, August 5, 1941, 211.

43. Andrew Delbanco, *Required Reading* (New York: Farrar, Straus, & Giroux, 1998), 104. Delbanco's statements also appeared in "The Political Incorrectness of Zora Neale Hurston," *Journal of Blacks in Higher Education* 18 (Winter 1997-1998): 103-108. Contemporary criticism on *Moses, Man of the Mountain* attempts to recuperate the novel even as it continues to draw attention to its failures. Lest I give the impression that the criticisms of Hurston's work are limited to male critics, less sympathetic to her feminist sensibility, I should note that Cheryl Wall applauds Hurston's experimentalism in *Moses* but sees the results as "disappointing," calling it a "very ambitious novel [that] fails in some respects [and] succeeds in others" (Cheryl Wall, "Zora Neale Hurston: Changing Her Own Words," in *American Novelists Revisited: Essays in Feminist Criticism*, ed. Fritz Fleischmann [Boston: G. K. Hall, 1982], 371-393). Likewise, in her introduction to the 1991 HarperPerennial reprint of *Moses*, black feminist critic Deborah McDowell deems it a "badly flawed novel" even as she argues for its importance in African American literary history (Deborah McDowell, foreword to *Moses, Man of the Mountain* [1939; repr., New York: HarperPerennial, 1991], viii). Perhaps the contention over *Moses* can best be summed up by Robert Morris's labeling of the novel as an "enigma." See Robert J. Morris, "Zora Neale Hurston's Ambitious Enigma: *Moses, Man of the Mountain*," *CLA Journal* 40.3 (March 1997): 305-335. Its enigmatic status has much to do with its form, as is often the case for Hurston's work. Like all of her fiction, *Moses* does not rest easily in a single aesthetic or political camp, but instead is driven by paradox. McDowell suggests that readers' bewilderment and frustration are a reaction to the novel's hybrid style, a "mélange of humor, conjure stories, folktales, and braided historical narratives" that "ultimately thwart[s]" Hurston's political position. Similarly attentive to form, both John Lowe

and Christine Levecq suggest that the novel has been overlooked because it unexpectedly employs humor to make its political statements. See John Lowe, *Jump at the Sun: Zora Neale Hurston's Cosmic Comedy* (Urbana: University of Illinois Press, 1994); and Christine Levecq, "'Mighty Strange Threads in Her Loom': Laughter and Subversive Heteroglossia in Zora Neale Hurston's *Moses, Man of the Mountain*," *Texas Studies in Literature and Language* 36.4 (Winter 1994): 436–461. Hurston's loyal defenders also measure her work against the minstrel tradition. Citing *Moses* as her "most ambitious work," Blyden Jackson argues that in this novel and her folklore collections leading up to it, Hurston "distanced herself . . . from blackface minstrelsy" (Blyden Jackson, "*Moses, Man of the Mountain*: A Study of Power," in *Modern Critical Views: Zora Neale Hurston*, ed. Harold Bloom [New York: Chelsea House, 1986], 152, 151).

44. Wall, "Zora Neale Hurston," 371–393. A number of critics target more specific aspects of this allegory, reading, for example, the emphasis on the character of Moses as a critique of black leadership. See Susan Meisenhelder, *Hitting a Straight Lick with a Crooked Stick: Race and Gender in the Work of Zora Neale Hurston* (Tuscaloosa: University of Alabama Press, 1999); and Ruthe T. Sheffey, "Zora Neale Hurston's *Moses, Man of the Mountain*: A Fictionalized Manifesto on the Imperatives of Black Leadership," *CLA Journal* 29.2 (December 1985): 206–220. In *Down Home* (New York: G. P. Putnam's, 1975), Robert Bone interprets it as an allegory for the Harlem Renaissance, and several other critics have pointed out that the depictions of Moses's siblings, Miriam and Aaron, are attacks on the black bourgeoisie and talented tenth.

45. See Mark Thompson, "National Socialism and Blood-Sacrifice in Zora Neale Hurston's *Moses, Man of the Mountain*," *African American Review* 38.3 (Fall 2004): 385–415; and McDowell, foreword to Hurston, *Moses*. In her study of the marketing of Hurston's fiction, M. Genevieve West notes that the source for this allegorical reading can be found in the advertising for *Moses, Man of the Mountain*; the back flap of the first edition reads: "The retelling of the story of Hebrew persecution and bondage in Egypt has special significance today because the modern Hebrew is undergoing a similar fate in some parts of the world at this time" (cited in West, *Zora Neale Hurston*, 155). Although the marketing does not specify Nazi Germany, the reference to "some parts of the world" directs the American audience away from the situation of Jews in the United States. Annie Nathan Meyer also made note of this parallel when she wrote to Lippincott in support of the novel.

46. McDowell, foreword to Hurston, *Moses*, xvi.

47. For histories of the NAACP that include some discussion of Jewish involvement, see Charles Flint Kellogg, *NAACP: A History of the National Association for the Advancement of Colored People* (Baltimore: Johns Hopkins University Press, 1967); and Patricia Sullivan, *Lift Every Voice: The NAACP and the Making of the Civil Rights Movement* (New York: New Press, 2009).

48. Daniel Itzkovitz, "Passing Like Me: Jewish Chameleonism and the Politics of Race," in *Passing: Identity and Interpretation in Sexuality, Race, and Religion*, ed. Maria Carla Sanchez and Linda Schlossberg (New York: New York University Press, 2001), 38–63.

49. See David Levering Lewis, "Parallels and Divergences: Assimilationist Strategies of Afro-American and Jewish Elites from 1910 to the Early 1930s," in *Bridges and Boundaries: African Americans and Jews*, ed. Jack Salzman (New York: George Braziller, 1992), 17–35.

50. Hurston, *Moses*, 11, 102.

51. Hurston, *Dust Tracks on a Road*, 237, 238.

52. Hurston's hypothesis that Moses is Egyptian resonates with that of Sigmund Freud, who published *Moses and Monotheism* in the same year. See Barbara Johnson, "Moses and Intertextuality: Sigmund Freud, Zora Neale Hurston, and the Bible," in *Poetics of the Americas: Race, Founding, and Textuality*, ed. Bainard Cowan and Jefferson Humphries (Baton Rouge: Louisiana State University Press, 1997), 15–29.

53. Boyd, *Wrapped in Rainbows*, 331–332.

54. Hurston, *Moses*, 2.

55. Henry James, *The American Scene*, in *Collected Travel Writings: Great Britain and America* (New York: Library of America, 1993), 464.

56. Hurston, *Moses*, 46, 28.

57. Ibid., 25.

58. Ibid., 35.

59. Ibid., 34.

60. See Lewis, "Parallels and Divergences," 17–35.

61. Hurston, *Moses*, 34.

62. Ibid., xxiv.

63. Hemenway, *Zora Neale Hurston*, 257.

64. Ibid.

65. Hurston, *Moses*, 200.

66. Ibid., 60.

67. Ibid., 42, 51.

68. Ibid., 60, 61.

69. Ibid., 63–65, 68.

70. Ibid., 70.

71. Ibid., 78.

72. Ibid., 114.

73. Ibid., 91.

74. Ibid., 98, 112.

75. Ibid., 134.

76. Diner, *In the Almost Promised Land*, 133.

77. On Spingarn, see David Levering Lewis, *W.E.B. Du Bois: Biography of a Race* (New York: Henry Holt, 1993), especially 484–500; Barbara Joyce Ross, *J. E. Spingarn and the Rise of the NAACP, 1911–1939* (New York: Atheneum, 1972); and Marshall van Deusen, *J. E. Spingarn* (New York: Twayne, 1971).

78. Hurston, *Moses*, 152.

79. Zora Neale Hurston, "The 'Pet Negro' System," in Wall, *Folklore, Memoirs, and Other Writings*, 921.

80. See Lewis, *W.E.B. Du Bois*, 486.

81. Hurston, *Moses*, 140, 268, 141.

82. Ibid., 204.

83. Ibid., 214, 131.

84. Ibid., 253, 205.

85. Ibid., 230, 243, 246.

86. Ibid., 246.

87. Ibid., 265.

88. Ibid., 282.

89. Cited in Lewis, *W.E.B. Du Bois*, 485.

90. Hurston, *Moses*, 288.

Conclusion

1. Danzy Senna, *Caucasia* (New York: Riverhead, 1998), 130, 140, 131.

2. Homi Bhabha, *The Location of Culture* (New York: Routledge, 1994), 89.

3. Rebecca Walker, *Black, White, and Jewish: Autobiography of a Shifting Self* (New York: Riverhead, 2001), 310, 311.

4. On "postethnic" identity, see David Hollinger, *Postethnic America: Beyond Multiculturism* (1995; repr., New York: Basic Books, 2000). For a discussion of Jews as representative of postethnicity, see David Biale, "The Melting Pot and Beyond: Jews and the Politics of American Identity," in *Insider/Outsider: American Jews and Multiculturalism*, ed. David Biale, Michael Galchinsky, and Susannah Heschel (Berkeley: University of California Press, 1998), 17–33.

5. Stanley Crouch, "Literary Conjure Woman," *New Republic*, October 19, 1987, 38.

6. Frank Rich, "It Still Felt Good the Morning After," *New York Times*, November 9, 2008.

7. bell hooks, "Eating the Other," in *Black Looks* (Boston: South End Press, 1992), 37–38. For an important reading of *Without You I'm Nothing* that considers how Jewishness and sexuality complicate Bernhard's representation of whiteness, see Ann Pellegrini, *Performance Anxieties: Staging Psychoanalysis, Staging Race* (New York: Routledge, 1997), 49–64.

INDEX

Abuza, Charles (Kalish), 26–27
Adler, Jacob, 25
African American composers, 17, 21, 33, 35, 40–41, 45. *See also specific names*
African American stereotypes: demand for abolishing, 108; "mammy," 38–39, 59, 62–63, 97, 120, 121–130, 139, 143; "tragic mulatto," 59–60, 63, 85, 86, 90, 97, 120, 121, 132–133; "Uncle Tom," 65, 89
"All Coons Look Alike to Me" (Hogan), 21
"All God's Chillun Got Wings" (spiritual), 91
"Angle Worm Wiggle" (Tucker's performance), 41
anti-Semitism: Ferber's experiences, 67, 72–73; Fitzgerald, 75; Hurston and, 149–150, 151; Hurst's experiences, 9–10, 117–118; Jewish self-hatred, 101; nazism and, 71, 111, 158, 161–162, 217n45; racism compared with, 161–162; stage Jew iconography, 187n17; vaudeville comics and, 21. *See also* nativist ideology
Antler, Joyce, 24, 28, 76, 212n107
assimilation, Jewish: anti-Semitism and, 9–10, 21, 67, 72–73, 109–110, 149–150, 199n31; blackface performance and, 4–6, 7, 180–182; civil rights advocacy and, 109–110, 154, 158, 168, 170;

consumerism and, 51–52, 135–137, 199n32; in entertainment industry, 21, 22, 53, 55–57; Hurst as exemplar, 106; Hurst's works on, 104, 137–138; middlebrow culture and, 74–75, 98; name-changing and, 137; passing and, 61, 68–70, 84–85, 86–87, 100, 118, 208n26; vaudeville performance and, 21, 22
"At the Yiddish Wedding Jubilee" (Tucker's performance), 55
"Aunt Jemima" image, 14, 63, 100, 123–124, 128–130, 211n82

Baker, Belle, 21
Baldwin, James, 11
Baraka, Amiri: *Blues People*, 44, 45
Barnard College, 114, 151–153
Barth, Belle, 23, 194n93
Batker, Carol, 61, 98
Bayes, Nora, 16, 21–22, 37, 60
Bellow, Saul, 71
Berg, Gertrude, 39, 53
Berlant, Lauren, 60, 85, 213n115
Berlin, Irving, 33, 35
Bernhard, Sandra, 24, 183
Bernhardt, Sarah, 22–23
Bhabha, Homi, 178, 206n9
Biale, David, 24
Birth of a Nation, The (film), 65

black arts movement, 44–45

blackface performances: African American, 19–20, 35, 145; empathy vs. exploitation, 4–5, 8–9, 28, 32, 53, 65–66, 77, 145, 181–182; evolution, 17–23; female impersonation, 19; homoerotics and, 19; Hurston's views, 144; Irish, 18; Jewish, 3–4, 16, 20, 32, 35, 146, 160, 172, 180–182; Jolson, 3–4, 146; in minstrel shows, 18–19; portrayed by Hurst, 6–10; *Show Boat* character Andy, 81–82; Tucker, 6, 16–17, 23, 28–30; in vaudeville, 19–23, 28–29, 35; women, 16, 57, 63, 179–182

"Bluebird, Where Are You?" (Tucker's performance), 56

blues: as African American culture, 44–45; African American singers, 42–43, 47–48; body type portrayed in, 49; female agency and empowerment in, 42–43, 47–48, 193n87, 194n90; "Some of These Days" as precursor to, 42; Tucker's performances, 33, 43–44, 45–47

Boas, Franz, 15, 115, 146, 148–149, 151–153, 160–161, 169

Bonner, Marita, 113, 210n56

Book-of-the-Month Club, 73, 75

Botshon, Lisa, 74, 75

Bourne, Randolph: "Trans-national America," 69, 70

Boyd, Valerie, 160, 215n16

Brice, Fanny: career, 49–50; Native American number, 30–31; performances in blackface, 16; Sochen's analysis, 61; as Ziegfeld Follies star, 21, 35, 42, 192n49

Brodkin, Karen, 13

Brooks, Shelton: "Darktown Strutters' Ball," 40, 194n93; "Some of These Days," 17, 40–43, 53–54; Tucker and, 33, 192n66

Brown, Jayna, 33

Brown, Sterling: criticism of *Imitation of Life*, 97, 119, 120–121, 123, 124, 133, 140; "Negro Character as Seen by White Authors," 132

Bruce, Lenny, 24, 183

Budick, Emily Miller: *Blacks and Jews in Literary Conversation*, 12

Bunche, Ralph, 39

Cahan, Abraham: as *Forward* editor, 105; Howells and, 207–208n24; writings, 76, 85, 191n42, 199n32

Cantor, Eddie, 21, 24, 35, 39

Carby, Hazel, 42, 43

Caspary, Vera: *The White Girl*, 84–85

Chopin, Kate: "Desiree's Baby," 187n15

Chung, Mom, 36, 192n55

civil rights: analogy with emancipation from slavery, 170–171; early twentieth-century efforts, 12–13, 109–111, 154, 158, 161–162; Frank's lynching and, 109, 154, 167; Hurst as champion, 110–111, 116–117, 151; Jews' leadership role in, 12–13, 109–110, 168, 170, 175; legal cases, 170; post–World War II movement, 12

Cohen, Sarah Blacher, 24, 48

coon shouting/singing/songs: Bayes's and Held's singing, 21–22; Brice's singing, 50; defined, 16; in *Show Boat*, 59, 60, 89, 91; Tucker's singing, 16, 21, 23, 25, 29, 32, 33; Yiddish songs as, 55

cosmetics industry, female entrepreneurs in, 136–137

Cosmopolitan magazine, 68, 102, 104, 105

"Crazy Blues" (Smith's performance), 43

Crisis, 111, 154

Danielson, Jacques, 101, 103

"Darktown Strutters' Ball" (Brooks), 40, 194n93

Davis, Angela, 43, 44

Delbanco, Andrew: *Required Reading*, 156–157

dialect comics, 20–21

Diner, Hasia R., 12, 109, 215n18

Dixon, Thomas: *The Clansman*, 65

double consciousness, 45, 165–166

Douglas, Ann: *Terrible Honesty*, 10, 78, 102, 207n16

Du Bois, W. E. B.: Hurston's criticism, 155; *The Souls of Black Folk*, 154, 174; Spingarn and, 170–171; Van Vechten criticized by, 209n36

"Eli, Eli": Baker's performance, 21; Waters's performance, 56

Elkins, Mollie, 36–40

Ellison, Ralph, 144, 156

Everett, Anna, 98, 124

Fauset, Jessie, 108; *Plum Bun,* 84, 132
femininity: blackface female
    impersonation and, 19; blackface
    performance's negation, 7, 28; cult of
    domesticity and, 10; Ferber's unsettling
    of, 62; "queer," 138–139; standards, 6,
    42, 56
Ferber, Edna: *American Beauty,* 72;
    anti-Semitism experienced by, 72–73;
    autobiography *A Peculiar Treasure,*
    58, 65–66, 67, 70–71, 72; *Buttered Side
    Down,* 67; childhood infatuation with
    minstrel shows, 58; *Cimarron,* 72, 74,
    92, 95; *Come and Get It,* 72; *Dawn
    O'Hara,* 67–68; Emma McChesney
    stories, 68, 73, 96, 198n17; fame
    and success, 66, 73, 102, 201n50;
    Fanny Herself, 60, 61, 67, 68–70, 71,
    76, 85–86, 90, 92, 96; *Giant,* 72, 73,
    92; "The Girl Who Went Right,"
    61, 85; "The Homely Heroine," 67;
    Hughes's views on, 95, 204–205n105;
    Ice Palace, 72; Jewish identity issues,
    70–71, 92; journalistic work, 67, 72,
    76–77; *A Kind of Magic,* 200n48; later
    works, 142; life and career, 67–73, 95;
    "middlebrow" label applied to, 66, 72,
    73–74, 145; midwestern upbringing, 67,
    76; *Minick,* 58–59, 62, 196n3; as New
    Woman, 11, 71–72; passing as theme in
    writings, 85–86, 176; racism issue and,
    64–65, 198n17; *Saratoga Trunk,* 92–94,
    204n103; *So Big,* 66, 72, 73, 74, 78, 95;
    Tucker and, 196n7. See also *Show Boat*
Fitzgerald, F. Scott: anti-Semitism, 75;
    denigration of women writers, 144–145,
    201n50, 207n24; Ferber viewed by, 73,
    75, 145; *This Side of Paradise,* 73–74
Five Kings of Syncopation, 43–44
Forsyne, Ida, 35
Frank, Leo, 109, 154, 167
Freedman, Jonathan: *Klezmer America,*
    5–6; *The Temple of Culture,* 75
Freud, Sigmund: *Moses and Monotheism,*
    218n52

Gabler, Neil, 56
Gardella, Tess, 62–63
Gates, Henry Louis, Jr., 64
Gershwin, George: as cultural
    intermediary, 33; Hurston's dislike,
148, 149, 214n5; *Porgy and Bess,* 79,
    144
"ghetto girl" stereotype, 50, 51
Giant (film), 73
Glenn, Susan, 22–23, 51
"Go Down, Moses" (spiritual), 91, 170
Goffman, Ethan: *Imagining Each Other,* 12
Goldsmith, Meredith, 74, 75
Goldstein, Eric: *The Price of Whiteness,*
    13, 110
Gone with the Wind (film), 39
Green, Paul: *In Abraham's Bosom,* 79
Green Mile, The (film), 89
Green Pastures, The (film), 172
Greenberg, Cheryl, 12, 109
Grossman, Barbara, 50
Gubar, Susan, 84, 133–134, 186n11

Hallelujah! (film), 172
Hammerstein, Oscar, II: *Show Boat,* 60,
    62–64, 79, 89, 95, 96, 144, 197n12,
    204n96
Handy, W. C.: "St. Louis Blues," 33, 43
Harlem Renaissance: African American
    writers' disappointment in, 145, 157;
    black-white encounters during, 113;
    Hurst's participation in, 14, 99, 105,
    107–109, 112, 121, 140, 151, 210n56;
    passing novels, 84, 108; race records
    and, 43; racial self-love during, 132;
    Show Boat and, 78; "talented tenth"
    elite, 172, 173–174, 217n44
Harrison, Daphne, 36, 43
Hawthorne, Nathaniel, 144, 201n50
Hearts in Dixie (film), 172
Held, Anna, 21–22, 60
Hemenway, Robert, 115, 164
Henry, O., 73, 200n46, 201n50
Herskovits, Melville, 148–149, 152
Heyward, DuBose and Dorothy: *Porgy,*
    79, 124
Hitler, Adolf, 71, 111, 158, 199n34
Hogan, Ernest: "All Coons Look Alike to
    Me," 21
Holiday, Billie, 56
"Hollywood Will Never Be the Same"
    (Tucker's performance), 57
Honky Tonk (film), 56–57
hooks, bell, 183
Howe, Irving: *World of Our Fathers,* 4, 6, 8,
    53, 77, 181

Howells, William Dean, 207–208n24

Hughes, Langston: *The Big Sea*, 107, 213n2; Ferber viewed by, 95, 204–205n105; Hurston viewed by, 143; "Limitations of Life," 127; "Negro vogue" term, 78; Van Vechten and, 209n36

Hunter, Alberta, 17, 33, 35, 36, 42, 63

Hurst, Fannie: activism and philanthropy, 8–9, 99, 101, 103, 105, 106–112; autobiography *Anatomy of Me*, 9–10, 101, 110; *Back Street*, 104, 207n22; biography, 99; causes supported by, 99, 101, 105, 107, 108–109, 111, 151; critical reappraisal, 102; exclusion from Jewish American literary canon, 104, 207–208n24; *Family!*, 104; fashion sense, 115–116; "The Gold in Fish," 137; *Humoresque*, 208n24; Hurston employed by, 114–115; Hurston's friendship with, 3, 15, 99, 106, 110, 112–120, 140, 143, 146, 149, 156, 176; "If I Were a Negro" essay, 140; "In Memoriam," 137–138; Jewish characters in works by, 104–105, 137–138, 207n22; Jewish identity issues, 105–106, 110, 118, 208n26; Jewish refugees aided by, 101, 110–111; as judge for African American and Jewish fiction contests, 105, 114; *Just Around the Corner*, 207n24; later works, 142; life and career, 100–106; *Lummox*, 102, 104, 207n22; marriage to Danielson, 101, 103; "middlebrow" label applied to, 73, 74, 98, 101–102, 145; midwestern upbringing, 98, 100–101; "Negrotarian" image, 106–112, 149; as New Woman, 11, 101, 103–105, 113–114, 149; *New York Times* obituary, 101–102; "The Other, and Unknown, Harlem," 140–141; as participant in Harlem Renaissance, 14, 99, 105, 107–109, 112, 121, 140, 151, 210n56; passing as theme in writings, 100, 120, 121, 122–123, 126–127, 130–139; popularity and success, 102, 104–105; "Roulette," 208n24; "Seven Candles," 104; "The Smudge," 1–2, 6–10, 16, 28, 99, 139; Stein compared with, 207n16; "Summer Resources," 103–104. See also *Imitation of Life*

Hurston, Zora Neale: African American characters, 145; artistic motives, 150; attempted novelization of Meyer's *Black Souls*, 154–155; autobiography *Dust Tracks on a Road*, 112–113, 115–116, 152, 159, 160, 213–214n2; at Barnard College, 114, 151–153; Boas's friendship with, 15, 115, 146, 148–149, 151–153, 169; criticism of white consumption of blackness, 143–144; double-voicedness, 112–113, 143–144, 147, 153; ethnographic fieldwork, 148–149, 152, 169, 215n16; "The Fire and the Cloud," 215n22; *The First One*, 215n22; "The Gilded Six-Bits," 215n22; "Glossary of Harlem Slang," 120, 130; "Herod the Great" (proposed project), 150; "How It Feels to Be Colored Me," 108, 152; Hughes and, 155; Hurst's employment, 114–115; Hurst's friendship with, 3, 99, 106, 110, 112–120, 140, 142, 143, 146, 149, 156, 176; Jewish inspirations and proposed projects, 150–151; *Jonah's Gourd Vine*, 108; Judaism viewed by, 147–148; Meyer's friendship with, 15, 114, 115, 146, 147–148, 149, 153–156, 176; minstrelsy charges against, 144–146, 148, 156; *Mule Bone* (with Hughes), 155; *Mules and Men*, 119, 149, 152, 169; "The 'Pet Negro' System," 170–171; "Polk County" collaboration, 214n5; relationships with Jews, 15, 145–146, 147–156; "Spunk," 114; "Sweat," 215n22; *Their Eyes Were Watching God*, 144–145, 146, 156; Tucker viewed by, 44; Van Vechten and, 209n36; "What White Publishers Won't Print," 150; white benefactors, 143, 147–156, 169; "You Don't Know Us Negroes," 143. See also *Moses, Man of the Mountain*

Hutchinson, George, 10, 78

"I Ain't Taking Orders from No One" (Tucker's performance), 46

"I Don't Want to Get Thin" (Tucker's performance), 48–49

"I Know That My Baby is Cheating On Me" (Tucker's performance), 41

"I'm a Yiddishe Cowboy" (Meeker's performance), 31

"I'm an Indian" (Brice's performance), 30–31

"I'm Living Alone" (Tucker's performance), 46–47

"I'm Wild About That Thing" (Smith's performance), 47

Imitation of Life (1934 film), 96, *122*; deviations from novel, 97–98, 130, 134, 212n99; ending, 133; "queer" femininity in, 138–139; African American reception, 121, 140

Imitation of Life (1959 film), 97, 134, 212n99, 212n108

Imitation of Life (Hurst novel): African Americans depicted in, 107, 111–112, 120–130, 143; alternative reading as parody, 120, 121–130; commodification of black culture as theme, 99–100, 120–130; cosmetics industry plotline, 135–137; critical reception, 97–98, 102, 120–123,130, 133–134; critical reevaluations, 98, 124, 133–134; female protagonist as working woman in, 99–100, 103, 123–127, 136; film adaptations' overshadowing, 96–98; gender passing in, 134–136; homoerotic undertones, 136–137; Jewish factors, 98–99; parataxis technique, 135; passing narratives, 84, 120, 121, 122–123, 126–127, 130–139; plot alterations in films, 97–98, 130, 133, 212n106; race issues, 96–99, 118–120; racism charges against, 13–14, 99–100, 127, 141–142, 143; reissue, 98; serialization, 96, 102, 122; title change, 96, 122–123, 205n1; treatment of gender, ethnicity, and assimilation, 134–139

Itzkovitz, Daniel, 84–85, 98, 159, 213n115

Jacobson, Matthew Frye, 13

James, Henry, 162

Jazz Singer, The: Jolson film, 4–6, 8, 56, 79, 146, 185n4; other versions, 185n4

Jessel, George, 21, 39

Jewface (compilation), 21, 190n15

"Jewish American Princess" stereotype, 51, 52

Jewish civil rights activism, 109–110, 158, 161–162, 170

Jewish Daily Forward, 105–106

Jewish identity issues: assimilation and, 4–5, 9–10, 11, 21, 22, 50, 53–57, 69, 74–75, 104, 106, 109–110, 168, 199n31, 208n26; blackface performance and, 4–5, 16, 20, 23, 29–30, 160, 180–182;

cultural mediation and, 26, 33, 60, 75, 159–160, 166, 170, 176; fashion and, 51–52, 115–116, 199n32; "ghetto girl" stereotype, 50, 51; Hurston's views on, 147–148, 150; intermarriage with gentiles, 104; "Jewish American Princess" stereotype, 51, 52; name-changing and, 137; negotiation of whiteness, 13, 20, 22–23, 29–32, 42, 44, 84–85, 192n49; passing and, 61, 68–70, 84–85, 100, 118, 135–137, 177–179; political activism and, 161–162, 168, 175; self-hatred, 101; vaudeville performance and, 21–22, 48, 49–51; women comedians, 23–24, 48, 179–183, 194n93; women's experiences, 6–7, 9–10, 11, 16–17, 23, 41–42, 49–52, 57, 61, 68–71, 133–134

Jewish literature: Ferber's place, 75–76, 92, 133–134; Hurst's place, 98, 104, 133–134, 137–138, 207–208n24; passing trope in, 84–85, 93–94, 100, 130–139, 212n107

Johnson, James Weldon: *The Autobiography of an Ex-Colored Man*, 84; *Book of American Negro Spirituals*, 108; endorsement of Meyer's *Black Souls*, 155; Van Vechten's *Nigger Heaven* and, 209n36

Jolson, Al, 3, 4, 21, 79, 146, 148, 149, 172

Jong, Erica, 24

Kallen, Horace, 10; "cultural pluralism" concept, 199n28; "Democracy versus the Melting-Pot," 69

Kaufman, George S., 58–59

Kern, Jerome: *Show Boat* adaptation, 60, 62–64, 79, 95, 96, 144, 202n63

Kibler, M. Alison, 22, 28

Koppelman, Susan, 102, 206n8, 207n23

Kroeger, Brooke, 99, 119

Lahr, John, 64

Larsen, Nella: *Passing*, 84, 108, 124, 132, 211n72

Lavitt, Pamela Brown, 21–22

Lewis, David Levering, 12; *When Harlem Was in Vogue*, 109

Lhamon, W. T., 18, 189n5

Live Entertainment Inc., 63–64

Locke, Alain: Hurston criticized by, 144; "The New Negro," 108, 121

Lott, Eric: *Love and Theft*, 19; Rogin viewed by, 5, 186n9
"Lovie Joe" (Brice's performance), 50
"Lucy Long" (minstrel song), 19

MacDonald, Dwight: "Masscult and Midcult," 66, 74, 75
Mailer, Norman, 71; "The White Negro," 11
"Make It Legal, Mr. Siegel" (Tucker's performance), 56
"Mama Goes Where Papa Goes" (Tucker's performance), 46, 56, 195n133
"mammy" stereotype: Elkins and, 38–39; Hurston's views on, 143; in *Imitation of Life*, 97, 120, 121–130, 139, 143; in *Show Boat*, 59, 62–63, 124
Mason, Charlotte Osgood, 146, 153, 214–215n16
Mayhew, Stella, 16, 29
McDowell, Deborah, 157–158, 216n43
McKay, Claude, 97
"Me and Myself" (Tucker's performance), 47, 52
Meeker, Edward, 31
Melnick, Jeffrey, 21, 33
"melting pot" ideology, 10, 55, 68–70, 106
Menken, Adah Isaacs, 190n15
Merwin, Ted, 21, 31
Meyer, Annie Nathan: advocacy for Hurston's *Moses*, 217n45; *Black Souls*, 154–155; Hurston and, 15, 114, 115, 146, 147–150, 151, 153–156, 176; as New Woman, 149; "The Shoe Pinches Mr. Samuels," 154; writings, 147–148
"middlebrow" label: applied to Ferber, 66, 72, 73–74; applied to Hurst, 73, 74, 98; critical reevaluation, 201n50; gendering of term, 74–75
Midler, Bette, 23, 190n21
minstrel shows: African American stereotypes in, 125, 172; all-black films as, 172; blackface performance in, 18–19, 45; Ferber's memories, 58; Hurston's views on, 144; *Show Boat* and, 59–60, 62–63, 64–65, 66, 76, 81–82; Stowe influenced by, 198n19
miscegenation: alluded to in Hurst's "The Smudge," 7, 9; Ferber's *Show Boat* treatment, 59, 81, 83–84, 86, 87–89, 91, 94; in O'Neill's *All God's Chillun Got*

Wings, 91; Production Code ban on representations, 133
Mizejewski, Linda, 42, 192n49
Morrison, Toni: "Africanist presence" claim, 5, 89, 116; *The Bluest Eye*, 131, 133, 212n99
Moses, Man of the Mountain (Hurston), 15, 156–176; Aaron character, 171–172, 217n44; allegorical levels, 146–147, 157–160, 175–176, 217nn44–45; anti-Semitism referenced, 91, 151; black folk dialect, 159, 163, 171, 173; call-and-response storytelling, 163–164, 168; conclusion, 174–175; criticism on, 216n43, 156–158; double-voiced technique, 147; Jethro character, 169; Mentu character, 165–166; Miriam character, 162–164, 170–171, 173–174, 217n44; Moses accused of rape in, 166–167; Moses as intermediary figure, 158, 160, 162–164, 166, 168–171, 174; Moses's identity issues, 165–168, 218n52; Moses's murder of Egyptian overseer, 166, 167; politics of cross-identification, 161–162, 164, 166, 172, 175–176; reviews, 156–157; skin color, 160, 173–174; structure, 161, 164–165; "talented tenth" elite satirized, 172, 173–174, 217n44
"mulatto, tragic" stereotype, 59–60, 63, 85, 86, 90, 97, 120, 121, 132–133
"My Handy Man": Hunter's performance, 36; Waters's and Spivey's performances, 47
"My Mother's Sabbath Candles" (Tucker's performance), 56
"My Southern Rose" (Tucker's performance), 38
"My Yiddisha Mammy" (Cantor's performance), 21
"My Yiddishe Mama": Holiday's performance, 56; Tucker's performance, 16–17, 21, 54–55, 56, 195n133

NAACP, 32, 109, 158, 170, 175
Nathan, Maud, 153
National Health Circle for Colored People, 111
National Urban League, 97, 111, 112, 120
nativist ideology, 10, 69, 147, 158, 161–162
nazism, 71, 111, 158, 161–162, 217n45

"Negro vogue," 78–79, 92, 99–100, 107–108
Newton, Adam Zachary: *Facing Black and Jew,* 12
New Womanhood: ethnic and racial dimensions, 11, 46, 51; Ferber and, 62, 67–68, 71–72, 96; flapper and vamp, 42; Hurst and, 96, 101, 103–105, 113–114, 149; Hurston and, 149; image, 10–11; Tucker and, 13, 23–24, 40–44, 54–55; vaudeville performances and, 11, 22–23, 40–41
"Nijinsky" (Brice's performance), 35
"No Man's Mamma Now" (Waters's performance), 46
"No One Man Is Ever Going to Worry Me" (Tucker's performance), 46
North, Michael, 10, 78

Obama, Barack, 182–183
"Oh! You Have No Idea" (Tucker's performance), 48
"Ol' Man River" (Kern and Hammerstein), 62, 79, 89, 144, 197n12
O'Neill, Eugene: *All God's Chillun Got Wings,* 91, 155; *The Emperor Jones,* 78–79, 124, 155
Opportunity, 97–98, 114, 120–121, 130, 153
"Oy, How I Hate That Fellow Nathan" (Brice's performance), 21

Parker, Dorothy, 50
passing, trope of: in Ferber's works, 61, 68–70, 85–86, 90–91, 93–94; in Harlem Renaissance novels, 84, 108; in Hurst and Hurston and, 118; in *Imitation of Life,* 100, 120, 121, 122–123, 126–127, 130–139; Jewish women writers' use, 84, 133–134, 212n107; in *Moses, Man of the Mountain,* 158, 160, 162–164, 167–168, 174; scholarly literature on, 84–85, 203n77; in Senna's *Caucasia,* 177–179; in *Show Boat,* 61, 77–78, 81, 87–89, 176
Philip, M. Nourbese: *Showing Grit,* 64, 89
Pictorial Review, 102, 122, 205n1
pluralism, cultural, 8–9, 10, 55, 66, 68–70, 106, 160, 164, 177–179, 199n28
Production Code, film studio, 97, 133
"Prove It On Me Blues" (Rainey), 194n90
Provincetown Players, 79, 155

Queen Latifah, 48

"queer" identity, 85, 100, 138–139

racial uplift, 99, 107, 109
racism: in 1920s, 161–162, 170; race as construction, 83–84, 87, 131–132; in minstrel shows, 18–19, 21, 45; politics of in *Moses, Man of the Mountain,* 161–162, 176; in vaudeville, 20. *See also* anti-Semitism and nativist ideology
Radway, Janice, 74
Rainey, Ma, 43, 45, 194n90
Raphaelson, Samson: "The Day of Atonement," 3–4
"red hot mama" image, 16, 42, 44
Redding, J. Saunders, 44–45
Rich, Frank, 64, 183
Rivers, Joan, 23
Robeson, Paul, 62, 197n12, 202n63
Roediger, David, 5, 18
Rogin, Michael: *Blackface, White Noise,* 4–5, 6, 8; cultural appropriation notion, 21, 22, 28, 29, 32, 53, 60, 61, 77, 142, 181–182, 186n9
Rosenwald, Julius, 148
Roth, Philip, 24; *The Human Stain,* 84
Rottenberg, Catherine: *Performing Americanness,* 85
Rubin, Joan Shelley, 74

"Sadie Salome, Go Home" (Brice's performance), 21
Saratoga Trunk (film), 204n103
Sartre, Jean-Paul: *La Nausée,* 52–53
Saxton, Alexander: *The Rise and Fall of the White Republic,* 18
Schuyler, George, 156
"Second-Hand Rose" (Brice's performance), 21
Senna, Danzy: *Caucasia,* 84, 177–179
sexuality: blackface female impersonation and, 19; blackface performers and, 18–19; blues and, 42–43, 47–48, 194n90; double entendres, 47–48; lesbianism, 43, 48, 192n55, 194n90; male homosexuality, 19; New Womanhood and, 11, 42, 46–47, 54–55; Tucker's independence, 13, 16, 17, 23–24, 27–28, 39, 40–42, 44, 47–49, 50; white portrayals of African Americans, 11; women in vaudeville and, 22–23, 28–29, 49–50

shimmy (dance), 33, 41

Show Boat (Ferber novel): adaptations' overshadowing, 13–14, 60, 96; African American characters, 59–60, 62–65, 124, 125; as Book-of-the-Month Club selection, 73; cultural intermixing and cross-racial performance, 78–79; ending, 92; female protagonist as working woman, 77–78, 89–90; Ferber's research, 76–77; Jews' absence from, 60–61; lack of critical writings on, 60, 66; miscegenation issues, 59, 81, 83–84, 86, 87–89, 91, 94; Mississippi-Nile equation, 77, 79–80, 91, 176; name-changing, 80; nuances, 66, 76, 83, 88–89, 95, 130; opening, 79–80; passing trope, 61, 77–78, 81, 85–86, 88, 176; plot differences from musical adaptation, 60, 83–84, 88, 89–92, 204n96; racial mixing and uncertainty as theme, 79–83, 86–92, 94, 95, 139; racism charges against, 64–65, 99, 141–142; sentimentality, 65; staying power, 74; success and reception, 78; use of word "nigger" in, 88, 90–91

Show Boat (films): 1936 version, 84, 204n96; 1951 version, 204n96

Show Boat (Kern and Hammerstein musical), 62–64; African American responses, 63, 64; changes to lyrics, 63, 197n12, 202n63; criticism, 63, 64, 144; as integrated book musical, 196n9; integrated cast, 62–63; Jewish factors, 60, 64, 98; motif of black suffering, 89–90, 95; opening, 79; plot differences from novel, 60, 83–84, 88, 89–92, 204n96; premiere, 62, 79; sentimentality, 89; updated version (1993), 63–64, 197–198n14; use of word "nigger," 63, 81, 87–88, 90

Silverman, Sarah, 24, 180–83, *181*

Sirk, Douglas, 97, 212n99, 212n108

Smith, Bessie, 17, 43, 45, 47, 192n52

Smith, Clara, 43, 47

Smith, Mamie, 43

Sochen, June, 24, 49–50, 61, 68

Sollors, Werner, 69

"Some of These Days" (Brooks), 17, 40–43, 53–54; Tucker's performance, 16–17

Spingarn, Joel, 170–171, 175

spirituals, 91, 108, 170

Spivey, Victoria, 43, 47

"St. Louis Blues" (Handy), 33, 43

Stahl, John, 97–98, 130, 133

"Stay at Home Papa" (Tucker's performance), 46

Stein, Gertrude: Hurst compared with, 207n16; *Three Lives,* 102

Stoddard, Lothrop: *The Rising Tide of Color Against White Supremacy,* 136

Stowe, Harriet Beecher, 201n50; *Uncle Tom's Cabin,* 65, 89, 198n19

"Strange Fruit" (Holiday's performance), 56

Streisand, Barbra, 23

Sundquist, Eric: *Strangers in the Land,* 12

Tanguay, Eva, 37

"There's Company in the Parlor, Girls, Come on Down" (Tucker's performance), 41

"There's Something Spanish in My Eyes" (Tucker's performance), 49

Thompson, Mark, 157–158

Thompson, Stephanie, 102, 124

Tomashevsky, Boris, 25

Trachtenberg, Alan, 30–31

transnationalism, 69, 70, 92, 147, 176, 199n29

Tuck, Albert, 25

Tuck, Louis, 25, 27

Tucker, Sophie, *34*; African American composers performed by, 17, 33, 35, 43, 53–54; African American women employed by, 35–40; autobiography *Some of These Days,* 17, 25–27, 36, 39–40, 51, 54; blues performances, 33, 35, 45–49; career path, 25–26; as feminist foremother, 23–24; factors shaping career and identity, 13, 16–17, 23–25; fashion, 51–52; Ferber and, 196n7; film career, 56–57; first performance out of blackface, 31–32, 37; Golden Jubilee, 39; Jewish causes supported by, 53–54; Jewish elements in performances, 29–30, 31–32, 41–42, 45–46, 49, 50–51, 53–56; misidentified as African American, 52–53; name changes, 25, 26–27, 37; as New Woman, 11, 27–28, 42, 45–47; performances in blackface, 6, 16–17, 23, 28–30, 65, 90; persona reinventions, 17, 23, 25–26,

30; as "Queen of Jazz," 43–44; "red hot mama" image, 42, 44; shimmy dancing, 33, 41; Silverman compared with, 183; Sochen's analysis, 61; success, 21, 25; vaudeville performances, 40–41; vocal sound, 16–17, 25, 52; weight, 23, 48–49, 56; Yiddish recordings, 56; Ziegfeld Follies appearance, 36–37

Twain, Mark: *Pudd'nhead Wilson*, 87

"Two-Fisted Double-Jointed Rough and Ready Man" (Hunter's performance), 36

"Uncle Tom" stereotype, 65, 89

unreliable narration technique, 124–125

Van Vechten, Carl, 150; Hurst and, 107, 108–109; Hurston and, 146; *Nigger Heaven*, 79, 108, 124, 209n36

vaudeville: anti-Semitism and, 21; blackface performances in, 19–23, 28–29; double entendres in, 47–48, 194n93; female performers, 21, 22–23; Ferber's *Show Boat* depiction, 59–60; heterogeneity, 20–21; immigration influx and, 20; integrated acts, 35; Jewish involvement in, 20, 21, 31; women's body images in, 42

Walker, George, 20

Walker, Rebecca: *Black, White, and Jewish*, 178–179

Wall, Cheryl, 157, 216n43

Waters, Ethel, 17, 35–36, 43, 46, 47, 56, 112

West, Dorothy, 113, 210n56

West, Mae, 23

Whale, James, 84

"Whip It to a Jelly" (Smith's performance), 47

White, Walter, 108; *Flight*, 84, 132

white identity issues: cross-racial contact as heightening, 108, 115–116, 118–119, 131–132, 183–184; immigrants' status, 26–27, 29, 51; instability and fragility, 5–6, 7–8, 9, 10, 13, 22–23, 30, 44, 55, 61, 80–81, 84, 86–92, 100, 133, 142, 160, 177–179; minstrel shows and, 18–19, 45; miscegenation and, 7, 9, 59, 81, 83–84, 86, 87–89, 94; passing and, 61, 68–70, 77–78, 81, 84–85, 88, 93–94, 100, 108, 126, 136–137; racism and, 18; vaudeville and, 20–21, 22, 29–30, 42, 192n49

"white negress": Bernhardt's self-description as, 22–23; explanation of term, 2–3; Ferber's Magnolia Hawks character as, 60, 82; Tucker seen as, 23, 52–53

Whiteman, Paul, 45

"Who Paid the Rent for Mrs. Rip Van Winkle When Rip Van Winkle Went Away?" (Tucker's performance), 48

Williams, Bert, 20, 35, 145, 192n49

Williams, Linda, 60, 88, 186n11

women's rights, 101, 149. *See also* New Womanhood

Wright, Richard: Hurston viewed by, 144, 148; *Native Son*, 145; *Their Eyes Were Watching God* reviewed by, 144–145

Yellen, Jack, 54

Yezierska, Anzia, 76, 85, 104; *Salome of the Tenements*, 199n32

Ziegfeld Follies, 21, 35, 36–37, 42, 50, 192n49

About the Author

Lori Harrison-Kahan received her A.B. Summa Cum Laude in English from Princeton University and her Ph.D. in English and comparative literature from Columbia University. She has taught at Boston College, Connecticut College, Harvard University, and the University of Pennsylvania. Among her publications are articles on Nella Larsen, Jessie Fauset, Edith Wharton, Anzia Yezierska, Spike Lee, and contemporary multiracial literature. She is currently co-editing a special issue of the journal *MELUS* on the future of Jewish American literary studies.

Breinigsville, PA USA
22 December 2010
251998BV00003BA/2/P